WITHDRAWN

FEMININE FICTIONS

A

A

A

ᵢ A

FEMININE FICTIONS

Revisiting the postmodern

PATRICIA WAUGH

ROUTLEDGE
London and New York

First published in 1989 by Routledge
11 New Fetter Lane, London EC4P 4EE
29 West 35th Street, New York, NY 10001

© 1989 Patricia Waugh

Typeset by J&L Composition Ltd, Filey, North Yorkshire
Printed in Great Britain by
Richard Clay, The Chaucer Press, Bungay, Suffolk

British Library Cataloguing in Publication Data

Waugh, Patricia
Feminine Fictions: revisiting the postmodern
1. Fiction in English. Women writers,
1900–1980 — Critical studies
I. Title
823'.912'099287

Library of Congress Cataloging-in-Publication Data

Waugh, Patricia.
Feminine fictions: Revisiting the postmodern / Patricia Waugh.
000 p.   cm.
Bibliography: p.
Includes index.
1. English fiction – Women authors – History and criticism.
2. English fiction – 20th century – History and criticism.
3. American fiction – Women authors – History and criticism.
4. American fiction – 20th century – History and criticism.
5. Feminism and literature. 6. Women and literature.
7. Postmodernism. 8. Sex role in literature. 9. Identity
(Psychology) in literature. 10. Woolf, Virginia, 1882–1941 –
Criticism and interpretation. I. Title.

PR116.W38 1988
823'.91'099287 – dc19   88–14887

ISBN 0–415–01546–4
ISBN 0–415–01547–2 Pbk

CONTENTS

v

CONTENTS

ACKNOWLEDGEMENTS

I should like to thank the following people who have contributed to this book: Sasha Brookes, who first introduced me to the work of Nancy Chodorow; Andrew Crisell, who read proofs and made many helpful suggestions; Leigh Davey, for looking after my children and giving me the time to write; my husband, Alec, likewise; Ann Clarke, for her typing skills; and my editor at Routledge, Sarah Pearsall, for her helpful suggestions.

Finally, I would like to dedicate the book to Matthew who was born as I conceived the idea for it, and to Jessica whose birth coincided with its completion. I could not have written it without them.

Chapter One

POSTMODERNISM AND FEMINISM: WHERE HAVE ALL THE WOMEN GONE?

POSTMODERNISM AND FEMINISM

Twenty-five years ago contemporary critical writers on recent fiction were busily proclaiming, celebrating, mourning, or heralding 'The Death of the Novel'. Today, with the novel still very much alive and kicking, it is 'The Death of the Self' that must occupy our critical attention. So we are told. In fact, fictional persons have also been dying for the past twenty or so years. As early as 1969, yet with all the fervour of later postmodernism, the narrator of Kurt Vonnegut's *Slaughterhouse-Five* announced:

> There are almost no characters in this story and almost no dramatic confrontations, because most of the people in it are so sick and so much the listless playthings of enormous forces. One of the main effects of war, after all, is that people are discouraged from being characters. (p. 110)

Judging by similar proclamations in novels by the 'recognized' postmodernists – Abish, Barth, Barthelme, Beckett, Borges, Brautigan, Burns, Butor, Calvino, Coover, Cortazar, *et al.*, – it seems that the human 'subject' has disappeared from post-modern fiction. There *are* no 'persons' any more. Indeed, Fredric Jameson has suggested that this can be read as postmodernism's most radical insight:

> Not only is the bourgeois individual subject a thing of the past, it is also a myth: it never really existed in the first place; there have never been autonomous subjects of that type. Rather this construct is merely a philosophical and cultural mystification,

1

which sought to persuade people that they 'had' individual subjects and possessed this unique personal identity. (Jameson 1985, p. 115)

Yet, although postmodernism's ontological disruption (its suggestion that textuality is the primary 'reality' of a world and a book fabricated through discourse) mediates a disintegration of belief in the full humanist subject, such a loss is usually cause for lament. It seems that the imagination longs nostalgically for, and thus in a sense continues to reproduce, the illusion of full subjective presence.

Or does it always?

> For what is this subject that, threatened by loss, is so
> bemoaned? Bourgeois perhaps, patriarchal certainly – it is the
> phallocentric order of subjectivity. For some, for many, this is
> indeed a great loss – and may lead to narcissistic laments about
> the end of art, of culture, of the west. But for others, precisely
> for Others, this is no great loss at all. (Foster 1984, p. 78)

Those excluded from or marginalized by the dominant culture – for reasons of class, gender, race, belief, appearance, or whatever – those Others referred to in Foster's essay, may *never* have experienced a sense of full subjectivity in the first place. They may never have identified with that stable presence mediated through the naturalizing conventions of fictional tradition. Such Others may, indeed, *already* have sensed the extent to which subjectivity is constructed through the institutional dispositions of relations of power, as well as those of fictional convention. Eg patriarchy

The problematization of the constitution of subjectivity mediated through narrative forms has become a central issue of post-structuralist and recent Marxist criticism. Traditionally, Marxists have tended to discuss literary texts either in terms of 'false consciousness', as a simple reflection of class interest which secures the reproduction of class relations, or in terms of 'transcendence', where the text somehow sees through to the 'real' social and historical determinations. In such terms, fictional characters function either as 'naïve' determined representations or as representations whose distance from such historical determinations thus exposes them. Althusser's work

2

represented a significant challenge to this dichotomy in its refusal to separate, absolutely, a domain of the 'real' from a domain of the 'represented'. Furthermore, he argued for the existence of the aesthetic as a material practice in its own right with its own conventions and techniques. Certainly, post-modernist writers have absorbed from this the anti-mimetic idea that 'characters' cannot be understood through comparisons with 'real people' but only by perceiving them through the generic and historical conventions that constitute our under-standing of 'character' at a particular time. What I wish to suggest in this book is that, for those marginalized by the dominant culture, a sense of identity as constructed through impersonal and social relations of power (rather than a sense of identity as the reflection of an inner 'essence') has been a major aspect of their self-concept long before post-structuralists and postmodernists began to assemble their cultural manifestos.

Vonnegut's postmodernist lament in *Slaughterhouse-Five* ex-presses not simply an existential identity crisis, but also the collapse of a particular set of historical and moral conditions which allowed for the reading and understanding of the conventions of character in nineteenth-century realist fiction:

> Rosewater said an interesting thing to Billy one time about a book that wasn't science fiction. He said that everything there was to know about life was in *The Brothers Karamazov*, by Feodor Dostoevsky. 'But that isn't *enough* any more,' said Rosewater. (*Slaughterhouse-Five*, p. 71)

It is clear, however, that contemporary *women* writers are unlikely to share the nostalgia for Dostoevsky's representation of 'life' and 'character'. It does not seem surprising, therefore, that the relationship of women writers to postmodernism (and, indeed, to modernism) should be ambivalent despite the fact that postmodernism is usually presented as an art of the marginal and the oppositional and as such would seem at last to offer women the possibility of identity and inclusion. There *are* strong points of contact, including, of course, historical situation, for the advent of postmodernism coincided with that of the women's liberation movement. In literary terms, both have embraced the popular, rejecting the elitist and purely formalist celebration of modernism established in the American academy

3

during the Cold War period through the influence of the New Criticism. Both movements celebrate liminality, the disruption of boundaries, the confounding of traditional markers of 'difference', the undermining of the authorial security of the 'egotistical sublime'.

However, glancing through almost any of the major theoretical postmodernist statements, one is forcibly struck by the total absence of reference either to women writers or, indeed, to issues of gender. Typical are statements like the following:

> The critical battles which have raged in this country over Barthes, Bloom, and Derrida, or the influence of Heidegger, hermeneutics and deconstruction, have bypassed feminist literary criticism. Postmodernism and even Modernism have not yet entered into female discussions of the feminine experience. ... The deconstructionist tenet that the ego must be eradicated or dismembered, that the text is all that counts, and that discourse must be at the level of language alone would be a form of death for the female experience. (Karl 1985, p. 439)

Or like Donna Gerstenberger's castigation for non-experimentation:

> in which feminist writers, particularly American, have participated very little. ... There has been, it seems to me, too ready an acceptance of the fact that since the world created and falsified by male intellect is complex, the antidote is to oversimplify. In this reaction there is a failure to conceptualise the complexity of modern existence in ways which only art can. (Gerstenberger 1976, pp. 143–4)

Even more insidiously revealing is an essay by Richard Harvey Brown entitled 'The position of the narrative in contemporary society' (Brown 1980), which begins with the announcement that 'Traditional Narrative is dead' and states an intention to 'explain its demise' (p. 545). His argument runs through the usual elucidations of postmodernist practice, suggesting that because of the breakdown of the individual and social order of meaning in which 'public action by moral agents was possible, in which a sense of lived connection between personal character and public conduct prevailed' (Brown 1980, p. 545), narratives, which

4

mediate chronology, causality, and continuity of identity, are now redundant. The world has been given over to textuality, so the novel can no longer articulate 'the history of ways in which the self can be told, a history of universal types for particular identities' (p. 548). With regard to the postmodern writer,

> Instead of reconstructing the world in terms of an earlier, conventional code, he deconstructs conventional experience through a new form of encoding. He is not focussed on objects as they are pregiven, but on how they might be made to reveal themselves as mediated by his own linguistic apparatus. The rules of his word games are made up as he writes. (p. 546)

The postmodern author here, as throughout the essay, is apparently represented through the 'universal' use of the pronoun 'he'. It is interesting, therefore, that in the paragraph following this quotation, where the discussion focuses on *traditional* (as opposed to postmodernist) narrative, the pronominal deictic shifts and Brown refers to the 'form through which the author realizes his or her intentions'. Authors may, it seems, be male *or* female, but *postmodernist* authors are, actually or necessarily, male.

However, it is true that a number of critics, while unable to account for the phenomenon, have expressed bewilderment at the paucity of critical accounts of the relationship between feminism, women's writing and postmodernism. Andreas Huyssen, for example, sees postmodernism in terms of a democratization of art in its 'meshing and mixing' (Huyssen 1984, p. 27) of popular and modernist (i.e. high) culture. He discusses the role in this of feminist writing, with its retrieval and recuperation of the marginal and the buried, its undermining of canonized forms, and its necessary though often implicit fracturing of the universal liberal subject through the introduction of an awareness of the social construction of gender. But he arrives ultimately at the conclusion that 'In light of these developments it is somewhat baffling that feminist criticism has so far largely stayed away from the postmodernism debate which is considered not to be pertinent to feminist concerns' (Huyssen 1984, p. 28). Why, then, have women writers, particularly *feminist* women writers, been excluded from considerations of postmodernist art?

My contention in this book is that feminism and postmodernism clearly *do* share many concerns as they each develop from the 1960s onwards. Both are concerned to disrupt traditional boundaries: between 'art' and 'life', masculine and feminine, high and popular culture, the dominant and the marginal. Both examine the cultural consequences of the decline of a consensus aesthetics, of an effective 'literary' voice, or the absence of a strong sense of stable subjectivity. Each expresses concern about the extension of relationships of alienation within a consumer society and the expansion of technological and scientific modes of knowledge which cannot be contained within traditional moral paradigms. In each case, too, there is a close relationship between theory and practice leading to an unprecedented aesthetic self-consciousness and awareness of the problematic situation of the contemporary writer in relation to historical actuality and fictional tradition.

Clearly, the reasons for the *absence* of women writers from postmodernist debates from the 1960s to the 1980s is similarly multiple and complex, overdetermined by economic, social, psychological, political, and aesthetic factors. *One* reason, in particular, however, is advanced here and will become the focus of the argument in this book. At the moment when postmodernism is forging its identity through articulating the exhaustion of the existential belief in self-presence and self-fulfilment and through the dispersal of the universal subject of liberalism, *feminism* (ostensibly, at any rate) is assembling *its* cultural identity in what appears to be the opposite direction. During the 1960s, as Vonnegut waves a fond goodbye to character in fiction, women writers are beginning, *for the first time in history*, to construct an identity out of the recognition that women need to discover, and must fight for, a sense of unified selfhood, a rational, coherent, effective identity. As male writers lament its demise, women writers have not yet experienced that subjectivity which will give them a sense of personal autonomy, continuous identity, a history and agency in the world.

SUBJECTIVITY, FEMININITY, AND THE POSTMODERN PERSON

There have been numerous attempts to define both post-modernism and feminism, and clearly neither constitutes a homogeneous category – nor should they. However, there is a striking set of opposed – yet complementary – issues around the questions of subjectivity and authority which occur again and again in separate discussions of each movement. The philosophical transition from a Hegelian or Marxian understanding of the subject in history to a structuralist or post-structuralist one is a shift fundamentally from consciousness to language. Postmodernism situates itself epistemologically at the point where the epistemic subject characterized in terms of historical experience, interiority, and consciousness has given way to the 'decentred' subject identified through the public, impersonal signifying practices of other similarly 'decentred' subjects. It may even situate itself at a point where there is no 'subject' and no history in the old sense at all. There is only a system of linguistic structures, a textual construction, a play of differences in the Derridean sense. 'Identity' is simply the illusion produced through the manipulation of irreconcilable and contradictory language games. In Raymond Federman's postmodernist fiction, *Double or Nothing* [1971], for example, 'narrators', 'characters', and implied 'readers' dissolve into the categorizations of grammar, where the play of proper names ridicules our nostalgia for stable identity:

FIRST PERSON
or
THIRD PERSON

FIRST PERSON is more restrictive   more subjective   more personal   harder
THIRD PERSON is more objective   more impersonal   more encompassing   easier

I could try both ways:
I was standing on the upper deck next to a girl called Mary ...
No Peggy
He was standing on the upper deck next to a girl called Mary ...
No Peggy.
(Comes out the same).

(*Double or Nothing*, p. 99)

One detects through the ridicule that nostalgia for the full subject also present in Vonnegut and Barth. The play with pronouns reminds the initiated (post-structuralist-informed) reader of Benveniste's analysis of the relationship between language and subjectivity: that the subject of the enunciation always exceeds the subject of the utterance, the 'I' can never be fully present in what it says of itself. Postmodernism's rejection of representation is premised on an acknowledgement of the necessary gap between subjectivities (grammatical and existential), yet for most postmodernist writers there is still a longing, a nostalgia for the discovery of an identity behind signification, a desire to close the gap and locate the 'self' in pure consciousness. Several commentators on postmodern art have drawn attention to this. As Hal Foster argues:

> To speak of a fragmented subject is to presuppose a prior moment or model in which the subject is whole and complete, not split in relation to desire or decentred in relation to language; such a concept, whether heuristic or historical, is problematic. On the Right this tendency is manifest in a nostalgic insistence on the good strong self, pragmatic, patriarchal, and ideological in the extreme. Yet the Left positions on the subject are only somewhat less troublesome. Diagnoses of our culture as regressive, one dimensional, schizophrenic ... often preserve this bourgeois subject, if only in opposition, if only by default. (Foster 1984, p. 77)

Women writers clearly occupy a rather different position in relation to such covert postmodernist nostalgia. Subjectivity, historically constructed and expressed through the phenomenological equation self/other, necessarily rests masculine 'selfhood' upon feminine 'otherness'. The subjective centre of socially dominant discourses (from Descartes's philosophical, rational 'I' to Lacan's psychoanalytic phallic/symbolic) in terms of power, agency, autonomy has been a 'universal' subject which has established its identity through the invisible marginalization or exclusion of what it has also defined as 'femininity' (whether this is the non-rational, the body, the emotions, or the presymbolic). The 'feminine' thus becomes that which cannot be expressed because it exists outside the realm of symbolic signification. Constituted through a male gaze and thus endowed with the mysteriousness of one whose *objective* status is seen as absolute and definitive,

8

One is not born, but becomes a woman. No biological, psychological or economic fate determines the figure that the human female presents in society: it is civilisation as a whole that produces this creature, intermediate between male and eunuch, which is described as 'feminine'. (de Beauvoir 1972, p. 249)

In the dialectical relationship between traditional humanism and the postmodern anti-humanism emerging in the 1960s, women continue to be displaced. How can they long for, reject, or synthesize a new mode of being from a thesis which has never contained or expressed what they have felt their historical experience to be? Feminist theory at this time thus focused less on deconstructing the discursive formations which position the subject than on analysing the socially constructed differences between the sexes as the chief source of women's oppression, and on examining sex roles as a mode of social control. Its emergent aesthetics drew not on structuralism or anti-humanist discourses but on humanist Marxism, liberal theories of inalienable rights, sociological role and social learning theory, and on theories of psychology which emphasized the need to 'actualize' and 'strengthen' the self-in-the-world. In particular, it emphasized the ideological production of 'femininity' as the 'other' of patriarchy and the need, therefore, for women to become 'real' subjects and to discover their 'true' selves. Thus, with a search for a *coherent and unified feminine subject*, began the deconstruction of the myth of woman as absolute Other and its exposure as a position within masculine discourse.

The practice of consciousness-raising, which aimed precisely at the forging of an individual and collective sense of identity and subjecthood in these terms, epitomizes the distance separating feminism from postmodernism. Postmodernism expresses nostalgia for but loss of belief in the concept of the human subject as an agent effectively intervening in history, through its fragmentation of discourses, language games, and decentring of subjectivity. Feminism seeks a subjective identity, a sense of effective agency and history for women which has hitherto been denied them by the dominant culture. Postmodernist writers express the disintegration of the potency of that 'individual vision' mediated through the 'unique' style of modernism and stress the inability of the contemporary subject to locate 'himself' historically. Ultimately, what has been lost is faith in the historically representative and ordering power of narrative itself and in the unified subject who believes 'he' is producing the world in producing a representation of it (see Jameson 1981). Feminist writers, in the meantime, *appear* to be pursuing the sort of definition of identity and relationship to history which postmodernists have rejected. For many women there can be no prior subject or self whose fragmentation becomes a political necessity, source of nostalgic regret, or hedonistic *jouissance*.

In fact, and for this reason, I would argue that women's writing, whether feminist or not, has largely existed in a highly contradictory relationship to both the dominant liberal conception of subjectivity and writing and to the classic 'postmodernist' deconstruction of this liberal trajectory. Much women's writing can, in fact, be seen not as an attempt to define an isolated individual ego but to discover a collective concept of subjectivity which foregrounds the construction of identity *in relationship*. Historically, such a concept of self appears strongly in women's writing well before 'postmodernism', though I shall argue that its emphasis has shifted more recently as the lessons of post-structuralism have been absorbed. This concept grows out of women's particular history and out of the collective politics of the women's movement. It appears in Virginia Woolf's writing, for example, (see chapter three), where the exploration of a dispersed/relational/collective concept of identity becomes a weapon in the killing of the 'Angel in the House'. Woolf seeks to become aware of the paralysing and alienating determinations of the myth of Woman, but equally to avoid embracing an identity articulated through an ideal of contained, coherent, 'proportioned' subjectivity which for her expressed the dominant cultural norm of masculinity.

Woolf desired that a woman writer should write *as a woman*, but as one who has forgotten this fact. To ask 'Who am I?' is to articulate a question which usually assumes an a priori belief in an ultimate unity and fixity of being, a search for a rational, coherent, essential 'self' which can speak and know itself. For Woolf, like many women writers positioned in a patriarchal society, a more appropriate question would be 'What represents me?' This question carries an implicit and necessary recognition of alienation: the phenomenological perception that 'I' am never at one with myself because always and ever already constituted by others according to whom, and yet outside of what, I take myself to be. For the woman writer, the further implication is that, if the 'I' is spoken or positioned in a discourse where subjectivity, the norm of human-ness, is male, then 'I' is doubly displaced, 'I' can never in any material or metaphysical sense be at one with myself. If 'I' can accept this, however, then I may be able to see the possibility of shifting from an identity defined necessarily through alienation to one defined potentially through relationship in a more equal society.

Woolf writes in *The Waves* [1931]:

> And now I ask, who am I? I have been talking of Bernard, Neville, Jinny, Susan, Rhoda and Louis. Am I all of them? Am I one and distinct? I do not know. We sat here together. But now Percival is dead, and Rhoda is dead; we are divided; we are not here. Yet I cannot find any obstacle separating us. There is no division between me and them. As I talked I felt 'I am you'. This difference we make so much out of, this identity we so fervently cherish was overcome. (p. 248)

It is the relational connection of being not simply an 'I' but also a 'you' in the eyes of others which stabilizes the shifter, the indexical deictic 'I', which thus *reassures* Bernard of his identity and rescues him from the feeling that he is 'a man without a self' (p. 245). Woolf has accepted and fictionally embodied the recognition that differentiation is not necessarily separateness, distance, and alienation from others, but a form of *connection* to others.

Other women writers, however, have been more concerned to express the inevitability of alienation in relations formed within the structures of a society which has only allowed women the position of 'other', there to confirm the subjectivity of the male but excluded from the subject position themselves. One image of this is madness, schizophrenia, paranoia:

> Sun and shade are tricks and I trust nothing and I understand why we fear the telephone, why, although we have cut the cables, we still lift the receiver and wait for the voice we dread; and I understand mirrors and try to track the point in their

11

depth when we become nothing – yes, I look in the tall mirror in the corridor outside the sister's office and I know it is set there to trap us, like the mirrors in the department stores, that the house detective may catch us picking over the haberdashery of ourselves and shoplifting. Who owns us now? Is it our crime that we steal from ourselves? (Janet Frame, *Faces in the Water* [1961], p. 201)

'We' have become commodities in a police state, 'possessed' by others, both alienated *and* criminal in our desire for *self*-possession. Mirrors offer an illusory image of wholeness and completeness, the promise of the security of possession, but they too are agents of oppression and control, enticing us with their spurious identifications. Telephones offer not the comfort of relationship through communication but an echo of the fragments and part-objects of our own minds which we obsessively project on to a dead world. If, for Woolf, women function like magnifying mirrors, reflecting back the male ego to itself, here the woman recognizes her cultural identification *as an image* and experiences herself as nothing. She knows that she cannot see herself with her own eyes:

> The tool for representing, for objectifying one's experience in order to deal with it, culture, is so saturated with male bias that women almost never have a chance to see themselves culturally through their own eyes. So that finally, signals from their direct experience that conflict with prevailing (male) culture are denied and repressed. (Firestone 1970, p. 157)

That way madness lies indeed.

If women have traditionally been positioned in terms of 'otherness', then the desire to become subjects (which dominates the first phase of post-1960s feminism) is likely to be stronger than the desire to deconstruct, decentre, or fragment subjectivity (which dominates post-1960s postmodernist practice and post-structuralist theory). They have not yet *experienced* this 'whole' or 'unitary' or 'essential' subjectivity. However, it seems to me that it is the gradual recognition of the value of construing human identity in terms of relationship and dispersal, rather than as a unitary, self-directing, isolated ego, which has fundamentally altered the course of modern and contemporary women's writing concerned to challenge gender stereotypes. It is this recognition, brought to full consciousness, which has led feminist writing closer to a 'postmodernist' conception of subjectivity. However, the pursuit of just such a unitary, essential self was a necessary phase in order that women writers might fully understand the historical and social construction of gender and identity. Certainly, for women in the 1960s and early 1970s, 'unity' rather than dispersal seemed to offer more hope for political change. To believe that there might be a 'natural' or 'true' self which may be discovered through lifting the misrepresentations of an oppressive social system is to provide nurturance and fuel for revolutionary hope and practice. Woolf, of course, was among the first feminist writers to emphasize the inauthenticity and the danger, for women, in adhering to this belief.

In fact, insights gained as feminism passed through a *necessary* stage of pursuing unity have produced an alternative conception of the subject as constructed through *relationship*, rather than postmodernism/post-structuralism's anti-humanist *rejection* of the subject. In many ways postmodernists have developed the modernist aesthetic of impersonality along the lines of Lacanian alienation, Derridean assault on presence and origin, and an Althusserian refusal of agency and determination as located in the individual. Much contemporary feminist fictional writing, however, has accommodated humanist beliefs in individual agency and the necessity and possibility of self-reflection and historical continuity as the basis of personal identity. It has modified the traditional forms of such beliefs, however, in order to emphasize the provisionality and positionality of identity, the historical and social construction of gender, and the discursive production of knowledge and power. What many of these texts suggest is that it is possible to experience oneself as a strong and coherent agent in the world, *at the same time* as understanding the extent to which identity and gender are socially constructed and represented.

For, while feminists have come to recognize acutely the *impersonal* social and historical determinants of women's oppression, that experience has itself developed in them strongly 'humanist' or 'personal' qualities: co-operativeness, nurturance, an awareness of self-in-relationship and of the relativity of fields of knowledge and totalizing systems which attempt to systematize individual and concrete human actions. Much recent feminist fiction and theory does indeed reflect a rejection and deconstruction of humanism in terms of its liberal contradictions and illusions which perpetuate women's marginalization and exclusion. Such writing, however, also preserves a belief that human beings *can* act upon the world as partially autonomous agents who can thus determine to some extent what they shall be. Many of the novels examined later in this book affirm a belief in the need for 'strong' selves without presenting the self as an unchanging, ahistorical essence or as an isolated ego struggling aggressively and competitively to define itself as unique, different, separate.

Thus the 'postmodernist' moment of feminist writing has, it seems to me, developed but modified an adherence to a fundamentally humanist concern with the subject in relationship. One of the most vociferous objections to postmodernism from both right and left (Graff, Jameson, Eagleton, Habermas) is that it has eschewed any potential oppositional power and simply added itself to the forms, surfaces, and obsessions of an anti-humanist, consumerist, and alienated culture. One of the critiques of early feminist and New Left rhetoric is that it was premised on naïvely opposed, distinct, and unified realms of the 'personal' and the 'social'. The latter was seen simply to distort, oppress, and repress the former in order to displace it from its 'natural' state. My argument is that most contemporary feminisms have refused to espouse an extreme anti-humanism but they have also recognized the contradictions in that liberal-humanist theory which posits a natural 'self' outside, or prior to, the social. What they have articulated instead is a core belief in a self which, although contradictory, non-unitary, and historically produced through 'discursive' and ideological formations, nevertheless has a material existence and history in actual human relationships, beginning crucially with those between infant and caretakers at the start of life.

Even in its 'essentialist' modes, in fact, feminism has radicalized the subject at least as much as postmodernism/post-structuralism. Although early feminism situated resistance at the site of the 'personal' and the 'experiential', consciousness-raising developed a deep understanding of how 'consciousness' itself, that liberal

centre of self, is produced within historically materialist practices and actual relations of power, and cannot therefore be seen
as simply productive and determining of the social world.
'Inside' and 'outside' ceased to be discrete; subjectivity was
recognized as a relative and shifting positionality. In these terms
there are striking similarities between the 'subjects' of feminism
and those of postmodernism, yet writers on each rarely make
explicit connections between them. Rachael Blau du Plessis,
defining a feminist writing practice, argues, for example:

> One may assert that any female cultural practice that makes
> the 'meaning production process' itself 'the site of struggle'
> may be considered feminist. These authors are 'feminist'
> because they construct a variety of oppositional strategies to
> the depiction of gender institutions in narrative. A writer
> expresses dissent from an ideological formation by attacking
> elements of narrative that repeat, sustain or embody the
> values and attitudes in question. So after breaking the
> sentence, a rupture with the internalization of the authorities
> and voices of dominance, the woman writer will create that
> further rupture ... breaking the sequence – the expected
> order. (Blau du Plessis 1985, p. 34)

Her definition emphasizes the discursive production of
meaning within institutionalized power relations and the need,
therefore, to 'break the sentence', fragment the hierarchies of
discourse which reproduce ideological formations. Her attack is
clearly, though not explicitly, focused on what post-structuralists
have referred to as the 'master narratives', the 'grand plots' of
history which produce and legitimate social practices and
relationships including those between men and women. Victor
Burgin sees the political import of postmodernism in terms
very similar to Blau du Plessis's understanding of feminism.
Criticizing left-oppositional criticism which develops out of
Romanticism and is the culmination of liberal-humanist conceptions of the autonomously expressive individual and the 'people'
as a projection of the dream of a pre-capitalist organic society,
he sees the political value of postmodernism in its insight that:

> What have expired are the absolute guarantees issued by
> overriding metaphysical systems. 'Certainties and necessities'

are now seen as inescapably *positional*, derived from, and applied within, complex networks of mainly local and contingent conditions; it is thus that Lyotard sees the great legitimating narratives, 'good for all time', as having given way to a proliferation of smaller narratives, 'good for the moment', or at best 'for the foreseeable future'. (Burgin 1986, pp. 198–9)

These statements reveal the commitment of feminism *and* postmodernism to the project of deconstructing both the subject and the 'master narratives' of history. In each case there will be nostalgia for their loss: from 'neo-conservative' postmodernists perhaps, and from feminists who have remained rooted in the earlier essentialist understanding of the subject. Any account of the relation between feminism and postmodernism must, however, acknowledge their historical differences. Postmodernism assumes or even rejects relationships which, as feminists have rightly argued, women have *never* experienced as subjects in their own right: relationships to the dominant literary and political institutions which legitimate and reproduce the 'master narratives', for example. Furthermore, the obvious fact remains that, historically, men and women have experienced both the world and their own selves in very different ways, and it is the central argument of this book, therefore, that despite common concerns the postmodern deconstruction of subjectivity is as problematic for women as the liberal construction of self.

IMPERSONALITY, MODERNIST AESTHETICS, AND WOMEN WRITERS

A similar case could be argued, of course, for women's relation to the definition of modernism. The central modernist pre-occupation with the transcendent artist, the impersonal author seeking 'objective correlatives' for 'his' state of mind, or paring 'his' fingernails in the background like an indifferent Deity, bears only a very partial resemblance to the fictional concerns of, for example, Woolf, Richardson, Mansfield, or Stein. In these writers, an emphasis on the relational embeddedness of artistic production in social and historical forms and experience and in personal relationships also gives rise to a very different conceptualization of subjectivity. In their writing, alienation is expressed not as a *necessary* condition of 'human existence' (a consequence of the opacity of the 'soul'), but as a consequence of the *social* and *historical* contradictions of women's experience (their constitution as 'others' who help to coalesce masculine subjectivity through the denial of their own). Mrs Ramsay's experience of nihilism, her sinking into the wedge-shaped core of darkness in Woolf's *To the Lighthouse*, resembles Kurz's perception of the dark absence at the centre of the human soul in *Heart of Darkness* or the echo of nothingness from the Marabar Caves in *A Passage to India*. Her experience, however, is presented as the consequence of her social situation, her positioning as a late Victorian wife and mother, a being so totally dependent on others for self-definition that solitude can only be experienced as disintegration of identity. Mrs Ramsay's experience is *not*, however, presented as a symbol of the essential solipsism of the human condition, as critics of modernism tend to assert. In my view, this misreads Woolf's aims and concerns by accounting for them in terms of *inappropriate* (though dominant) cultural and literary paradigms.

Judith Kegan Gardiner (1982) has argued that fictions by male writers in the modern period are often characterized by splitting, fragmentation, and atomization, particularly of character. The more characteristic mode in women's writing is dissolution and mergence, again particularly of characters. It is as if the axiomatically *masculine*, integrated subject of nineteenth-century fiction has fragmented under the weight of its own idealizations, undermined by developments in twentieth-century culture and history. The alienated hero of modern fiction is simply the other side of the coin of a self conceived in terms of containedness, difference, autonomy. Similarly, the breakdown of the 'master-plots' of nineteenth-century history reveals the repression and exclusion required for their mediation through the conventional fictional linear (male) quest. Thus both modernism in its obsession with 'impersonality' and postmodernism with its persistently 'decentred' subject displace order and fixity from the 'personal' and the 'human' to the *impersonal* structures of language and history conceived as an essentially static and synchronic order.

Eliot's essay 'Tradition and the individual talent' (1919) asserts the separation of the mind which suffers from the mind which creates, and calls for a fully 'impersonal' art. His essay on *Ulysses* (1923) asserts the need to substitute myth for history. Ortega y Gasset talks of the 'dehumanization' of art. Clive Bell seeks to displace human feeling and experience on to a universal 'significant form' which resembles Joseph Frank's later definition of modernism in terms of 'spatial form' (1947). Critics such as David Lodge explain postmodernist fictions as radically indeterminate texts which foreground the arbitrariness of all interpretative constructs, while for John Barth formal exhaustion and parody provide a common definition. In all of these critical accounts and explanations of modernism and postmodernism, each movement is constituted in predominantly *formal* terms; each is viewed as seeking, in different ways, to displace subjective experience on to *objective* forms or structures.

Of course, impersonality or formal distance as the basis of an aesthetic is neither *intrinsically* reactionary *nor* progressive in political terms. I am not suggesting that the significantly different *aesthetic* emphases in postmodernist fiction compared to contemporary women's writing bear an intrinsic and *necessary* relationship to their political implications. Indeed, 'impersonality' has much to offer, aesthetically and ultimately politically, to women writers. Patricia Meyer Spacks, for example, has argued that the early twentieth-century aesthetic retreat from personal authority as a rhetorical pose allowed women writers (whose relation to this had always been deeply problematic) to be free at last from the label of 'sensibility' (Spacks 1976, p. 27). Woolf, herself influenced by Bell's aesthetic of significant form as a mode of projecting the personal on to the sphere of objective forms, also welcomed those historical changes which were enabling women writers to shift away from the personal. In 'Women and fiction' (1929) she argued:

> The change which has turned the English woman from a nondescript influence, fluctuating and vague, to a voter, a wage-earner, a responsible citizen, has given her both in her life and in her art a turn towards the impersonal. Her relations now are not only emotional; they are intellectual, they are political. The old system which condemned her to squint askance at things through the eyes or through the interests of husband or brother, has given place to the direct

18

and practical interests of one who must act for herself, and not merely influence the acts of others. Hence her attention is being directed away from the personal centre which engaged it exclusively in the past to the impersonal, and her novels naturally become more critical of society, and less analytical of individual lives. (In Barrett 1979, p. 50)

Here it is evident, however, that 'impersonality' may mean different things to different writers. For Roger Fry, 'impersonality' corresponds to the aesthetic need for distance from the immediate impingement of psychology and emotion. Although Woolf was influenced by the concept of 'significant form', Fry's and Bell's ideas bear more resemblance to Eliot's concept of an 'objective correlative' and to his distinction between 'feeling' and 'emotion', than to the 'impersonality' espoused and advocated by Woolf in the above essay. 'Autonomy theory', 'significant form', 'impersonality' emphasize above all the virtues of distance, separateness, objectivity, independence. These are the values of nineteenth-century science and of Cartesian rationalism. The construction of modernism almost *entirely* in such terms was reinforced, of course, by the popular spread of the New Criticism, with its emphasis on objectivity, rigour, and intrinsic meaning. The New Critics developed Eliot's ideas about impersonality in their concern with the 'poetic persona', the speaker in the literary work being necessarily a dramatic construction who bears no relation to the person who writes the poem. 'Irony', 'wit', 'paradox', 'ambiguity' define literary discourse in terms which further prise the poetic 'I' away from any identification with the actual poet or of the words of the poem from reference to the world outside. As in the theorization of modernist literature in Ortega y Gasset's work, there is the recurrent proposition that literature – here, the novel – 'cannot propagate philosophical, political, sociological or moral ideas: it can be nothing beyond a novel' (Ortega y Gasset 1968, p. 94).

The common thread running through these theories of impersonality is that separation of the object of knowledge from the mind which perceives it pursued in twentieth-century phenomenology. As far as possible, the object must be perceived in relation to itself, rather than in relation to the experiences/feelings/thoughts of the perceiving mind. Outside itself, it may

19

be perceived only in relation to the system of literature itself, so that an impersonal elitist 'tradition' substitutes for the personal and collective experience of all those human beings – including women – who have been written out of history in its very construction.

My argument is that women writers, on the whole, have not felt comfortable with an aesthetics of impersonality as it appears in many modernist and postmodernist manifestos. The reason for this is the overvaluation in the first instance of exclusive objectivity, of distance, autonomy, separateness, discrete form, and the disappearance in the second instance of human connection via meaningful affection, communication, or ethical belief. Furthermore, although post-structuralism has rejected the modernist ideal of art in a closed field, it has attempted to reconstruct modernism in the broadly postmodernist terms of ludic transgression, refusal of representation and totalization, and dispersal of subjectivity. In both readings, what disappears are the relations of human subjects engaged in meaningful historical action.

A blank refusal of the subject simply reproduces the effects of capitalist relations at the level of the text. One can see in much modernist, postmodernist, and post-structuralist writing an obsessive desire to displace human experience entirely by the substitution of intellectual categories and formal, 'impersonal' structures. Marx emphasized that contradictions within capitalist society are not simply impersonal constructs; they are lived out through experience and do not have an independent existence outside people. In many ways, the influence of Althusser (though central in the understanding of the construction of subjects) has been to reinforce a traditional western *rationalist* suspicion of the personal and the experiential. For feminism the emphasis on 'impersonality' in all of these theories is problematic because deeply at odds both with the practices of consciousness-raising and with women's own experience of subordination and objectification as *lived realities*.

Perhaps more politically effective than deconstructing subjects would be their *reconstruction*, the production of alternative modes and models of subjectivity. It is their mediation of a subject constructed historically through relations with other subjects, rather than a subject positioned through discourse in terms of 'alienation' or *'jouissance'*, that distinguishes the concerns of many recent women writers from those of the dominant modernist or postmodernist aesthetic. Their work cannot therefore be read in terms of the literary canon, for it presents a fundamental challenge to both its institutionalized reification of 'form' as the 'essence' of the work and its liberal heritage of 'expressive realism': literature as the expression of a universal unity which is 'human nature'. For these reasons, among others, it is vitally important that feminist critics *refuse* the reading of twentieth-century writing by women in terms of a narrow (but dominant) 'modernist' or 'postmodernist' aesthetics of impersonality, autonomy, and dehumanization.

What has generally been overlooked here is the connection between the 'impersonality' advocated in such an aesthetic and the popularized psychological conception of the construction of identity. In most psychoanalytic theories, selfhood is achieved predominantly by *separation*. The dependent infant is regarded as having achieved autonomous subjectivity when, regarding the primary caretaker (almost always the mother or another *woman*) as simply an object against which it defines its subjectivity, an instrument of its needs, it becomes a 'self' by breaking free of her and asserting its own separateness, its difference, its boundaries. That 'otherness' analysed by feminists from de Beauvoir onwards thus becomes (from the male point of view) the *necessary* condition of women, so that separation and objectivity rather than relationship and connection become the markers of identity. Thus Jessica Benjamin suggests that 'women's own denial of their subjectivity corresponds to the male perception of the mother. She becomes in her own mind, instrument, earth mother. Thus she serves men as their Other, their counterpart, the side of themselves they repress' (Benjamin 1980, pp. 44–5). Furthermore, for a self perceived as constructed in terms of difference, continuity of subjective identity depends upon the objectification of all others. Individuality is thus established, in this model, through the denial, imaginatively and emotionally (if not cognitively), of the existence of others as 'subjects'. Thus can one understand the disintegration of the rational, autonomous, nineteenth-century ego into the alienated, tortured solipsism of the modernist 'self': a self which fears relationship and communication but is locked into a chess game where control of the other becomes a prerequisite for subjective definition. Such control, however, destroys both the basis of human affection and also self-respect itself: 'My nerves are bad tonight. Yes bad. Stay with me. Speak to me. Why do you never speak. Speak' (Eliot, *The Wasteland* [1923], p. 31).

In my view, many twentieth-century women writers (whether consciously feminists or not) have sought alternative conceptions of subjectivity, expressing a definition of self in relationship which does not make identity dependent axiomatically upon the maintenance of boundaries and distance, nor upon the subjugation of the other. However, for the most part, the institution of literary criticism has ensured, through the marginalization or misinterpretation of their works (in the terms of the dominant aesthetic theories), that this potentially radical aspect of their work is silenced through its non-representation. This is as true of Virginia Woolf as of more recent writers like Anita Brookner or Grace Paley:

> Both in theory and practice our culture knows only one form of individuality: the male stance of over-differentiation, of splitting off and denying the tendencies towards sameness and reciprocal responsiveness. In this 'false differentiation' the other subject remains an object rather than emerging as a person in her/his right. This way of establishing and protecting individuality dovetails with the dualistic, objective posturing of western rationality. To be a woman is to be excluded from this rational individualism, to be either an object of it or a threat to it. To be a man is not merely to assert one's side of the duality, the supremacy of the rational subject. It is also to insist that the dualism, splitting and boundaries between the male and female postures are upheld. (Benjamin 6–7)

FEMINISM AND REALISM: THE 'LIBERAL SELF'

Much early feminist writing, however, simply pursued the desire to *reverse* this duality rather than to deconstruct it (as in the so-called 'novel of liberation' by, for example, Alther, Jong, Rossner, French). Many of these texts adhered fundamentally to a liberal-humanist belief in the possibility of discovering a 'true' self, and simply substituted female for male heroes and preserved more or less traditional quest plots. The concept of a 'person' can only ever be constructed out of available ideologies and discourses, and the dominance in the novel tradition of a liberal consensus offered to these writers a vindication of the apparent 'naturalness' of personal experience. The traditional realist mode of the romantic quest plot seemed the obvious structure through which to portray the self as an essence which might be 'discovered' or as a unity which might be 'willed' into existence. Such fictions thus set out to *deny* difference, to insert women into a fundamentally unchallenged social and fictional structure (usually quest or picaresque) where sexual conquest and self-realization were, however, to be pursued by a *female* protagonist. Alternatively, difference could be *celebrated*. In this instance, the traditional designations of rationality as masculine and 'emotionality' as feminine were accepted, but the priority which has invariably been accorded to the former was simply shifted to the latter in order to construct an alternative women's tradition and perspective.

Feminist intervention here, therefore, largely took the form either of a simple reversal of existing stereotypes or of exploring the difficulty of discovering and acting upon a 'true' self, given the social roles available to women (Marilyn French's *The Women's Room* [1977], for example, explores this problem). Such fictions did little to challenge the dominance of expressive realism with its consensus aesthetics: its assumption of the authority of omniscience or the veracity of personal experience in first-person narration; its coherent, consistent characters whose achievement of self-determination signifies a new maturity; its assumption of a causal relationship between the 'real' inner essence of a person and the ultimate achievement of selfhood through acts in the world. Nor did they challenge the dominant liberal view of subjectivity, with its belief in the unified self and a universal human nature. Such writing can, however, be seen as a necessary phase, a point of crisis and contradiction which allowed for the self-conscious development of fictional modes which would more radically challenge dominant concepts of gender and identity. The 'celebration of difference' novel, for example, though 'essentialist' in its conception of the unity of woman and naïve in its reversal of the liberal theory of the subject (so that women simply become the moral, spiritual, and psychological superiors of men, who are all characterized in terms of denial of emotionality, over-rationalization, competitiveness, and even brutality), did suggest the necessity for what Adrienne Rich (1972) has called a 're-vision of literature': a return to the traditional preoccupations of the psychological and domestic novel, but self-consciously from the perspective of writing as a woman. This emerges strongly in the 1970s in some of the writing of Margaret Drabble, Doris Lessing, and Alison Lurie. The quest for the basis of a female 'unity' further led to the exploration of myth, symbol, and archetype, which has since been developed in more radical directions (in the work of Margaret Atwood and Emma Tennant, for example) in order to explore the role of symbolic systems and unconscious factors in the construction of subjectivity. In other writers, the gradual recognition of the naïvety of such an imagined 'unity' reinforced their growing awareness of the heterogeneity of women (in terms of class, race, sexuality) and the intransigence of desire at unconscious levels (as in the work of Doris Lessing, Fay Weldon, Alice Walker).

Shulamith Firestone, in 1971, recognized the necessity for such an 'essentialist' feminist phase:

> The development of 'female' art ... is progressive: an exploration of strictly female reality is a necessary step to correct the warp in a sexually biased culture. It is only after we have integrated the dark side of the moon into our world view that we can begin to talk seriously of universal culture. (Firestone 1971, p. 167)

It is a stage in the recognition of oppression: if one has always been defined as an 'object' in someone else's gaze or discourse, then full identity will be conceived in the terms of adopting their subject position for oneself, asking the question 'What am I?' Such a question posits oneself as both a sovereign subject and one's own object, but it does allow women to experience the subject position (whatever its illusoriness) which the sexual differential man/subject: woman/other has never allowed them in relation to men. Gayatri Chakravorty Spivak, herself a deconstructionist feminist, has argued that such a gesture must, indeed, 'continue to supplement the collective and substantive work of "restoring" women's history and literature' (Spivak 1983, p. 186). Once women have experienced themselves as 'subjects', then they can begin to problematize and to deconstruct the socially constructed subject positions available to them, and to recognize that an inversion of the valuation of 'maleness' and 'femaleness' will not in itself undermine the social construction of 'masculinity' and 'femininity':

> It still remains *politically* essential for feminists to defend women *as* women in order to counteract the patriarchal oppression that precisely despises women as women. But an 'undeconstructed' form of [such] feminism, unaware of the metaphysical nature of gender identities, runs the risk of becoming an inverted form of sexism. (Moi 1985, p. 13)

Recognizing the inauthenticity of the liberal ideal of a unified self has not, however, been easy for women novelists. Prevailing twentieth-century aesthetic norms have emphasized concepts of 'organic wholeness', unity, vision, coherence (properties of the historical world in realism, of the human mind in modernism, and of language in structuralist aesthetics). It is difficult to give up the belief in a 'real' or 'natural' world which can be discovered outside the 'social' or 'cultural' or 'socially constructed' one and which can be discovered through quest, altered states of consciousness, different lifestyles, political action, or mystical belief. It is tempting to believe that characters in fiction can be constructed to provide positive role models by reflecting the 'true self' of woman as opposed to the 'false self' of patriarchal ideology (conceived often as a concerted conspiracy). But what is this 'true self'? Where does it reside? In the 1960s and 1970s surely it is a construct of dominant concepts of subjectivity drawn, for example, from liberal theory, popular Freudianism, moral philosophy, and the new psychologies and theories of human rights, all of which emphasize a potentially free, autonomous, self-directing, non-contradictory, consistent essence which is 'self'. For writers like Alther and Jong, the self is seen in relation to a concept of internalizing something situated outside it, 'the social', and is shaped out of sex roles and sex stereotypes which distort its true nature. Becoming a 'person' involves, simply, throwing off these roles and struggling to discover the 'inner essence'. Such novels often begin with a comic hedonism (as in *Fear of Flying* [1974], for example) but end with irresolution or inauthenticity, their liberated women 'integrated into British life at its roots', as parodied by Doris Lessing (*The Golden Notebook* [1962]) and with the 'zipless fuck' exposed as the chimera it has always been.

Particularly prominent in such fiction is ego psychology's version of the liberal self. Here the 'unified self' has to be willed, created, put together through a struggle with numerous social obstacles involving sacrifice, loss, and conflict. Such narratives often take a confessional form where the implicit split in first-person narration between the narrating 'I' and the narrated 'I' (the experiencing self) is explicitly foregrounded. The mature 'full self', represented by the narrating 'I' situated at the temporal end of the events to be told, is the subject which has discovered itself, come to knowledge of its 'true' nature. This 'I' records its own progress as an experiential 'I' struggling to throw off the false social roles and attain the present position of unity and liberation. As with the use of this form in Defoe's *Moll Flanders* (1722), however, the reader often has the impression that the author is more interested in the celebration of the exploits (usually sexual) of the experiencing 'I', than in the enlightened justifications and rationalizations of the narrating 'I'. The widespread use of this narrative form by women writers in the early 1970s coincided with feminist ideas about women becoming 'authors' of their own lives, struggling to express and define themselves through coming to terms with their past experiences. Ironically (and pertinently for this argument), at more or less the same moment, structuralists and post-structuralists like Barthes and Foucault were beginning to proclaim *their* liberation in theories of the '*Death* of the Author', where 'Notions of originality, authenticity and presence ... are undermined' (Hutcheon 1987, p. 17).

Unfortunately, the publicity received by novels like *Kinflicks* and *Fear of Flying* fostered a popular (and academic) image of feminist fiction in the above terms. The consequence of this was that the more subversive (though less ostentatious) re-examination of plot and construction of subjectivity in fiction by writers such as Margaret Drabble, Ann Quin, Brigid Brophy, Muriel Spark, and Ann Tyler, for example, was on the whole ignored or misrepresented by the literary establishment. The literary academy might recognize a distorted image of its own favourite obsessions – self-discovery, quest, unity – in novels like *Kinflicks*, but it complained that apart from the reversal of sex roles there was little else which was innovatory in such fictions. Typical of the (male) academy's response, therefore, to nearly *all* fiction by women writers in the post-1960s period, is Frederick Karl's view:

> I think that the lack of experiment, the paucity of narrative daring, the stress on traditional storytelling ... is connected to the failure of the women's experience to be projected onto the larger world. That desire to resolve old wounds through love and bonding, that forsaking of achievement in the larger world, is reflected in the unadventurous use of narrative, plot details, character. The 'female experience', like all other experiences, must be handled in modern or postmodern terms, and yet repeatedly novels limning this experience are old-fashioned in structure, based on Edwardian models. (Karl 1985, p. 424)

Again, however, the assumption is that there are only two alternatives for the writer: the continuation of traditional realist concerns or the espousal of a radical 'postmodernist' refusal of totality, the subject, morality, and history. The above texts represent in their writing and reception the tenacious continuation of a preference for 'expressive realism' which mediates fundamentally liberal-humanist concepts of subjectivity. To attack such a conception, moreover, is often assumed by literary critics (feminists included) to be an attack on humans themselves. Derrida has shown the pervasiveness and inescapability of our tendency to refer all questions about the meaning of representations to a singular founding origin – 'human nature', 'common sense', 'God' – or presence, which we imagine lies behind them. The confessional form of novels such as *Kinflicks* and *Fear of Flying*, in particular, reinforces such a 'metaphysics of presence': the self appears, directly, to be telling, 'speaking', its own story. Speech, as Derrida has also emphasized in his critique of Saussure, seems more 'direct' than writing, appears to reflect immediately a 'presence' which lies in the speaker's head or heart or experience. 'To thine own self be true' was a piece of advice which ushered in the 'new' humanism. Yet, despite our

27

sociological awareness of the construction of subjectivity and our psychoanalytic perception that consciousness cannot know its own unconscious, we still adhere to assumptions about the individual which are tied historically to this earlier phase.

In fact feminist critiques of the liberal conception of self have appeared increasingly over the last few years (see, for example, Cora Kaplan 1986; Lloyd 1984; Belsey 1985a), and all have analysed the ways in which the 'subject' produced through this version of humanism is, explicitly or implicity, a masculine subject. Above all, liberalism depends upon 'consent and this in turn depends on the autonomy of the subject. My choices spring out of what *I am*, and only a speaker entitled to mean these words is free to make a deliberate decision ... women have only a sporadic, precarious hold on such autonomy' (Belsey 1985a, p. 200). Similarly, recent feminist criticism has examined the way in which the realist novel, particularly in the nineteenth century, articulated the liberal division of public and private through a 'consensus' aesthetics, denying subjectivity to women through their confinement to a contracted and imaginary realm of 'sensibility' (Rabine 1985; Ermarth 1983; Jehlen 1983). Indeed, it has been argued that the identification of women with 'interiority' or 'sensibility' in the realist novel tradition precludes 'their becoming autonomous, so that indeed they would do so at the risk of the novel's artistic life' (Jehlen 1983, p. 89). The male hero may act in the world to assert his subjectivity and autonomy, but the woman character may only provide the domestic world of feeling in which he may, as long as it remains under his ultimate control, recognize his *own* inner life. Either the woman remains the object of the hero's own classically romantic search for identity (i.e. as a reflection of his own ego-ideal), or she becomes the 'object' of a domesticated romance structure whose aim is the rationalization of and justification for marriage in terms of 'love' and 'women's nature' rather than economic reality.

That such structures essentially deny subjectivity to the woman character, who functions in effect as an image of the 'lost' interior self of the male hero, is amply illustrated by the development of realism in much twentieth-century British and American fiction. What this suggests is that women writers can have only a contradictory and problematic relationship to postmodernism because they occupy a similar relationship to the aesthetic forms against which postmodernism has reacted and defined itself. If the dominant realist plots of nineteenth-century fiction function through silencing the voice of women's resistance, those of the twentieth century (particularly its latter half) show a deep hostility and misogyny which, at times, verge on the pathological (Kesey and Roth, for example). Although the romance quest plot still dominates, its promise of identity, transcendence, and self-presence has collapsed. Whereas some writers have responded to this with a postmodernist rejection of such totalities, many adherents of the so-called 'liberal tradition' have instead projected the *fear* and *loathing* produced by such fragmentation on to the female. Thus, instead of functioning as the ideal *object* of the masculine quest for self, she now becomes the *cause* of the failure of masculine transcendence. Leslie Fiedler, in 1960, was one of the first (of the very few) male critics to note the absence in male twentieth-century fictions of 'any fully-fledged, mature women, giving us instead monsters of virtue or bitchery, symbols of the rejection or fear of sexuality' (Fiedler 1984, p. 24).

This development seems to me to be a logical outcome of a view of identity which projects the inner life, 'sensibility', and thus *emotionality* entirely on to women, retaining rationality, authority, and independence as the core of 'male' identity. Once projected, such qualities are perceived by the male as threatening the very basis of selfhood and beyond his control. In much post-1945 fiction, the feminine further develops to become the bearer of more general masculine fears about destruction. In a technological age, images of the castrating female are often overlaid with the almost literal presentation of women as machines which have outstripped and threaten the technological but *controlled* and rational dominance of the male. Sensibility plus power is seen to equal an irrational will to triumph. Images of romantic desire are easily transposed into those of paranoia, as women, once the source of freedom and unity, become, explicitly, that 'Other' which entraps and threatens. Kesey's Nurse Ratched, of course, in *One Flew over the Cuckoo's Nest* [1962] most obviously epitomizes this process, constructed as she is out of a whole panoply of masculine projections, idealizations, and objectifications of the feminine. The dehumanized world of technology and systems analysis is microcosmically expressed in the asylum. Presiding over this world, its Great and Terrible Mother, is the Nurse, who programmes her machine through the control panel and the drug cupboard, 'nurturing' her 'offspring' with her cannon-like breasts and shots of chlorpromazine. Hope and life lie outside her dehumanizing maternal possession; death and annihilation are all she offers inside. In effect, she carries, projected on to her simultaneously weapon-like and exaggeratedly maternal breast, the blame for the contemporary 'death of the self'.

It seems to me that women writers cannot simply reverse the gender positions constructed through such plot structures. Attempts to do this offer no real alternative to the imaginary, unified (masculine) self of liberal humanism and traditional realism, nor to the deeply split, alienated, nostalgia-ridden, decentred subject of much postmodernist fiction. During the twentieth century, however, there has been an increasing number of women writers whose work does not easily 'fit' into the dominant aesthetic categories of realism, modernism, or postmodernism, and whose exploration of gender and identity does not conform, either, to the liberal-humanist construction of self. Their work, implicitly or explicitly, recognizes the construction of woman as 'other', but refuses the unitary concept of self which appears to be its self-evident opposite: the achieving, rational, autonomous, transcendent, successful 'self'. Some of these writers (Angela Carter, for example) have been influenced by post-structuralist theory and postmodernist experiment, but all refuse the 'impersonality' central, in different ways, to this and other twentieth-century aesthetic theories. A conception of self which involves the possibility of historical agency and integration of ego is necessary for effective operation in the world and must be experienced before its conceptual basis can be theoretically deconstructed. Thus the Althusserian argument that agency is simply an effect of the subject's self-delusion is a concept which many of these writers effectively struggle against through their fictions.

As the social psychologist Rom Harré has argued, we *need* at one level to believe in the theories in which concepts like self have a place, and we structure our experience so as to create them. In order to function effectively, as 'selves', we need to discover our histories (a sense of continuity in time), a sense of agency (how we can act upon the world), and to be able to reflect self-consciously upon what we take ourselves to be. Thus 'one who is always presented as a person, by taking over the conventions through which this social act is achieved, becomes organized as a self' (Harré 1983, p. 106). The 'novel of liberation', in this sense, reflects a necessary stage of awareness. I would argue, however, that it has been the *failure* of the premises of such fiction which has been most productive for feminists and has enabled women writers attempting to work outside dominant aesthetic forms and concerns to become more self-conscious about their aims and strategies. In particular, the pursuit of 'unity', the idea of the category 'man' subordinating the unitary category of 'woman', was problematized. The *heterogeneity* of social practices, discourses, ideologies, and subject positions began to be recognized, yet without necessarily being mediated through the extreme 'schizophrenia' and 'nostalgia' which, as Jameson has argued, characterizes the classic post-modernist text.

The schizophrenic, indeed, is one who, unable to organize language (according to Lacan), has no stable sense of identity, time, or memory and 'experiences isolated, disconnected, discontinuous material signifiers which fail to link up into a coherent sequence' (Jameson 1985, p. 119). There is no persistence of 'I' and 'me' over time, only an 'undifferentiated vision of the world in the present'. Jameson connects this to the loss of historicity, to postmodern culture's conversion of reality into images, and of history into perpetual presents which are thus dominated by nostalgia rather than a true sense of the past (for a critique of this, see Hutcheon 1987). Yet it is precisely the quest for history, agency, and self-conscious identity, as aspects of relationships with socially situated others, which has motivated much women's writing in the twentieth century, fictional or otherwise. I would suggest that the 'schizophrenia' of the postmodern text, a condition identified as the splitting of thought and feeling, is simply a *fin-de-siècle* caricature of the western tradition of Cartesian dualism in its liberal-humanist version (defining the 'self' in terms of a transcendent rationality which necessitates splitting off what is considered to be the 'emotional' on to what is considered to be the feminine).

31

Increasingly, in the twentieth century, this 'rational' self has been unable to make sense of the world in which it finds itself (Kafka's novels, for example, reveal the absurdity of the obsessive application of reason to a world where the consensus about what constitutes rationality has broken down). When 'transcendence' fails, the dominant systems of rational thought are not, however, blamed. Instead, the threat is seen to come from the split-off aspects of the psyche which have been projected on to the 'non-rational', on to women, children, the sick, non-whites, psychotics, the 'masses', sexual 'deviants', etc. As scapegoats for, rather than subjects of, the twentieth-century loss of self, women have not fictionally constituted their experience in the terms either of 'schizophrenia' or of 'nostalgia'.

Much women's (and not necessarily feminist) twentieth-century writing has explored a different vision of human change and possibility from the alienation and failure of relationship at the level of intimacy and nurturance prominent in much mainstream modernist and postmodernist fiction. Writers like Lessing, Atwood, Piercy, Walker, Tyler, Brookner, and Drabble show less concern with 'splitting' and disintegration than with merging and connection; are less interested in the quest of isolated individuals than in positing an individual whose maturity will involve the recognition of her construction through the collective. Their work is more contextualized in terms of historically situated personal relationships, often residing at the borders of 'life' and 'art', rather than obsessed with maintaining distance, formal abstraction, systematization: 'impersonality'. There is a much less acute manifestation of paranoia (and in particular of the experience of the loss of rigid boundaries between inner and outer as necessarily *threatening*) than in the work of writers such as Barth, Hawkes, Pynchon, Barthelme. Not necessarily *explicitly* feminist, these writers do, however, challenge dominant social and aesthetic constructions of identity and gender. Unlike the self-proclaimed feminism of the 'novelists of liberation', therefore, their work may constitute a '"vibration" available only to the consciousness of those men and women already at odds with the strictures of gender' (Pratt 1982, p. 178).

Before turning to psychoanalysis to seek alternative formulations of subjectivity and gender, I wish to end this chapter by quoting Hal Foster's hopes for postmodernism. If his desires are realized, my belief is that it will largely be through the efforts of the writers yet to be discussed, rather than those whose expressions of despair and pessimism have been the subject of this chapter:

> But what must be stressed is the need to *connect* the buried (the nonsynchronous), the disqualified (the minor) and the yet-to-come (the utopian, or better, the desired) in concerted cultural practices. For finally it is this association which can most fully resist major culture, its semiotic appropriations, normative categories and official history. (Foster 1985b, p. 179)

Chapter Two

PSYCHOANALYSIS, GENDER, AND FICTION: ALTERNATIVE 'SELVES'

THE LIMITS OF CONSCIOUSNESS

In order to connect 'the buried', the 'disqualified', and the 'yet-to-come', one must come to terms with the repressed, the feared, and the desired, with that which is *unknown* because outside the dominant signifying order. This is as true for postmodernism as it is for feminism, and in both a shift away from theories of role-play, self-as-agent, actualization, to an exploration of the unconscious and the irrational, has emerged strongly in the last ten or so years. Again, there are significant differences. Postmodern fiction has appeared to explore and been theorized in terms of the alienated, fissured subject of Lacan, whose aim is to dislocate not simply the subject as centre, but the very concept of 'centring' itself as the locus of significance and value:

> But where does this being [the subject], who appears in some way defective in the sea of proper names, originate? We cannot ask this question of the subject as 'I'. He lacks everything needed to know the answer, since if the subject 'I' was dead, he would not, as I said earlier, know it. (Lacan 1977, p. 317)

Here, the liberal subject has disintegrated into the postmodern subject, caught up in the systems of language and exchange, betrayed by the category of 'experience'.

Although many feminists have been influenced by Lacanian psychoanalysis and have recognized the need to deconstruct the subject of liberal theory, I would argue that in the work of many women writers, from Woolf to Lessing, we are given more than a simple choice between an essential unified self on the one hand and a radically fissured 'decentred' subject on the other. The relational, dispersed, collective concept of identity which emerges in this work is derived neither from liberal ego theory nor from Lacanian psychoanalysis (though some influence from these is inevitable) but is much closer to that posited by *object-relations* psychoanalysis. (Recently, this approach has been developed in *feminist* terms by writers like Chodorow, Dinnerstein, Flax, Gilligan, Ruddick, Baker Miller, and Chesler.) Unfortunately, the work of such writers has generally been misread through a critical appropriation of theories of subjectivity (derived from either ego theory or Lacanianism) which provide an obvious correlation with the dominant aesthetics, respectively, of realism and postmodernism. Writers like Woolf, Atwood, Lessing, and Weldon, for example, combine a strong awareness of 'personal experience' with an equally committed examination of the impersonal and historical determinants of human behaviour, which has facilitated interpretations of their work in both expressive realist *and* post-structuralist terms. The connection explored in their work between the 'personal' and the 'political' can be approached, however, in entirely different terms.

A shift towards psychoanalysis within feminist theory during the 1970s was, perhaps, inevitable, once contradictions began to emerge in assumptions about the unified subject. Psycho-analysis begins where cognitive-developmental and role-theory models of identity leave off. It focuses on the irrational, the functioning of the unconscious, on desire, on contradictory ways of experiencing oneself as a subject and behaving as a person. The decision, in itself, to focus on an 'un-conscious' immediately undercuts the very concept of a 'unitary' subject:

The psychology of consciousness was not better capable of understanding the normal functioning of the mind than of understanding dreams. The data of conscious self-perception, which alone were at its disposal, have proved in every respect inadequate to fathom the profusion and complexity of the processes of the mind, to reveal their interconnections and so to recognise the determinants of their disturbances. (Freud 1940, pp. 195–6)

Such a focus also undercuts any simple 'reflectionist' view of the relationship between literature and 'reality', or essentialist construction of the 'individual' in relation to the 'social'. If none of these is pre-given, then their potential for change is dramatically increased.

For feminism, the limitations of the rational explanations of the sources of women's oppression, explored through consciousness-raising, clearly emerged from the mid-1970s onwards. Consciousness-raising had failed to elucidate the sources of the intransigence of desire, people's resistance to change, and their compulsion to repeat patterns of behaviour non-conducive to their wellbeing or happiness. As Jane Flax has argued:

> Women who joined the early women's liberation movement achieved euphoric pleasure in the company of women. 'The personal is political' ideology allowed women to discuss their female experiences within a relatively safe context: consciousness-raising groups were considered both political (rational) and personal (emotional). Hence, some of the potentially threatening aspects of disclosing oneself to another woman were muted by the context. Nevertheless, feelings of anxiety, of competition, and of unmet needs often arose within these groups and were both unexpected and difficult to resolve. Some women felt that to uncover buried feelings and to reconstruct the meaning of life experiences was sufficient. Others argued that the groups should serve as preludes to more formal politics and political action or political study and analysis. (Flax 1978, p. 184)

'The personal is political' is a statement fraught with contradiction because of the pervasiveness of the assumption that 'the personal', the realm of 'feeling', is separable from the 'political', that of reason and action. Feminist theory and practice early revealed their interconnections, for, 'while alienation reduces the man to an instrument of labour within industry, it reduces the woman to an instrument for his sexual pleasure within the family' (Foreman 1977, p. 151). Personal relationships, however, cannot be altered simply by rationalization of the social structure. Nor is one's experience of being a 'woman' or a 'man' simply the consequence of a 'false consciousness' which can be rationally deconstructed and thrown off. The basis of one's subjectivity as 'masculine' or 'feminine' is formed out of real needs and desires which are constructed outside of one's consciousness. Thus psychoanalysis is particularly well equipped to deal with this area of experience. As David Ingelby suggests, 'It is the psychological problem which Marxists after World War I, and feminists after the 1960s, turned to psychoanalysis to solve. Why was it that when the conditions for social change seemed ripe that people seemed emotionally incapable of accepting a new order?' (Ingleby 1984, p. 69).

Marxism, in particular, had failed adequately to theorize the subject, and yet, as Janet Sayers points out, it is precisely 'women's subjective experience of the conflicting demands of home and work, of family and society – that constitutes the major impetus of today's women's movement' (Sayers 1984, p. 76). It is not surprising that the impetus to connect the personal and the political should come from women, nor that prevailing rationalist theories should be perceived as an inadequate basis for this attempted connection. The human infant, as many psychoanalysts have pointed out, is less instinctual and more dependent upon social environment and cultural norms than any other, and the group on which its survival and development has depended is women. Political readings which ignore the construction of subjectivity within actual human relations (pre-dominantly, in the west, within the traditional family) continue to oppress women by marginalizing their experience and history. Women writers who explore subjectivity through domestic or familial relations may be just as 'political' as those who analyse issues of war, state control, and foreign policy. However problematic their view of sexuality and the un-conscious as a basis for political change, psychoanalytic theories do 'dissolve in great part the binary divide between reason and passion that dominates earlier concepts of subjectivity. They break down as well the moralism attached to these libidinal and psychic economies' (Cora Kaplan 1985, p. 174).

Women writers in the 1970s discovered that deeper insights were needed, for example, into how women are positioned within sexual discourses whose repressiveness is often recognized, yet which offer such powerful emotional investments that resistance proves virtually impossible: romantic love, the desire

37

to conform to dominant images of feminine attractiveness, the misrepresentations of the experience of motherhood as simple 'joy'. As early as 1895, Freud had, of course, argued that 'hysterics suffer mainly from reminiscences' (Freud and Breuer 1895, p. 7). His clinical work aimed to free people from neurotic compulsions and repetitive behaviour, to free the present from the past, and encourage a more productive and constructive way of life. Yet what he discovered above all was the sheer difficulty of this process and of the huge expenditure of psychic energy on resistance to change or 'cure'.

Freud's work on sexuality and the unconscious undermines traditional conceptions of subjectivity, in particular the opposition of 'reason' and 'feeling'. Despite his emphasis on the 'anatomical distinctions' between the sexes, his work ultimately denies any indissoluble link between 'femininity' or 'masculinity' and the anatomical female or male, and he argued that the attraction between the sexes is not an inevitable result of chemistry (Freud 1905a). There are, however, difficulties in drawing on psychoanalysis for a feminist aesthetics and theory of the subject. In particular, although Freud's early work (1900) saw no difference in the oedipalization of the little girl and boy, his cultural 'norm' of subjectivity remains centred on the male. By 1925, he argued that feminine sexuality is not developed along the same path, but is related to masculine sexuality in terms of negative absence, lack (Freud 1925). (As with all *apparently* equal binary oppositions, one term is *actually* privileged over the other.) He formulated the distinction as a shift of love object and object of identification. Both sexes begin by relating to the mother as first love object. For boys, therefore, the primary attachment is, from the start, to a member of the opposite sex. At the oedipal phase, however, when the father comes to be seen as a rival, the desire for the mother is repressed through fear of castration, the boy identifies with the father and seeks a substitute for the mother, his 'own' woman, so that one day he may also become a father. According to Freud, feminine sexuality is not so easily resolved. The little girl has, first of all, to shift her primary erotic attachment from mother to father, to a different sex, yet simultaneously has to accept her identification with the mother as a woman, a member of the same sex. The passage to femininity is thus premised on irresolution and defeat: the little girl learns that she can never possess the mother sexually because, unlike her father, she has no penis. She turns to the father, therefore, in *resentment against* the mother, yet still has to identify with her as a woman if she is to take up her feminine position. The girl, therefore, has to accept her 'lack', her anatomical inferiority, to repress her active sexuality and accept a role as passive receptor. The penis thus takes on the symbolic values of masculinity emphasized in the rationalistic philosophical tradition discussed in chapter one: visible achievement, 'presence', possession, aggression, material success, activity. It comes to symbolize in the eyes of the little girl all that she seems not to have: autonomy, independence, freedom. Thus penis envy is at the centre of her oedipalization, just as castration fears propel the little boy's.

The obvious problems for feminism in this account are those of sexist bias, universalism, biological determinism, ahistoricity, privileging of the visible. Any account of subjectivity in psychoanalytic terms is likely to present problems, however, for 'the problem of keeping theory separate from ideology is especially acute in both psychoanalysis and feminism, for both attempt in different ways to make a science of subjectivity – to make subjective experience itself the object of scientific or historical study – and both lend themselves to normative or valuational thinking at every turn' (Strouse 1974, p. 8). So Freud argues for the superiority of the penis, while Horney sees this as a rationalization of the male's envy of the womb. What matters is the contextualization and mode of appropriation of the ideas of psychoanalysis for feminism. After all, whereas psychoanalysis 'interprets our consciousness of the world, feminism seeks to change it' (Sayers 1986 p. x).

Traditionally, psychoanalysis has on the whole functioned more powerfully to *support* normative practices and agencies rather than to subvert them. Moreover, its model of the relationship between patient and analyst is one based on inequality, subordination, and professional mystification:

A theory which relegated the patient's own views about what was going on to the status of fantasy, and which took disagreement, or 'resistance', as a sure sign that the professional was in the right, did wonders for professionals anxious to secure their cognitive authority as experts in the field of human subjectivity. (Ingleby 1984, p. 46)

For women, in particular, psychoanalysis has served to reinforce myths of femininity and the 'naturalness' of mothering. The good mother (or even Winnicott's 'good enough' mother) is characterized above all by her self-sacrificial absorption in the welfare of the child (an extension of her feminine masochism) and ideally, as Alice Balint argued, has no interests of her own. Although Klein's infant feels deeply ambivalent about its mother, experiencing violent hate *and* idealizing love, Klein's mother seems to share none of its ambivalence. As Adrienne Rich has written of her own experience of being a mother,

> psychoanalysis has assumed that the process towards individuation is essentially *the child's* drama, played out against and with a parent or parents who are, for better or worse, givens. Nothing could have prepared me for the realization that I was a mother, one of those givens, when I knew I was still in a state of uncreation myself. (Rich 1977, p. 17)

Once again the woman is simply the source of *another's* subjectivity.

'Women's liberation' in fact drew on a particular version of psychoanalysis in the 1970s which, in effect, simply reinforced the contradictions of the liberal definition of the subject. The theories of ego psychologists and the cognitive-developmental models of Erikson, Piaget, and Kohlberg hover behind the pages of the 'novels of liberation' and of feminist literary histories like Elaine Showalter's. The extension of Freud's later work on the ego was first taken up by Anna Freud, who focused specifically on the emergence of a sense of identity and emphasized adaptation and independent ego functioning rather than the irrational or the unconscious. For ego psychology, although the ego does develop largely out of past experiences and contexts, there is a central 'core' ego which moulds the available conceptions of self into a personal identity. The subject is finally, therefore, an essence which constitutes or determines experience. The subject is

> The domain of an inner 'agency' safeguarding our coherent existence by screening and synthesizing, in any series of

40

moments, all the impressions, emotions, memories and impulses which try to enter our thought and demand our action and which would tear us apart if unsorted and unmanaged by a slowly grown and reliably watchful screening system. (Erikson 1968, in MacCabe 1981, p. 124)

This suggests that it is possible for us to organize all of our self-conceptions. It thus avoids the issue of how the ego is itself a *product* (of past identifications, experiences, beliefs) and not simply a *producer*. If the ego fails in satisfactory organization, then this is seen as grounds for social intervention through the agencies of education, welfare, and health, to facilitate the necessary adjustment between individual and society. Freud's liberal pessimism is replaced with a liberal optimism which ignores his 'tragic' view of the inevitable loss and pain involved in entering the existent culture. Society is viewed as simply facilitating or obstructing individual development towards identity, which can, in any case, be monitored and 'put right' if failures occur.

Erikson's 'self' is the unified liberal subject approached in terms of 'struggle' rather than 'transcendence', crisis and resolution rather than a natural 'flowering'. It is still, para-digmatically, a *masculine* subject, concerned to achieve autonomy and separation. For women:

The stage of life crucial for the development of an integrated female identity is the step from youth to maturity, the stage when the young woman, whatever her work career, relinquishes the care received from the parental family in order to commit herself to the love of a stranger and to the care to be given to his and her offspring. (Erikson 1968, p. 265)

She simply trades one form of familial dependency for another. Erikson's 'universal subject' may seek autonomy as the mark of maturity, but women (non-subjects or non-mature, therefore) simply seek men to fulfil and 'complete' them. Furthermore, all of this is ultimately a consequence of their anatomy, their need to protect the unique 'inner space' of the womb, which must be protected and made safe by the male through the institution of the family. In fact, in Erikson's description of this 'inner space', one can see how he might appeal also to an essentialist feminism viewing liberation as simply the reversal of the valuation of essential male and female attributes:

> man's ultimate has too often been visualized as an infinity which begins where the male conquest of outer space ends, and a domain where an 'even more' omnipotent and omniscient being must be submissively acknowledged. The Ultimate, however, may well be found also to reside in the immediate, which has so largely been the domain of woman and of the inward mind. (Erikson 1974, pp. 1,318–19)

This is simply a restatement of the Victorian concept of the domestic world of interiority as the haven, the place of moral virtue outside the public realm.

However, clearly to assign all rationality, intellectual capacity, and urge towards autonomy to the male, and emotionality, intuition, and urge towards connection to the female, is to validate both traditional stereotypes and the dominant social order. This is why the deconstructive concept of 'difference' is useful in seeking a psychoanalytic account of subjectivity which might form the basis of a feminist aesthetics:

> Difference, in this context, is not simply defined by reference to a norm – the masculine norm – whose negative side it would be while remaining inscribed within the realm of identity. Rather difference is to be thought of as other, not bounded by any system or any structure. Difference becomes the negation of phallogocentrism, but in the name of its own inner diversity. (Féral 1980, p. 91)

Most psychoanalytic theories of identity emphasize the urge to independence, autonomy, separateness, as the goals of maturity and, specifically, the development of analytic and decision-making capacities which form the basis for moral action in the world and constitute one's uniqueness as a 'self'. Such qualities are, indeed, important in achieving a sense of self, but the way in which they monopolize definitions of identity reflects an individualist conception of subjectivity which is closer to the historical experience of white middle-class males than to that of any other social group. It is a definition which subtly reinforces the liberal separation of public and private, emphasizing those

42

qualities which western society sees as necessary to the effective *public* self. A woman's 'different' characteristics are produced not as a consequence of her innate 'narcissism', or 'masochism', or anatomical difference, but as a consequence of her history of economic dependency (necessitating her attention to *physical* attractiveness to secure a husband, compelling her to seek identity in definition or relationship through others). Men look to women to confirm a subjectivity defined in terms of separateness and autonomy (though their need for its recognition continually undermines its autonomous status). Women's experience, historically, has been defined almost entirely through interpersonal, usually domestic and filial, relationships: serving the needs of others. In existential terms her identity exists largely as being-for-others (needing to please; narcissistic vanity; mothering as institutionalized in western social practices; deriving security from intimate relations with others) rather than being-for-herself.

If one's identity is dependent on being-for-others, one experiences that self as perceived *by* others: hence, women's physical 'narcissism' and self-reflexive concern with the body:

> A woman must continually watch herself. She is almost continually accompanied by her own image of herself. . . . She has to survey everything she is and everything she does because how she appears to others, and ultimately how she appears to men, is of crucial importance for what is normally thought of as the success of her life. Her own sense of being in herself is supplanted by a sense of being appreciated as herself by another. . . . Men act and women appear. Men look at women. Women watch themselves being looked at. . . . The surveyor of woman in herself is male: the surveyed female. Thus she turns herself into an object – and most particularly an object of vision: a sight. (Berger 1972, pp. 46–7)

According to most post-Freudian psychoanalytic theory, however, female 'narcissism' is a consequence of penis envy. The woman compensates for her 'lack' by an overestimation of or an excessive concern with her body, and through defensive displacements may thereby regain her wounded self-esteem. Female 'masochism' derives from the same source: here, her genital 'inadequacy' is turned on herself with the failure of the defence of narcissistic vanity. The question of why a penis should be superior, and of how relations between the sexes are socially regulated (particularly through parental gender expectations), is not addressed. Moreover, if a woman reads Freud she will discover, also, that she has little 'sense of justice', less capacity for sublimating her instincts, and is 'weaker' in her social interests; all of this 'no doubt related to the predominance of envy in [her] mental life' (Freud 1933, p. 134). If she attempts to resist such definition and to pursue a masculine ('universal') trajectory, then she is perceived as 'unfeminine' and hence unnatural. Not surprisingly, by adolescence, her self-representation may be tied more strongly to the narcissistic gratifications associated with presenting a non-threatening 'feminine' image to those she depends on, than to the continued pursuit of an independent, autonomous subjectivity. Narcissism is not an inevitable consequence of her anatomy, but a pathological disorder consequent upon her exclusion from power and subjective definition.

Yet the fact that women identify themselves to such a great extent through others results in pathology only in a society where such relationships are unequal and where 'uniqueness' is valued over connection. In fact, a shift away from viewing identity *necessarily* in terms of uniqueness, transcendence, and separation may form the basis for a more significant feminist assault on liberal individualism than simply reversing or denying the valuation of its sexual stereotypes or rejecting the category of the subject altogether. The definition of self through relations with others, identity as mutually defined, and the centrality of primary affectional relationships are not, in fact, pathological positions, but essential for the survival of the human race. Freud emphasized that the development of the ego is the work of culture. If that culture's norm of individuality, however, is exclusively that of the rational, independent, contained self whose relational and emotional needs are split off and relegated to the 'feminine' (viewed predominantly in terms of masochism and narcissism), then that culture will inevitably produce incomplete and unhappy human beings.

An adequate psychoanalytic account of subjectivity will view gender as largely a *social* product rather than a biological fact, and the product of a society in which the division of labour is neither mutually beneficial nor equal, and which denies full humanity to both sexes. In the work of feminist psychoanalysts who have drawn on object-relations theory (Chodorow, Dinnerstein, Orbach, and Eichenbaum, for example) gender is seen as produced and maintained through *cultural* arrangements rather than anatomical ones. For Freud, gender is established around the fact of having or not having a penis. For Chodorow's infant, object- and therefore relationship-seeking rather than simply instinctually *pleasure*-seeking, gender is produced through the earliest construction of a sense of self in the identifications and values learned through relationships within the western family. It is through this institution, rather than through anatomical difference, that the ability to mother will be reproduced in little girls and the nurturant capacities of little boys will be curtailed and repressed. Because women carry almost the sole responsibility for childcare, they are inevitably associated with the period of primary socialization and constitute the first significant 'other' through whom both sexes define their sense of self. To some extent, therefore, they will inevitably remain identified with the intensely ambivalent feelings, desires, and fears of this period. Fathers, increasingly in western society, are absent or peripheral figures who appear much more centrally in the infant's life during secondary socialization. Perceived under the sway of the reality principle, therefore, they are seen as separate people, as subjects in their own right. Once males begin to matter to the child, the process of individuation which has depended so exclusively on the mother will be developed, so that the child can perceive others (especially males) as subjects without threat to its own sense of subjectivity.

Chodorow, in particular, emphasizes how this process is different for boys and girls. Daughters, because they are perceived by the mother in terms of 'sameness', are viewed more as extensions of her. The mother's identifications with her daughter will thus be fraught with her own ambivalence about being a woman in a society which devalues women. Clinical findings support Chodorow's assertion that daughters tend to remain in a much longer pre-oedipal symbiotic relationship with the mother than do sons, and refute Freud's view that girls must renounce the mother in order to resolve their oedipal complex. In this view, girls continue to derive their sense of identity from the mother (with the concomitant sense of the social inferiority of the feminine) rather than primarily through a desire to give the father a baby as a substitute for the missing penis.[1]

For boys, the process is different, for, if 'the basic feminine sense of self is connected to the world, the basic masculine sense of self is separate' (Chodorow 1978, p. 169). The boy establishes his gender and identity through separation, emphasizing his *difference* from the mother, who will herself encourage this perception. The difficult shift of object here (unlike Freud's account) is that of the boy's shift from identification with the mother to the father. His sense of identity is formed through a *denial* of the early connection with the mother and extended to the denial of those aspects of himself which he learns, culturally, to associate with 'femininity'. The maternal world of infancy, with its emphasis on nurturance, connection, and blurring of self/other distinction, must rigidly be denied or devalued, and the world of secondary socialization, of school, work, success, and autonomy, comes to be viewed as superior and as *masculine*. Primary relationships thus remain caught up with the intense ambivalence of the early period – acutely desired and acutely feared. Women, all women, become the carriers and focus of this projected masculine ambivalence, not subjects in their own right, but simply the receptacles of masculine desire.

Chodorow argues further that girls emerge from this with a basis for empathy built into their primary definition of self, and without the masculine need to define themselves through denial or disavowal of primary affective relationships. Girls 'come to experience themselves as less differentiated than boys, as more continuous with and related to the external object-world and as differently oriented to their inner object-world as well' (Chodorow 1978, p. 167). They thus grow up with more ongoing preoccupations with both internalized and externalized object relations and, though desiring autonomy, they also fear it. They do, however, retain a stronger core gender identity than boys because of the continued connection with the pre-oedipal, but their sense of secondary identity is more likely to be tenuous and vulnerable. These psychological characteristics are both culturally produced and culturally productive: women internalize a sense of 'femininity' as the central core of their self-concept derived from their particular connection to their mothers:

46

Women's early mothering, then, creates specific conscious and unconscious attitudes or expectations in children. Girls and boys expect and assume women's unique capacities for sacrifice, caring and mothering, and associate women with their own fears of regression and powerlessness. They fantasize more about men and associate them with idealized virtues and growth. (Chodorow 1978, p. 83)

Children of both sexes will fail to see women as 'subjects' and will project on to them their own ambivalence about the infantile experience of dependency and impotence. Women will feel deeply ambivalent, therefore, about their own identity because of the cultural perception and construction of femininity, not because of their lack of a penis. *This* is the 'bedrock' of feminine psychology, not penis envy as Freud argues:

> we often have the impression that to wish for a penis and the masculine protest we have penetrated through all the psychological strata and have reached bedrock, and thus our activities are at an end. This is probably true since, for the psychical field, the biological field does in fact play the part of the underlying bedrock. The repudiation of femininity can be nothing else than a biological fact, a part of the great riddle of sex. (Freud 1937, p. 252)

Similarly, women take up social positions of subservience and dependency, not because of innate passivity or inferior moral awareness, but because the economic structure which has rendered them powerless has also ensured, through the agency of family relations, its own reinforcement. As Chodorow argues:

> a girl continues to experience herself as involved in issues of merging and separation, and in an attachment characterized by primary identification and the fusion of identification and object choice. Boys are more likely to have been pushed out of the pre-Oedipal relationship, to have had to curtail their primary love and sense of empathetic tie with their mother. A boy has engaged, and been required to engage, in a more emphatic individuation and more defensive firming of experienced ego boundaries. (Chodorow 1978, p. 167)

Just as women are defined primarily through domestic relationships (as daughters, wives, mothers) and men by position in the social world of work, so too women's occupational roles are generally conceived as an extension of the domestic (requiring nurturance, affective behaviour, diffuseness rather than goal orientation), and men's are conceived in terms of efficiency, profit production, individual talent. The affective ties of the family, rather than the impersonal capitalist world of work, are more likely to provide women with the definition of self-in-relationship they have been programmed to seek. Because men are likely to have had such relational capacities curtailed, they are more likely to seek identity and satisfaction through individual achievement and success in the more impersonal world of work. Such 'productive' activities are perceived as having greater value, reflected in the low esteem of the woman who says 'I'm just a mother' and the refusal of the man who believes it is below his dignity to clean a house or care for a child.

Chodorow's work reveals that women can respond and relate to others' needs without feeling that this detracts from their own sense of identity. However, if such responses equal the total sum of that identity, then she is likely to perceive herself as a shadow, a negative, an object:

> When one is an object, not a subject, all of one's own psychical and sexual impulses and interests are presumed not to exist independently. They are to be brought into existence only by and for others – controlled, defined and used. Any stirrings of physicality and sexuality in herself would only confirm for a girl or woman her evil state. This is one of the most striking and tragic examples of how inequality enlists some of a woman's own marvellous qualities in the service of her enslavement and degradation. (And then a term like inherent masochism is used.) (J. B. Miller 1983, p. 63)

The masculine self-image is clearly not constructed around a compulsion to serve the needs of others, nor to define itself in relationship. Men are actively discouraged early on from such identifications. Prevailing models of subjectivity, which perceive maturity as exclusively involving ego development, separation, and self-enhancement, thus define 'human nature' (i.e. men *and* women) as fundamentally selfish. The struggle is for survival in a world of competing egos, each defining its own interests *against* those of others.

FREUD ON SEXUALITY: HUMANIST PSYCHOLOGY AND FEMINIST DEBATES

For Freud, the basic human instinct is to satisfy biological needs through hallucinatory wish-fulfilment, which is regulated through the intervention of the ego and the reality principle. Neurotic symptoms exist when, in the conflict between the unconscious or instinctual impulse and the opposition to it of the conscious mind or reality principle, the libido has become fixated to the unconscious fantasy and its provision of hallucinatory gratification. Thus it cannot respond to developments in the 'real' world and seek gratification in the present:

> the hysteric instead sought an alternative form of gratification by reviving infantile forms of satisfaction that is by regression to the phantasies that constructed 'the psychical reality' of the unconscious. The hysterical symptom served to recapitulate this form of gratification in somatic form – in a form that is termed 'hysterical' because its basis was not real and organic, but unreal and phantastical. (Sayers 1985, p. 79)

Because the pleasure principle thus seeks impossible 'imaginary' pleasures (and not just infantile ones), the human mind *necessarily* stands in a tragic and contradictory relationship with reality itself 'at loggerheads with the whole world, with the macrocosm as much as with the microcosm' (Freud 1930, p. 13). The idea of an intrinsic opposition between nature and culture is at bottom an extension of conservative liberalism, and similarly posits a view of the *inherent* competitiveness and aggression of human beings, which must be curbed or coerced into co-operation by laws and the state. Just as the 'natural' state of things is aggressive conflict, so the 'natural' desire of human beings is for self-enhancement. Relational tendencies, needs, and capacities enter very little into this picture. Human society is begun by an act of murder, people are inevitably isolated and anti-social, and their identity and sexuality are resolved oedipally through *fear*. These are innate and inevitable characteristics of the 'human condition' rather than tendencies produced by the social formation. Moreover, the pursuit of pleasure *cannot* bring happiness because, in its innate interconnection with the death instinct, the pleasure principle will ultimately produce masochism or sadism. Rationality cannot bring happiness either, because it will, inevitably, be in conflict with this irrational pleasure principle.

Freud's infant, from the first, is not a *relating* being but an auto-erotic isolated being, seeking to discharge libidinal impulses which can only produce conflict between itself and others. Only later is adaptation to the environment and to others learned, but this is a secondary development which only superficially affects the primary instinct. The 'other' is simply 'the object of an instinct ... through which it can achieve its aim ... it is not originally attached to it but becomes attached to it only in the consequence of being peculiarly fitted to provide satisfaction' (Freud 1925, p. 65). For ego psychology (which was influential in early women's liberation thought and writing), development thus depends upon *mastering* such impulses and instincts (innately anti-social though they are), *adapting* to the environment, and acquiring a sense of identity in terms of independence and separation.

If, however, the human infant is seen as fundamentally *object*-seeking rather than *pleasure*-seeking, then our basic desire is for *human relationship* rather than for the discharge of impulses or self-aggrandizement. Our basic fears would centre not on the loss of *pleasure*, but on the loss of *people* to whom we are attached and from whom we derive our sense of identity. Moreover, as Guntrip has argued:

> Freud arbitrarily equated unpleasure with increase and pleasure with diminution, of excitation, without taking into account the *total situation* of the satisfaction of a need in and for object-relationship.... If tension *qua* tension were unpleasant in itself and the aim were simply its reduction, then any method of relieving excitation would be as good as any other, i.e. autoeroticism would be as satisfactory as object-love and much more easily come by. (Fuller 1980, p. 65)

Freud's infant was only interested in the mother, however, in so far as she served, precisely, its auto-erotism (its desire for food, for example). Sexual desire arises through attachment to a vital somatic function (eating, for example) which is essentially *auto-erotic*, and does not arise in relation to an object. The first love object is thus the developing ego itself, and this primary narcissism is reflected even in the parents' regard for the child as well as its regard for them. Thus Freud can argue that parental love is 'nothing but the parent's narcissism born again, which transformed into object-love unmistakably reveals its former nature' (Freud 1914, p. 91).

Though clearly inappropriate in many ways to the experience of women, in particular, Freud's model has been assimilated to the dominant cultural perception of the constitution of identity. Erikson's view of maturity as increasing separateness, for example, suggests that, if the desire for attachment is an impediment to this, then women (whose historical experience has located them primarily in the domestic sphere of primary attachments) are simply less 'mature' than men. Certainly in much twentieth-century fiction (Pynchon, Barth, Kesey) women characters either are presented as infantile in their emotional possessiveness or are represented through projections of infantile images of the all-powerful mother. Attachment is viewed as regressive and as destructive of the independent self, to be transformed into 'romantic' or sexual conquest, or rejected in favour of worldly success, the 'man at the top' syndrome.

Interestingly, the only human relationship which Freud saw as free of hostility was that between mother and son – but even this is not reciprocal. For the mother, the relationship is near perfect, but unless the son repudiates this primary connection it will lead to his own self-destruction. The assumption, again, is that the only alternative to individuation as separation is a regressive tendency to fusion with the mother. It is surely possible, however, to see connection not simply as infantile fusion but as a means of recognizing one's own individuality in that subjectivity is indissolubly bound up with our sense of relationship to others. Such relatedness does not *have* to threaten identity, nor, therefore, result in the splitting of subject and other in the 'normal' sado-masochistic relationship, where the stronger (usually male) partner punishes the weaker for her mute reminder of his need for her recognition; nor, furthermore, would the deconstruction of this complementary concept of gender destroy the identity of and desire between men and women.

Significantly, Freud had so little to say, in general, about the early infant–mother relationship that several commentators have referred to his 'matrophobia'. He consigns to pre-culture (i.e. nature) the whole pre-oedipal period (see Eisenstein and Jardine 1980, p. 25), making it 'possible to deny the most fundamental proof of human bonding, the sociability and interdependence which characterize early infantile experience' (Eisenstein and Jardine 1980, p. 30).[2] Charles Rycroft, for example, comments on Freud's analysis of Little Hans's dream that his mother had gone, suggesting that instead of being an incestuous sexual dream it was probably a self-confrontation with the fact that one day, indeed, 'his mother would be gone' (Rycroft 1985, p. 87). It is *fathers* who dominate Freud's interpretations ('Dora', 'Little Hans', 'The Rat Man', 'The Wolf Man'), just as they dominate most nineteenth-century *fictional*, 'oedipal' plots (mothers are often absent or ineffectual). The theory of sexuality, itself, focuses on the intervention of the father at the moment of entry into culture, gender, and identity. This is rationalized in terms of the assumed superiority of the penis, whose sense of lack in the little girl 'develops like a scar, a sense of inferiority' (Freud 1925, p. 253). Thus even the desire to mother is seen as a conversion of penis envy whereby the baby functions as a substitute for the male possession of the penis.[3]

Freud acknowledged, however, his uncertainty about feminine sexuality, and this hesitancy increased markedly between 1905, when he argued that libido is necessarily masculine (in *Three Essays on the Theory of Sexuality*), and 1930 and after, when he suggested that, perhaps, we too readily identify femaleness with passivity and maleness with activity. Increasingly, he became more uncertain of the relationship of women to his theory of oedipalization, though he did persist in the view that femininity is precariously resolved, resulting in a weaker ego, deficient moral sense, and a tendency towards masochism and narcissism: 'Their superego is never so inexorable, so impersonal, so independent of its emotional origins as we require it to be in men' (Freud 1925, in Strouse 1974, p. 25). Women's development is seen to be prematurely curtailed because of their regressive fixations, so that they never resolve infantile conflicts. (Again, nineteenth-century fiction reveals the extent to which such curtailment is rooted in economic necessity and the suppression of feminine development through Victorian marriage.)

What emerges here does, in fact, seem to be a 'dread' of women. Penis worship itself can be seen to express a deep male anxiety about reabsorption into the female: the penis is *the* sign of difference and must thus function as the supreme weapon in the devaluation of the feminine. As Joel Kovel has argued:

> Civilization, built out of repression, provides a real counterweight to men's deepest fears by placing great value on male achievements, thus vindicating the craziness that went into its making. By structuring itself according to the male castration complex civilization sets the conditions under which women are forced to define themselves as castrated. The psyche is hemmed in then, not by biology, but by the social processing of biological givens. (Kovel 1974, p. 139)

Freud did, however, perceive the extent to which neurotic conflict is partly a consequence of the exclusiveness of the relation between mother and child in early infancy. Moreover, his theory of the unconscious actually undermines his model of the ideal autonomous self and emphasizes the fundamental role of emotionality, fantasy, and desire in constructing subjectivity. In deconstructionist terms, it is evident that Freud's texts repeatedly undo their rationalist and universalist assumptions.[4] If ego psychology in its optimistic liberal version has suppressed such knowledge of contradiction, Lacan has placed it at the forefront of his reading of Freud. It is also necessary briefly to examine the limitations of this Lacanian extension of Freudianism for a feminist theory of the subject. As we shall see, neither 'liberal' nor 'post-structuralist' accounts of the subject seem to explain the concerns of many recent women writers; nor can these concerns be adequately expressed through the classic forms of realism or postmodernism.

LANGUAGE AND DESIRE: FROM FREUD TO LACAN

Lacan insisted that the notion of rational self-determination was simply an illusion produced through ideology. He felt that ego psychology, in particular, had misunderstood the alienated and contradictory nature of Freud's subject and his emphasis on the role of idealism and representation in mental life. Juliet Mitchell summarizes his position thus:

> Humanism believes that man is at the centre of his own history and of himself; he is a subject more or less in control of his own actions.... The matter and manner of all Lacan's work challenges this notion of the human subject: there is none such. (Mitchell and Rose 1982, p. 4)

Humanist ego psychology (and the liberal novel tradition) views the human being as endowed with a capacity for self-determinations which ultimately transcends social, if not biological, determination. Lacanian psychoanalysis (and much postmodernist fiction) views human agency, determination, and identity as simply the illusory effects of the individual's discursive positioning within a necessarily patriarchal culture. In Lacan's view:

> the subject (the individual in its social relations) finds its place as a sexed subject according to the structure of the pre-existing familial and ideological configuration. Thus ideology is not a cloud of ideas hanging over social relations but has a materiality that structures the subject's development. For example, an expected baby in a family already has a 'place'. There is simply no way in which he or she can freely chose to interpret their sexuality or culture as individuals. (Coward, Lipschitz, and Cowie 1982, p. 279)

In particular, Lacan returns to Freud's work on narcissism, emphasizing that the ego *cannot* be centred on itself, self-determining and integrative (as in ego psychology), because it is formed in alienation in an identification with an 'other' which produces only the *illusion* of wholeness. The ego cannot 'master' the primary processes because it is, itself, founded on illusion. Identifications are made not through actual people but through insertion into the pre-existing symbolic order. Entry into this order is the precondition for the construction of both subjectivity and the unconscious (contrary to the liberal reading of Freud, which argues for the unconscious as the site of 'freedom', the bit of biology 'free' from cultural encroachment; see Trilling 1967). Lacan makes a crucial distinction between need and desire which elaborates on Freud's original insights. Freud argued that the baby hallucinates that it is at one with the original object of desire: the mother's breast. When it is hungry it recalls a memory-trace of the actual breast in an attempt to gratify its biological needs, but, on discovering that the hallucination does not bring gratification, it represses it into the unconscious. Identification thus occurs in terms of what is *absent*, rather than with the breast of the actual mother. The infant becomes human through *absence* and the creation of *desire* rather than presence and the discovery of satisfaction. Desire cannot be satisfied. We search not for the lost object but for its substitute by displacement. The object which has been lost can never be the same as that which we seek to rediscover.

In *The Ego and the Id* (1923), Freud developed some tentative ideas about the formation of the ego out of the early period of auto-erotism, suggesting it is first, in effect, a mental projection of the body experienced as a separate object which can be observed, experienced, loved. Lacan's theory of the mirror stage situates the necessary alienation of the subject precisely here. If 'I' perceive my own bodily actions, this body or person appears to be myself, but 'myself' as perceived is not identical with my subjectivity as a position in the symbolic system which 'I' *cannot* perceive. By accepting the illusion that this is 'myself', however, I can believe that I am in control of myself and can direct my actions in the world. These beliefs make up the 'imaginary order', but, in fact, our confidence that we are the source of our beliefs and values is an illusion. This is what Lacan means when he argues that the subject is determined by the chain of signifiers, and this signifying chain is itself the structure of the unconscious. Thus the unconscious determines our behaviour, not in terms of innate biological drives, but through the cultural formations of the symbolic order.

Despite the problems for women in Lacanian theory, his writing has been of value to feminists attempting to understand the social construction of gender. His concept of the mirror phase as central to the construction of an alienated subjectivity echoes the feeling present in much women's writing that feminine subjectivity is simply the mirror of another's (masculine) desire.

In Sylvia Plath's *The Bell Jar* [1963], for example, Esther's extreme sense of self-alienation increases as she becomes aware of the contradiction between her desire to conform to a cultural ideal of feminine passivity and physical attractiveness, and her ambition to be a creative writer, a person who *does* rather than one who is simply *looked* at. She resolves the conflict by withdrawing into a state of catatonia, unable to experience her body as part of 'herself' or her words as expressive of personal meaning. Recovering in hospital from the subsequent suicide attempt, Esther demands a mirror. As she surfaces from what she experiences as a birth, Esther wishes to see her new 'infantile' self:

> At first I didn't see what the trouble was. It wasn't a mirror at all, but a picture. You couldn't tell whether the person in the picture was a man or a woman, because their hair was shaved off and sprouted in bristly chicken-feather tufts all over their head. One side of the person's face was purple, and bulged out in a shapeless way, shading to green along the edges, and then to a sallow yellow. The person's mouth was pale brown, with a rose-coloured sore at either corner. The most startling thing about the face was its supernatural conglomeration of bright colours.
>
> I smiled.
>
> The mouth in the mirror cracked into a grin. (*The Bell Jar*, p. 185)

What Esther sees in the mirror is the conflation of a distorted image of a newborn baby, downy, genderless, and bruised from birth trauma, and a horrible caricature of the painted face of a cosmeticized 'femininity' with its monstrous and garish 'supernatural conglomeration of bright colours'. Esther thus 'recognizes' simultaneously both her desire to be reborn into a state of sexual neutrality and a mocking reminder of the unavoidable cultural image of femininity within which her 'other' self remains imprisoned. She sees the inevitability of self-division, the subject caught between the hallucinatory desire for imaginary wholeness, a new origin, and the necessary dispersal produced through the arrangements of the cultural order. Later, Esther is transferred to a psychiatric ward. Here she deliberately breaks a thermometer when its registration of her normal temperature reinforces her sense of division, reminds her that she is a 'sick' mind in a 'sound' body. She scoops up a ball of mercury:

I opened my fingers a crack, like a child with a secret, and smiled at the silver globe cupped in my palm. If I dropped it, it would break into a million little replicas of itself and if I pushed them near each other they would fuse, without a crack, into one whole again. I smiled and smiled at the small silver ball. (*The Bell Jar*, p. 194)

Esther's intense fascination with the ball of mercury (the original material of mirrors) is again a perception of human illusion. She, Esther, can control the image reflected by the mercury. She can drop and fragment the silver ball or push its fragments into a whole again. That she *knows* this to be an illusion, however, is implied in the next sentence (which closes the chapter): 'I couldn't imagine what they had done to Mrs Mole' (p. 194). 'They' have locked away Mrs Mole for registering a victim's protest by throwing her food on the floor. 'They' are the ones who control, and, if 'you' are female, old, poor, non-white, then only 'their' definition of subjectivity and sanity is legitimized through the institution.

Lacan's theory of the mirror phase attempts to explain, without recourse to innate biological presuppositions, the unification of instincts which Freud saw as the beginning of ego development and primary narcissism. Drawing on clinical evidence of the infant's fascination with its own image, Lacan represents this mirror stage as the first formulation of identity. Like Freud, however, because he sees the oedipal phase as initiating the child into the system of culture and gendered sexuality, this pre-oedipal phase is similarly viewed as asocial and 'natural' (it could be argued, in fact, that this 'mirror' is most obviously, at first, the *mother's face*, and that her response will be largely ideologically determined: it will be 'social'). Because the baby still experiences itself as fragmented and lacking boundaries of self, Lacan argues that it is fascinated with the unified image presented in the mirror. Thus the baby identifies with the wholeness of the reflected image (as Esther wishes to): 'we have only to understand the mirror-stage as an identification, in the full sense that analysis gives to the term: namely the transformation that takes place in the subject when it assumes an image' (Lacan 1977, p. 94). Once it can identify itself with a whole image, the child can then project from this a series of equivalences between the objects of the surrounding world which now appear to be fixed and permanent. Thus Esther seeks the 'lost' (in fact illusory) primordial totality which is 'herself'. That her discovery is of the fragmented and the brutalized is a consequence of the ambivalence of such 'mirror' identification functioning as both a confirmation of subjectivity and a negation of it, an *image* not a presence. All identifications are, in fact, according to Freud, ambivalent:

> It can turn into an expression of tenderness as easily as into a wish for someone's removal. It behaves like a derivative of the first, oral phase of the organization of the libido, in which the object which we long for and prize is assimilated by eating and is in that way annihilated as such. (Freud 1920, p. 105)

Interestingly, as Esther struggles to identify with her culture's image of femininity, heightened and focused through the fashion magazine and the sophisticated Doreen whom she meets there (and who makes Esther feel like 'the negative of a person I'd never seen before in my life'; *The Bell Jar*, p. 10), she finds herself driven by a desire to eat, to consume. Significantly, her first brush with death comes not through her own seeking, but through eating poisoned crabmeat at a fashion public-relations lunch. Sitting down for the meal, Esther experiences an illusory sense of her own new sophistication: 'I folded the linen napkin and laid it between my lips and brought my lips down on it precisely. When I put the napkin back on the table a fuzzy pink lip-shape bloomed right in the middle of it like a tiny heart. I thought what a long way I had come' (p. 41). Some hours later, recovering consciousness, Esther's stomach pains subside after she has vomited the whole meal. She has consumed (introjected) an image of tenderness and sophistication which in reality has poisoned her body and nearly killed her. On being informed of the source of the poison:

> I had a vision of the celestially white kitchens in *Ladies Day* stretching into infinity. I saw avocado pear after avocado pear being stuffed with crabmeat and mayonnaise and photographed under brilliant lights. I saw the delicate, pink-mouthed claw-meat poking seductively through its blanket of mayonnaise and the bland yellow pear cup with its rim of alligator-green cradling the whole mess. Poison. (p. 50)

Esther discovers that the sophisticatedly 'feminine' wholeness with which she has identified (eaten) is the image of an overdressed culinary delicacy served up for the brutal consumption of the camera and the appropriation of the photographic image. The vivid colours of the food repeat those of the little make-up kit with its built-in mirror which is her first promotional 'gift' on arrival at the magazine. These are the colours which become a part of her 'natural' body as she is 'reborn' after the suicide attempt. It is at this moment that Esther dimly perceives that there can be no pure white baby-self, that the image in the mirror is all.

Lacan's refusal, in clinical practice, to work towards strengthening his patients' illusion of themselves as unified subjects represents a critique of that Cartesian individualism and liberal humanism which has deluded both men and women into believing they are self-determining and 'free' through their identification with images which promote such a reflection of themselves. As with Freud's theory, however, the implication is *Silence* that women can do nothing within the symbolic order to change their position, and if they speak outside this order they will either not be heard or be heard as insane. However,

> It is because the obstacles to women realizing the individual freedom promised by capitalist society are not eternal but are historical and social that the struggle of feminists over the last three hundred years to overcome these obstacles in order to realize their needs as individuals have not been as futile as Lacan's theory of the mirror stage implies them to be. (Sayers 1986, p. 84)

According to Lacan, it is still the phallus (as symbol here of the Law of the Father) which is the sign of difference, fixing meaning and identity in language, signifying a human desire which positions women in a universal system of exchange. Through the castration complex, girls come to identify themselves as objects of male desire and boys take up their place as representatives of the Law of the Father. What Lacan emphasizes, however, is that desire can only exist by virtue of alienation. The object longed for (fantasized) only comes into existence when it is lost to the infant, and any subsequent satisfaction will thus contain the loss within it. During the

59

oedipal phase, the little girl comes to desire, not the mother, but the phallus as a symbol of the missing object of desire which can never be rediscovered. Thus the relationship with the mother takes on meaning only through the introduction of the Name of the Father, the symbolic order which breaks up the mother–infant dyad to form the oedipal triangle. Language and symbolization begin when the child first experiences desire, recognizes that something is missing or lost and that words can *stand in for objects*. Women's sexuality is thus seen as inseparable from the phallocentric symbolic order through which it is produced:

> That the woman should be inscribed in an order of exchange of which she is the object, is what makes for the fundamentally conflictual, and I would say, insoluble, character of her position: the symbolic order literally *submits* her, it transcends her. ... There is for her something insurmountable, something unacceptable, in the fact of being placed as an object in a symbolic order to which, at the same time, she is subjected just as much as the man. (Lacan, in Mitchell and Rose 1982, p. 45)

In Lacan's system one cannot become a speaking subject at all, however, without entering the symbolic order and accepting the phallus as the representation of the Law of the Father, repressing the desire for 'lost' wholeness which creates the unconscious. As desire moves in the unconscious ceaselessly from one signifier to another, seeking the impossible original lost object, the only hope of change offered to women by Lacan is through the impermanence of linguistic signifiers. 'Man' and 'woman' are not necessarily tied to the same objects, the same signifieds, because the meaning of any linguistic element is given by its relationship to all the other elements of language and has no inherent meaning of its own. Jacqueline Rose sees this as important for feminism because it calls into question 'the register of the absolute fixity ... of the category of woman' and 'challenges other notions of the political which require a total identity of the group to which they refer'; 'certain aspects of feminism ... demanded a theory which challenges the category of woman in that way' (Rose 1983, pp. 15–16).

Certainly the essentialist assumptions of much liberal feminism can, usefully, be addressed through Lacan's refusal of unity. The limitation of his writing for feminists, however, lies in the fact that his system seems to offer no way in which the primacy of the phallus can be displaced or undone. If culture is dominated by the Law of the Father (symbolized by the phallus, signifying difference), and if difference is necessary to acquire a position in this symbolic order, then how can women be positioned other than in negative terms in relation to it (even if signifiers/identity continuously slide and shift)? The subject is denied *all* agency, and human affection is simply the product of alienation and illusory desire. How, then, are social relations to be changed or improved? Ultimately Lacan's theories seem to offer as bleak a view of the possibility of human co-operation and love based on mutual respect as do those schools of ego psychology whose model of the innateness of human aggression and competitiveness is derived in part from liberal theory. Moreover, Lacanian psychoanalysis provides no analysis of the material structures of human life, where the hope for change must be situated. Again, such avoidance of particularity and specific historical context and experience appears to preserve an impersonal and 'masculine' ideal of knowledge. According to Lacan, women either remain in the dyad of the mother–infant bond, accepting madness or invisibility, *or* allow their identification within the symbolic order and 'masquerade' within the terms of an alien rationality. Either way, their capacity for historical agency and self-determination is virtually nil. Like Freud, Lacan fails to investigate as *cultural* the pre-oedipal period or to examine the mother's position as a subject in her own right. She remains necessarily 'other'. Desire is for *possession* (of the missing phallus) rather than for mutual affection and participation. Desire is thus power for men and 'lack' (being appropriated or exchanged) for women. Even in a text like *The Bell Jar*, however, where Lacanian insights seem so fully endorsed by the fictional structure (Esther refuses the masquerade and, therefore, goes mad), there are moments of resistance which do suggest possibilities outside Lacan's pessimistic alternatives. After the incident with Marco, the sadistic misogynist, Esther signals her first refusal of the 'masquerade' in a gesture not of depressed withdrawal but of exhilarated though desperate defiance. Climbing high on to the hotel window, she gathers the markers of acceptable femininity and:

piece by piece, I fed my wardrobe to the night wind, and flutteringly, like a loved one's ashes, the grey scraps were ferried off, to settle here, there, exactly where I would never know, in the dark heart of New York. (*The Bell Jar*, p. 117)

WOMEN, MOTHERING, AND IDENTITY: THE PRE-OEDIPAL AND LITERARY IMPLICATIONS

Melanie Klein's work shares many of the assumptions of Freud and Lacan, particularly in the tendency to ignore the mother as a subject, but she does focus on the primacy of the mother's role in ego formation and on the pre-oedipal period. Coupled with her emphasis on the innateness of human behaviour, however ('nobody has understood the full depth and vigour of the instincts of aggression innate in each individual'; Klein 1932, p. 257), such a focus has generally been interpreted to justify extremely conservative views of the traditional family and mothering role. Her subject, like Freud's, is essentially isolated and driven by instincts which remain largely unmodified by the impact of the cultural environment. Oddly, however, despite her theoretical focus on the pre-oedipal, the mother as a person 'remained curiously invisible and almost irrelevant: a cloud behind the "good" or "bad" breast. Since the infant would endure hell whatever she did or did not do, it followed that there was a sense in which she was hardly responsible for its well-being at all' (Riley 1983, p. 75). Once the mother–infant attachment was seen as the most crucial phase of development, however, Klein's ideas could be used to emphasize the absolute necessity of the all-sacrificing mother whose own needs must be suppressed for the good of the infant and who will, in any case, find her 'true' nature realized through its care. Theories of 'maternal deprivation' thus went far in reinforcing the 'feminine mystique' of the 1950s in America and Great Britain. Yet, as several commentators have pointed out (see Mead 1962), it is only in societies which combine production of food outside the home with the practice of contraception to limit child numbers that the sort of exclusive and continuous relationship with one, two, or three children (advocated by Bowlby (1951), for example) is possible. Klein's emphasis on the naturalness of mothering, on psychological innateness, and (in the theory of reparation) on reconciliation to the status quo has involved precisely those definitions of identity which feminists have sought to resist in their separation of biological 'sex' from socially constructed 'gender'. Some feminists, of course, *have* embraced an essentialist view of women's 'nature', and very often this involves an idealization of the maternal function in terms of Kleinian and post-Kleinian theory. I would argue, however, that this is a *misreading* of Klein for feminism. In Janet Sayers's words:

> the phantasy of the positively fused mother and infant daughter is an illusory basis on which to found the unity and solidarity of women. This can only be forged on the basis of recognizing the real factors (both material and psychic) that at the same time unite and divide women as a sex – a recognition that will be obstructed as long as there is defence against acknowledging the contradictions that inhere in relations between women. (Sayers 1984, p. 240)

Despite the possibility of feminists reading Klein 'against the grain', as it were, fundamental problems will persist in attempting to transpose a predominantly 'universal' theory into historical and provisional terms (see Timpanaro 1976, p. 12). Sayers's article (1984) suggests two possible areas for potential development, however: Klein's concept of 'splitting' as the earliest defence against the recognition of the contradictions in social relations, and her perception of the conflicts existing in relationships between mothers and daughters. Klein's emphasis on the *ambivalence* of the early mother–infant relationship is a useful corrective to those theories which idealize relations between women on the model of the mother–daughter bond. Most men and women in this society will have been 'mothered' in early infancy in terms of a fairly exclusive emotional attachment (though the actual *forms* of this will differ according to variations determined by historical factors including class, education, region, state intervention, etc.). 'Father' tends to appear as breadwinner/support though not as a primary pre-oedipal figure; so, while mother *appears* (as in Freud and Lacan) to be part of the 'natural' order, father is conceived in the terms of the 'cultural'. 'Mother' will thus carry our ambivalence not only about dependency but about the 'natural', and she will continue to be experienced in part as tied to regression to a pre-social, primitive state whose emotional uncertainties undermine our 'sophisticated' secondary socialization. This is as true for women as for men, and a simple return to an 'ideal' model of mother–infant nurturance will not provide adequate theoretization for an alternative feminist model of human relations. In an article significantly entitled, 'Our own worst enemies', Jane Temperley reminds feminist readers:

> Given the profoundly ambivalent attitudes that all of us are bound to have towards our mothers, the person on whom we were so dependent, in relation to whom we felt our earliest, most primitive love and hate and whose task was to help us negotiate our first social frustrations, we need to examine very carefully how far our perception of men's aggression may be overlaid by our own projection onto them of our own hostility towards the role and function of women. (Temperley 1984, p. 29)

As chapters three to five will attempt to demonstrate, it should be a reminder, too, of the dangers of founding a feminist aesthetics on a simplistic regression to an idealized pre-oedipal sphere unhampered by the cultural, and existing through structures of bonding, interchangeability, and fusion. However, Klein's focus on the pre-oedipal period made it possible to view the human infant in a new light as *object*-seeking rather than *pleasure*-seeking, thus implicitly *social* rather than isolated and alienated. Her emphasis, too, on the creative and reparational aspects of the construction of subjectivity through others, while not denying the loss, anger, and pain involved, does produce an image of human growth which stresses elements of co-operation and care rather than those of competitiveness and fear.

For Klein, the infant's ambivalence towards the mother, however, was not a cultural consequence of the western style of exclusive mothering (as for later theorists such as Dorothy Dinnerstein), but an innate disposition arising from the instinctual endowment in the human of love and hate. The mother is the person who gratifies or frustrates as she offers or withholds the satisfactions of the breast as the source of food and comfort. She is all-giving and all-punishing, an all-powerful being who contains within her the means of satisfying every desire (the phallic mother), and thus intensely idealized as the source of good and feared because of the dependency that this creates and the envy to which it gives rise. At the earliest stage, the mother is not an integrated person but a 'good' and 'bad' breast.[5]

Klein's theory is concerned with the creation of an internal fantasy world rather than with the infant's interaction via the mother with the social world. Her infant 'takes in' the 'good' breast (the part-object first experienced as good) and internalizes it in fantasy as a good object within. Similarly, the 'bad' breast (the object which frustrates) is experienced as internalized. Because this bad object threatens internal psychic equilibrium, however, it is projected out through a process of primitive splitting so that the mother is herself experienced as hating and wishing to destroy the infant. This 'Terrible Mother' becomes the source of the persecutory anxiety which gives rise to hatred and aggression. Such feelings must be split off from the feelings of good in order to preserve the latter. The Kleinian ego thus develops through a continuous process of projection and introjection where external objects are experienced as part of the internal world and internal fears and desires are treated as parts of objects in the world outside. Representations of objects which are introjected may themselves already carry projections. Thus the infant projects its aggression on to the mother and then introjects the mother as an object which is invested with its *own* aggression. The distinction between the internal object world of fantasy and that of external objects and relations becomes more crucial and problematic, in this model, than the distinction between the conscious and unconscious processes (so that later object-relations theorists like Charles Rycroft could argue for the need to dispense altogether with the latter distinction). For Klein, *aggression* dominates the process rather than libido. Love, however, is born through the need to idealize the mother as all-giving in order to protect against the fear that aggressive feelings will cause the disintegration of the fragile and developing ego. Fantasy becomes an inevitable part of reality, rather than an 'escape' from it:

> The baby, to whom the mother is primarily only an object which satisfies all his desires – a good breast, as it were – soon begins to respond to these gratifications and to her care by

developing feelings of love towards her as a person. But this first love is already disturbed at its roots by destructive impulses. Love and hate are struggling together in the baby's mind; and this struggle to a certain extent persists throughout life and is liable to become a source of danger in all human relationships. (Klein 1937, p. 308)

This paranoid-schizoid position, dominated by part-objects, splitting, and fear of persecutory objects, was not, for Klein, a developmental stage, but a configuration of object relations which persist into adulthood. It is partially solved through both internal and external events. The strengthening of the internal 'good breast', through the provision of food and containment by the 'external' mother, increases the security necessary to resist the threat of the persecutory 'bad breast'. Splitting is connected to the idealization of the 'good' breast, the ideal object, and, if the persecutory anxieties become overwhelming, idealization may increase or be projected on to the persecutor. If this fails, the ego may disintegrate and parts of it be projected on to objects in the world (as in phobias, extreme paranoia, or hypochondria). If the good internal objects, reinforced by external experience, are strong enough, however, then the ego develops a sense of its own and the external world's goodness, defensive projections and introjections decrease, and a movement towards integration begins. Once the infant is relieved of the need to project on to the mother parts of itself and to introject into itself parts of her, it can begin to perceive her as a whole and separate person, outside its fantasies. Similarly, it begins to perceive itself as separate and, therefore, to attempt to control its destructive impulses for fear that they will drive the mother away. Fear of *annihilation* by the persecutory object is gradually replaced by the fear of the *loss* of the loved object on whom the infant now recognizes its dependency.

This recognition of the mother as a whole person who is the source of *both* good and bad experiences constitutes the 'depressive position', according to Klein. It also involves recognition by the infant that it too is the source of both good and bad feelings towards the same object, and thus allows the development of the ability to tolerate ambivalence rather than splitting off unwanted 'bad' feelings. New feelings arise here: of *mourning* for the loved object felt to have been destroyed by the aggressive instincts, and of *guilt* for such destruction. At the height of these feelings, the infant believes it has destroyed both the external loved object and its own inner world, and thus begins the process of resolving such feelings through *love* – not *hate* – in the experience of reparation:

> Side by side with the destructive impulses in the unconscious mind both of the child and of the adult, there exists a profound urge to make sacrifices, in order to help and to put right loved people who in phantasy have been harmed or destroyed. In the depths of the mind, the urge to make people happy is linked up with a strong feeling of responsibility and concern for them, which manifests itself in genuine sympathy with other people and in the ability to understand them, as they are and as they feel.... . This *making reparation* is, in my view, a fundamental element in love and in all human relations. (Klein 1937, pp. 311–13)

Defences against the pain of the depressive position, however, may involve regression to paranoid-schizoid mechanisms or a denial or rejection of the intensity of the bond with the loved object which may take the form of the need to control, triumph over, or devalue that object. Klein discusses, for example, the existence of 'Don Juanism', where erotic feelings are split off from those of love in order that the original intensity of the relationship with the mother may be denied. The Don Juan figure thus strives to prove, in his compulsive superficial relations with women, his independence of the need for mother substitutes while simultaneously gratifying his need to return at some level to the relationship with the mother: 'In reality he is driven from one person to another, since the other person soon comes to stand again for his mother. His original love object is thus replaced by a succession of different ones' (Klein 1937, p. 323). Alternatively, the male may express affectionate feelings towards a partner whose familial position (for example, wife) replaces that of the mother, but he may feel compelled to split off his sexual instincts and turn them towards another. Here, argues Klein, 'The loved and highly valued woman, who stands for his mother, has to be saved from his sexuality, which in phantasy is felt to be dangerous' (p. 324). Other women are simply objects on to which he projects his own self-disgust and ambivalence about sexuality.

There are several implications here for a feminist theory of subjectivity and gender. First, the emphasis on the formation of identity in relation to the mother explains the intense ambivalence to which such dependency gives rise, particularly as these feelings are not yet under the sway of the reality principle. Klein argues that we retain in our minds these earliest images or *imagos*, repressed but always part of us. They are the product of the intense defense mechanism of splitting – idealization and denigration – and are directed for the most part against the first object of love and hate, the mother, because it is she who is most associated with this pre-oedipal period. The father is not generally subject to the same degree of irrational and intensely cathected splitting. This helps to account for the modes of representation of women characters in much recent fiction.

The women characters of writers like Barth, Bellow, Kesey, Pynchon, Mailer, or even Fitzgerald and Hemingway, for example, are in large measure projections of primitive masculine fears and desires, very often close to myth. The manic defence (against depressive loss) of control is useful in analysing the prevalence of jokes which 'hate women' or the extreme objectification of the female body in pornographic literature. In genres such as gothic and romance, particularly, women must be seen as not only economically dependent upon men, but emotionally dependent and sexually exchanged (there is some *self-conscious* exploration of the psychoanalytic basis for this in McKewan's *The Comfort of Strangers* (1982), Coover's *Pricksongs and Descants* (1969), and Bellow's *Herzog* (1964)). The 'splitting' of women characters into idealized and asexual *or* highly sexualized objects is the norm in much modern fiction. In Fowles's *The French Lieutenant's Woman* (1969), for example, Sarah paradoxically functions in both modes (ostensibly the 'French Lieutenant's Whore', and actually discovered at the climax of the plot – effectively a rape scene – to be a virgin). Moreover, although she appears to be the carrier in the novel of existential meaning and the possibility of freedom, she functions predominantly as the romantic ideal object of Charles's own quest for self-identity. Interestingly, too, the extreme *formal* fragmentation, dispersal of subjectivity, and splitting of narrative modes which dominates mainstream postmodernist writing has been, on the whole, significantly *absent* from much contemporary fiction by women. Consequently women writers have, in the main, been excluded from the postmodernist debate.

In drawing on Kleinian theory, however, the view taken here is that psychological tendencies which manifest themselves in writing are not a consequence of anatomy or innate drives but of the specific historical formation of the family and the disposition within it (and the larger culture) of men and women. Similarly, instead of seeing human relations as the product of innate aggression, and artistic production as a means of transcending sexual failure, one may see artistic work as expressing the human subject's deep, culturally formed need for, and ambivalence towards, other human beings. Ultimately hope and love rather than individualistic aggression may be seen to form the basis of human subjectivity.

In terms of a feminist theory of the subject, Klein's work suggests that, because of our system of parenting, it is women who are most intensely idealized *and* objectified, just as they are most caught up in our fundamental ambivalence about love and dependency. If women exclusively mother, then the earliest, most intense and repressed human experiences which form the basis of identity are mediated through the relationship with, and separation from, a woman. Separation involves a profound sense of loss and desire to return to the imaginary whole security of the pre-oedipal state, but also a profound *fear* of the loss of identity which such regression would entail. This is likely to be more acute for men, whose identity is culturally dependent upon denying association with the feminine in order to separate as masculine, and is thus part of the cultural reproduction of femininity as 'lack', weakness, dependency. It is a cultural norm for both men and women to assume 'women's unique capacity for sacrifice, caring and mothering, and to associate women with their own fears of regression and powerlessness', whereas men, who are seen to facilitate separation and entry into the wider society, are associated with 'idealized virtue and growth' (Chodorow 1978, p. 83). However, it is likely that men will subscribe more to such a view of women for obvious reasons of vested interest and also because women's own subjective experience of femininity and motherhood will involve them in a more realistic assessment of this position and identity. Most women know that, if they themselves are not saints or monsters, then it is unlikely that other women fall simply into these stereotypes.

For men, the fact of beginning life merged with a woman is, potentially, a terrifying assault on masculine identity and involves the compulsion (reinforced by economic and cultural reasons for the devaluation of femininity) to project on to women aspects of their own experience which are regarded as displaying 'weakness'. In a rationalist, individualist, profit-oriented society such characteristics will include emotionality, relational impulses, dependency needs, and nurturant behaviour. Invested with the intensity of such split-off feelings, women will thus be seen as emotionally insatiable and voracious, scheming to trap men into commitments such as marriage and parenthood which threaten the independence, freedom, and self-expression of the male. As Len tells Peter in Atwood's *The Edible Woman* [1969]: 'you've got to watch these women when they start pursuing you. They're always after you to *marry* them. You've got to hit and run. Get them before they get you and then get out' (p. 66). Overhearing this and listening to their vicious description of hunting a female animal ('I took her by the hind legs and gave her one hell of a crack'; p. 69), Marion runs blindly out of the bar and down the street. Peter, who has chosen her for his girlfriend because 'she was the kind of girl who wouldn't try to take over his life' (p. 61), pursues her in his car – and, ironically, proposes to her. The chapter ends with a storm: 'As we stared at each other in that brief light I could see myself, small and oval, mirrored in his eyes.' The consuming woman has been safely captured and herself consumed.

If femininity is thus enveloping, threatening, possessing, then men are justified (so it appears) in their emotional distance, rationalism, and need for control of the female. Thus Sartre, for example:

> The obscenity of the feminine sex is that of everything which 'gapes open'. It is an appeal to being as all holes are. In herself woman appeals to a strange flesh which is to transform her into a fullness of being by penetration and dissolution. Conversely woman senses her condition as an appeal precisely because she is 'in the form of a hole'.... Beyond any doubt her

sex is a mouth and a voracious mouth which devours the penis
– a fact which can easily lead to the idea of castration. The
amorous act is the castration of the man; but this is above all
because sex is a hole. (Sartre 1958, pp. 613–14)

Absence, lack, inchoateness, insatiability, nothingness: it is a
monstrous image of the feminine, yet it is also, astoundingly, the
normative view presented in Freud (the castration complex),
Lacan, Erikson ('inner *space*'), in Kesey's nurse, Roth's mothers,
and Barth's female computer. Thus distance, separateness,
objectivity, and rationality are the haven and 'escape' of
masculinity. So Descartes glorifies abstract knowledge as a 'truth'
which rises above the provisional and contextual truths with
which women deal in the everyday; Freud argues for the
superior abstract powers of the masculine superego; and
Kohlberg argues that, out of a possible score of six in moral
reasoning, women tend to reason at a conformist stage three
while men reach a 'legalistic' fourth stage superior in its
abstraction and objectivity. Masculine 'impersonality' comes to
be seen not only as superior, but as a necessary defence against
the inferior feminine qualities of emotionality and subjective
impressionism.

Evelyn Fox Keller's work on the theory of science is interesting in this respect. Arguing that the identification of scientific
thought with masculinity is deeply embedded in our culture
as the 'new religion', she suggests that the hegemonous view
of science as necessarily involving distance, separation, and
objectivity is also linked to its gender basis. 'Objectivity' has
become our highest goal, and, despite the outmoded nature of a
strict separation of 'subject' and 'object', she suggests its
persistence is the consequence of an institutionalized defence
against masculine anxieties about autonomy:

The scientific mind is set apart from what is to be known, i.e.
from nature, and its autonomy is guaranteed (or so it has
traditionally been assumed) by setting apart its modes of
knowing from those in which that dichotomy is threatened. In
this process, the characterization of both the scientific mind
and its modes of access to knowledge as masculine is indeed
significant. Masculine here connotes, as it so often does,
autonomy, separateness, and distance. It connotes a radical

71

rejection of any commingling of subject and object which are, it now appears, quite consistently identified as male and female. (Keller 1978, p. 415)

In the development of selfhood, the necessity for separation is balanced against the process of individuation which occurs in the relationship with the parenting figure (almost always the mother). The ability to conceive of oneself as separate from and mutually independent with the mother develops with the ability to accept one's dependency and to feel secure enough to be able to relax the boundary between self and other, to allow for the ambiguity which resides at the *interface* between subject and object. Traditional psychoanalysis has, however, over-whelmingly emphasized autonomy and separation. Again, one can connect what Keller sees as the 'masculine' obsession with 'objectivity' and 'separation' in science to our cultural parenting arrangements. If selfhood is conceived in terms of disidentifi-cation with the mother and identification with a father who symbolizes the larger culture, it is the father who is seen to carry the reality principle. For a boy, the disidentification with the mother will be more radical and selfhood more likely to be defined absolutely in terms of autonomy and objective distance. 'Truth' in the 'real' world of knowledge will thus be seen in such terms, involving a necessary devaluation of the 'personal' and provisional 'truths' of the familial world. Science thus becomes over-masculinized, adhering often to an out-moded positivism or a pursuit of technological goals which no longer serve human interests and needs. Keller recommends that:

The disengagement of our thinking about science from our notions of what is masculine could lead to a freeing of both from some of the rigidities to which they have been bound, with profound ramifications for both. Not only, for example, might science become more accessible to women, but, far more important, our very conception of 'objectivity' could be freed from inappropriate constraints. As we begin to understand the ways in which science itself has been influenced by its unconscious mythology, we can begin to perceive the possibilities for a science not bound by such mythology. (Keller 1978, p. 431)

Similarly, once 'literature' became an acceptable *male* academic profession, a parallel development occurred whereby it was no longer fashionable to conceive of the literary work as 'self-expression' (or even 'life'), but only in the formalist/structuralist terms of aesthetic distance and objectivity (New Criticism), impersonality (T. S. Eliot), autonomy theory (Fry, Bell, Ortega y Gasset), estrangement (Russian formalism), the linguistic system (structuralism), the 'death of the author' (Barthes), the free play of the signifier (deconstruction). Rigour and precision *must* be an important aspect of literary analysis, but to ignore that the text is part of a human and historical process which exists in a context of actual *social* relations is surely to impoverish it.

In 1941 Otto Rank argued: 'the gradual masculinization of human civilization, in my opinion, probably the most enlightening clue to history, is borne out by mythical and religious tradition as well as by the development of social concepts and artistic creation' (Rank 1941, p. 237). More recently, Dorothy Dinnerstein has explored this idea, drawing implicitly on Kleinian theory to articulate the view that, because of our cultural situation of almost exclusive mothering, children in fact never work through their ambivalent infantile feelings. They retain into adulthood a powerful sense of the mother as engulfing and tend to associate *all* women with the not-self, the inchoate, the natural. Dinnerstein describes the early dependency:

It is in a woman's arms and bosom that the delicate-skinned infant – shocked at birth by sudden light, dry air, noises, drafts, separateness, jostling – originally nestles. In contact with her flesh it first feels the ecstasy of suckling, of release from the anguish of hunger and the terror of isolation. Her hands clean, soothe and pat its sensitive bottom. Her face is the first whose expression changes reciprocally with its own. Her voice introduces it to speech: it is the first voice that responds to the voice of the child, that signals the advent of succour, whose patterns of rhythm or pitch correspond to events the child notices or body sensations it feels. She is the one who rocks or bounces it when it feels tense, who thumps it when it needs to burp. She comes when it feels anxious or bored or provides the sense of being cared for, the interesting

73

things to look at, touch, smell and hear, the chance to use growing powers of back-and-forth communication, without which the human intellect and personality – and indeed the body itself – cannot develop. (Dinnerstein 1976, p. 33)

Moreover, this state persists long after the child has become cognitively aware of its dependency.

In the very early pre-oedipal period, the infant has little sense of the boundaries between self and other, and Dinnerstein argues that once a sense of self has developed the mother will still be associated with the state of non-identity. Thus she will remain associated with fears of loss of identity, of being consumed, and will remain the focus of our ambivalence about existence, mortality, and the flesh itself:

female sentience, for this reason, carried permanently for most of us the atmosphere of that unbounded, shadowy presence towards which all our needs were originally directed. And the intentionality that resides in female sentience comes in this way to carry an atmosphere of the rampant and limitless, the alien and unknowable. It is an intentionality that needs to be conquered and tamed, canalled and subjugated. (Dinnerstein 1976, p. 164)

It is unlikely that the human being will again experience the same degree of dependency as on this all-powerful controller of life and death. It is not surprising that we thus develop defences against acknowledgement of the terror of sinking back into this sort of helplessness: the defences of splitting, manic denial, repression, disavowal, which psychoanalysts have observed. For the male, in particular, it seems that fears of reabsorption (always coupled with *desire* for such a state) are projected on to women, who are seen as insatiable, engulfing, desiring control. Often, such fears are associated specifically with the flesh, the female body viewed as sexually voracious, castrating, or dangerously seductive (the 'kiss of the spiderwoman', the smile of the Medusa, Woody Allen's parodic engulfing breast, the witch of *Hansel and Gretel* waiting to eat the children in her gingerbread house). Men are not subject to the same intense degree of splitting because their presence tends to be registered by the infant once it is coming under the sway of the reality principle and has, therefore, already formulated a rudimentary sense of identity and separateness. The 'splitting' of representations of the male tends to derive from masculine positional roles in the larger culture and is usually detached from the ambiguous sexuality which distinguishes the primary processes ('Superman' as the redeemer of law and order, Christ the saviour, 'the doctor' as trusted healer or authority figure rather than the ambiguity of the 'Angel of Death' image attached to nurses).

The male has a much greater psychic investment in the need to emphasize boundaries and distance and to represent subjectivity as a moral rationalism which splits off the unbounded, the inchoate, and the emotional on to women, thus constituting the definition of 'femininity' in such terms. Women thus carry not only the affiliative and domestic human ties because of their economic position within the family; they also carry the deep human ambivalence about the flesh and mortality (about that which cannot be ultimately controlled). Not surprisingly, women experience their bodies in a much more alienated way than men, draw more on the defences of narcissism and depersonalization, and suffer neurotic illnesses such as anorexia nervosa which are connected to feelings, specifically, about the female body as human, mortal, *flesh*. While women seek desperately to control their own bodies, men, too, feel compelled to control, triumph over, denigrate, or idealize (i.e. distance) the female body. Male control of the female body is culturally endorsed and carries none of the implications of 'castration' and 'annihilation' which are attached to female control over the male. Exclusive 'possession' of a female body both provides access to the physical and emotional security of the pre-oedipal period and guards against a recurrence of the boundlessness and dependency of this time:

> What is reflected in man's unilateral possessiveness, then, is not only the original monolithic infant wish for ownership of a woman but also a second, more equivocal feeling, rooted in early boyhood: that attachment to a woman is emotionally bearable, consistent with solidarity among men which is part of maleness, only if she and one's feelings towards her remain under safe control. (Dinnerstein 1976, pp. 49–50)

Dinnerstein sees both sexes as experiencing a deep 'rage' towards the feminine. The male uses this to consolidate his

masculine identity (expressed ultimately through sadistic attitudes to women). Women also use it to loosen the tie with the
mother, but because of their inescapable 'sameness' and thus
need to *identify* with her, however, they experience such rage
masochistically turned on themselves. For both sexes, the father is
idealized as the figure who provides the possibility of separation,
the release from ambivalence, and the access to a reality outside
the confines of the family.

I would argue that the earlier separation from the mother of
the boy, with his intense investment in defences (such as
splitting) against recognizing her as a whole being, results in a
tendency to represent women in terms of the idealization and
denigration, the fear and desire, the *fragmentation* of Klein's
paranoid-schizoid position. For women, however, the mother is
seen in more realistic, less sexually ambivalent terms because of
the longer pre-oedipal attachment and the later, more mature,
recognition of sameness with difference. The longer attachment
means that ambivalence may be more successfully resolved
through the reparations and integrations of the depressive
position. Instead of splitting/fragmentation/intense idealization
and denigration, her internal representation of the mother is
more likely to be in the terms of this later position, tied to the
feelings of loss, responsibility, guilt, reparation, merging, and
connectedness, with a reduction of the compulsion to split off
parts of the mother. Inevitably, the little girl will share the
dominant cultural devaluation of femininity, and *this* ambivalence will be passed on to her own daughter and defended
against through narcissistic or masochistic behaviour. For
women, however, the maintenance of relationship and connection will remain central to their sense of identity, though
displaced, as a consequence of their cultural inferiority, on to
the traditional requirement that they *serve* others, seek to please,
and suppress any anger or resistance that they may feel about
such enslavement.

In terms of literary expression it is evident that, to a large
extent, women writers have not revealed the same obsession
with formal abstraction, aesthetic distance, autonomy, and
'objectivity' which has dominated modernist aesthetics and much
twentieth-century literary theory. Nor have they adopted the
postmodernist version of 'impersonality': subjective dispersal,

splitting, fragmentation. From Woolf, Mansfield, and Stein to Drabble, Lessing, and Atwood, although their writing clearly bears some relationship to these movements, such women writers have, typically, explored human subjectivity and history in terms of non-systematized particulars, forms of collective expression, formal principles which suggest connection rather than fragmentation, history conceived as an ongoing human process. There is no 'absolute' women's style, of course, and, for each writer, gender is only *one* historical determinant among many and constituted in a variety of ways. There does, however, seem to be a marked tendency in this direction.[6] Classic modernism searches for the ultimate objectification of mind in the external world or in the system of language which would offer the possibility of discovering a set of formal principles which might connect the human and the natural worlds. Postmodernism rages against the collapse of such hope or celebrates its indifference to the possibility of fixity of meaning in a hedonistic play of signifiers. Women writers like Woolf, Lessing, Atwood, and Walker search instead to connect 'the small personal voice' with the collective human experience. Woolf thus experiments with multiple points of view, extensive use of free indirect speech, and shifting symbolism which emphasizes unexpected connections and resemblances between things and people. Alice Walker explores how the subjective experience of history in the everyday lives of black women is not what the 'objectification' of the history books would have us believe. One critic has written generally of post-war fiction, 'the problem is that although the responses may be powerfully rendered, the concrete events and specific social circumstances that induced them are seldom identified' (Aldridge 1983, p. 140). That this is not generally true of post-war writing by women does not simply mean that these writers have failed to challenge the assumptions of realism, as other critics (Karl 1985, for example) have argued.

David Lodge, writing on modernism, has offered the following definition:

Formalism is the logical aesthetic for modernist art, though not all modernist writers accepted or acknowledged this. From the position that art offers a privileged insight into

77

reality there is a natural progression to the view that art creates its own reality and from there to the position that art is not concerned with reality at all but is an autonomous activity, a superior kind of game. (Lodge 1977, p. 48)

The view of Oretega y Gasset, which agrees with Lodge's last position, is often linked with the work of Virginia Woolf, yet it is clear that such an interpretation not only marginalizes her feminist politics but also ignores the connection between her modes of formal innovation and her political refusal of patriarchy. Similarly, Dorothy Richardson's work has been interpreted through such a formal aesthetic, but again her concern to explore the possibility of a communal consciousness and plural identifications arose from an awareness of gender differences and a desire to explore the capacity of the feminine psyche to 'do what the shapely normalities of men appear incapable of doing for themselves, to act as a focus for divergent points of view' (quoted in Blau du Plessis 1985, p. 150).

THEORIZING MODERN FICTION:
THE CHALLENGE FROM FEMINIST PSYCHOANALYSIS

Psychoanalytic theory clearly provides *some* of the reasons for the problematic relationship to modernism and postmodernism of many women writers. Postmodernism has generally been discussed by critics in terms of its dislocation of subjectivity, hermeneutic meaning, history, and identity. Fredric Jameson sees its basic mode as involving 'nostalgia' plus 'schizophrenia'. Discussing the impact of Lacan's work on modern aesthetics, he refers particularly to the way in which Lacan has shown the experience of time, history, memory, and identity to be an effect of language. We have a sense of time as lived because language has a past and a future and sentences unfold in time. For the schizophrenic, language articulates not temporal continuity but the sense of a perpetual present with no causal relation to a time conceived of as before or after:

in other words, schizophrenic experience is an experience of isolated, disconnected, discontinuous material signifiers which fail to link up into a coherent sequence. The schizophrenic thus does not know personal identity in our sense, since our feeling of identity depends on our sense of the persistence of the 'I' and the 'me' over time. (Jameson 1985, p. 119)

For the schizophrenic, everything is vividly *present*, and the experience of the sheer *materiality* of words becomes more and more acute and obsessive.

One could argue that this tendency is present, in fact, in modernist writing, with its emphasis on formal autonomy, identity as transcendence of history through *symbol* (Eliot, Yeats), and self as a construction of language (particularly in Joyce and Conrad). Increasingly, modernists discovered that as the linguistic system shifts, as words take on meanings in new and startling contexts, then human identity is also positioned through the disconnected and arbitrary associations of the verbal image. These tendencies are foregrounded in postmodernist work, from the early exploration of dissolution of identity through the past and present voices in a text like Beckett's *Krapp's Last Tape* [1959], to the 'full' postmodernist *bricolage* of disembodied 'voices' and signifiers in, for example, Donald Barthelme's fictions. The shift from modernism to postmodernism is from an aesthetics of impersonality ('schizoid') to one of extreme de-personalization ('schizophrenic'). In the first, the subject is displaced on to the 'objective' world and, in the second, both collapse into fragmentary part-objects. Once 'impersonality' fails as a means of control, there is a relapse into the primitive defences of splitting and fragmentation characteristic of Klein's paranoid-schizoid position. For Klein, the fragmentation of subjectivity (conceived as ego) is the final defence against the fear of annihilation by the object and the *desire*, therefore, to destroy the object oneself. As Chodorow has shown, an overemphasis on masculinity is, in fact, a defence against the fear of and desire for a regressive return to the pre-oedipal mother which offers the recovery of an imaginary lost wholeness only at the expense of an annihilation of identity. Thus the strategies of both modernism and postmodernism can be related to masculine ambivalence towards the mother as first love object (and thus towards all women) and what she has culturally come to represent, which has necessitated the overemphasis of certain developmental aspects of the human subject at the expense of others.

Women writers, as a consequence of *their* oedipalization, are unlikely to show the same formal and thematic obsession with issues of 'objectivity', distance, separation. As Chodorow has argued, women's gender identity, far from being threatened by a relational view of self, is *strengthened* by such a view. What *is* problematic for them is the shared cultural devaluation of femaleness and thus the mother's ambivalence towards her daughter. A female child will seem both an extension of herself and therefore a confirmation of her own identity, but will also function as someone who, by virtue of this sexual sameness, reinforces the mother's own low cultural valuation of herself as a woman. Given these differences, it seems likely that the mobilization of the paranoid-schizoid defences of splitting (intense idealization and denigration), fragmentation, projection, and introjection is more likely to occur in the formal strategies of male writers. An expression of 'depressive' concerns and anxieties – the struggle to cope with ambivalence without splitting; fear of loss; recognition of guilt; desire for reparation and relationship – is more likely to occur in women's writing. For girls, the longer pre-oedipal connection to the mother (extending well into the depressive position) results in a sense of her as, more realistically, a whole person, a subject. For the boy, however, precociously pushed out of the early pre-oedipal dyad, pressured culturally to accept an identity emphasizing his sexual 'difference', the mother is much more likely to remain bound up with the projections and the introjections of the early period, identified with the imago figures and part-objects of the paranoid-schizoid position. She thus remains an object, but one which, overwhelmingly, threatens masculine subjectivity.[7]

If women share men's rage towards women because they too were mothered (as Dinnerstein argues), it is more likely to be expressed as masochistic self-disgust and guilt, and fear of the betrayal of the mother (emotions which again dominate the 'depressive position'). The feeling of loss and the need to seek reparation will be stronger, I would argue, than the fear of regressive reunion and the desire to control and separate. In formal aesthetic terms, breaking down boundaries, loosening distinct outlines, merging the individual with the collective, and exploring the ambiguity of identity at the interface of subject and object are likely to be stronger in women writers than the search for autonomy, impersonal formal systems, 'hard, dry objects', or the final desperate defence of disintegration. Again I must emphasize that these distinctions are neither absolute nor universal. The work of Iris Murdoch is interesting, for example. In her distinction between the 'crystalline' and the 'journalistic', she seems to recognize that a predilection for the crystalline ('a closely-coiled carefully constructed object wherein the story rather than people is the important thing'; Murdoch 1977, p. 113) can function as a psychological defence: 'There can be a tendency too readily to pull a form or structure out of something one's thinking about and to rest upon that. The satisfaction of the form is such that it can stop one from going more deeply into the contradictions or paradoxes or more painful aspects of the subject matter' (p. 113). However, the alternative she proposes is a return to the traditional 'moral' sense of character and contingency.

I have already argued against the tendency among critics to assume that formal impersonality and postmodernist decon-struction of the subject, on the one hand, and the old liberal 'moral' and unified subject, on the other, are the only aesthetic alternatives remaining to writers (see chapter one). Acceptance of such a restrictive binary opposition can only lead to the misinterpretation of writers attempting to express alternative models. In her own fiction, Murdoch strives to embody the catastrophic effects of approaching the world in a 'crystalline' fashion. Discussing her novel *Under the Net* (1954), for example, she says: 'The problem which is mentioned in the title is the problem of how far conceptualizing and theorizing, which from one point of view are absolute, essential, in fact divide you from the thing that is the object of theoretical attention' (Murdoch 1977, p. 115). However, her obsessive concern with the self-conscious presentation of this dilemma in her fiction often precludes the possibility of developing the 'opaque' or 'contin-gent' characters which she desires. Her protagonists are usually artist/magician/trickster figures who attempt to manipulate other people into conformity with a projection on to the world of their own aesthetic theories or rationalized desires. However, the internal structures of subjective desire are repeatedly shown as unable to connect with the structures of the 'other', with language, the social order, with the people needed to confirm identity. Her characters, though, continue to struggle, endlessly, towards connection, hoping to free themselves from the net of linguistic convention and the stalemate of the Hegelian master—slave relationship of mutual dominance and dependency which is the product of an unequal society. Most of them lose faith in the attraction of aesthetic distance and order, in the 'crystalline', but continue to require its consolations as a basic form of defence. Charles, for example, in *The Sea, The Sea* [1978], comes to recognize at the end of his journal:

> Life, unlike art, has an irritating way of bumping and limping on, undoing conversions, casting doubt on solutions, and generally illustrating the impossibility of living happily or virtuously ever after .... Human arrangements are nothing but loose ends and hazy reckoning, whatever art may otherwise pretend in order to console us. (p. 477)

Neither the resolution of the nineteenth-century fictional ending nor the 'cold pastoral' of autonomous form seems adequate to mediate the diffuseness of human subjectivity: at least Charles ends his journal recognizing that there *must* be aesthetic possibilities outside this restrictive choice.

The American novelist and philosopher William Gass has expressed a similar view of the consolatory aspects of art: 'Very frequently the writer's aim is to take apart the world where you have very little control and replace it with language over which you have some control. Destroy and then repair' (in LeClair and McCaffery 1983, p. 27). The substitution of an arbitrary linguistic order for the perception of reality as a fragmentary chaos accords with Jameson's analysis of the 'schizophrenic' character of much postmodernist writing. It is as if such writers, unable to tolerate ambiguity of boundaries or the possibility that subjectivity grows out of connection and not simply separation, seek systems of total but arbitrary order whose non-representativeness endows them with an infinite malleability. The attitude to this may be semi-ludic. In *Finnegans Wake* [1939], for example, the impossibility of seeing through the elaborate self-conscious construction of arbitrary systems of order to a mimetically consistent world suggests that *all* systems are equivalent, and that we should simply give up our anxiety about the failure to 'connect'. Similarly, the 'chosisme' of the French New Novel, Abish's strict adherence to alphabetical order as a substitute for plot in *Alphabetical Africa* (1974), or Barthelme's collapsing of the pretensions of a high literary tradition into the 'dreck' of contemporary culture are 'ludic' in the relationship which the text offers the reader. More often, though, such strategies are a defence against rage, fear, and the terror of annihilation.

The psychoanalyst D. W. Winnicott has argued that the roots of creativity, artistic expression, play, and symbol formation lie in what he calls the 'transitional phase'. He describes this as a point of subjective development which is situated between the mergence of the very early pre-oedipal period, where no boundaries between self and other appear to exist, and the point where we experience ourselves as subjects and others as objects outside ourselves:

> From birth, therefore, the human being is concerned with the problem of the relationship between what is objectively perceived and what is subjectively conceived of, and in the solution of this problem there is no health for the human being who has not been started off well enough by the mother. The intermediate area to which I am referring is the area between primary creativity and objective perception based on reality-testing. The transitional phenomena represent the early stages of the use of illusion, without which there is no meaning for the human being in the idea of a relationship with an object that is perceived by others as external to that being. (Winnicott 1982, p. 13)

According to Winnicott, this stage is characterized by feelings of ambivalence, particularly about mergence and separation, about what is self and other, and about loss of the other. Modern literature has, in many ways, been caught up with precisely this ambivalence and blurring (from James's perspectivism, for example, to John Hawkes's menacing nightmare landscapes where subjective projection and introjection dissolve all boundaries between inner and outer). Yet it is evident that the emphasis of modern aesthetic theory has been on separateness, distance, *exaggeration* of the boundaries between self and other. As the conceptual basis of the liberal notion of an essential 'unified' self was eroded by historical events, modern physics, Freudianism, and the philosophical undermining of positivism, a new 'perspectivist' awareness entered twentieth-century writing – but it is as if the full implications of this conceptual shift were too disturbing, psychologically, to be acknowledged. One can see the development of autonomy theory, the emphasis on *aesthetic* distance and formal unity, as strategies which substitute for a *subject* conceived in terms of independence, separateness, autonomy. It was too threatening to place the ambivalence of 'potential space', the blurring of subject and object, at the theoretical centre of a new aesthetics and conceptualization of the subject. Instead there developed that defensive over-emphasis on 'impersonality' which characterizes modernism, and the regression to defences of splitting and fragmentation as in postmodernism.

The art historian Adrian Stokes has usefully extended Winnicott's discussion of 'potential space' and the transitional phase, to suggest:

> Our relationship to all objects seems to me to be describable in terms of two extreme forms, the one a very strong identification with the object, whether projective or introjective, whereby a barrier between self and not-self is undone, the other a commerce with a self-sufficient and independent object at arm's length. In all times except the earliest weeks of life, both of these relationships, in vastly different amalgams, are in play together, as is shown not only by psychoanalysis but by art, since the work of art is *par excellence* a self-sufficient object as well as a configuration that we absorb or to which we lend ourselves as manipulators. (Stokes 1961, pp. 10–11)

To argue that, in terms of recent psychoanalytic theories of gender, the first aesthetic option here is likely to be less threatening to women and the second more attractive to men is *not* to lay down absolute categories for the distinction between masculinity and femininity. These are not static, nor do they lie in a fixed relationship to biological sex. Each writer is likely to articulate forms and themes which can be related to her or his particular history, although that history *can* to some extent be theorized in the broader terms of the cultural development of gender.

At present, it is evident that women's greater sense of identity in relationship and need for connection functions, on the whole, to reproduce their psychological problems and oppression. Dependency, insecurity about self-concept, feelings of 'loss' and depression, the desire to please, a sense of inadequate boundaries, and therefore vulnerability to criticism or attacks on the 'self', are conditions present more often in women than in men, and arise out of their economic and cultural situation. What is needed is social change which would facilitate the development of a subjectivity based on a relational identity where sameness *and* difference are not mutually exclusive or split into categories of gender, but are recognized as *equally* important aspects of an effective sense of self. Indeed, I would then be able to experience myself as both part of and merged with other people and, simultaneously, as independent of them, occupying my own subjective space and 'small, personal voice'.

Many twentieth-century women writers, struggling to express and explain their dissatisfaction with available aesthetic norms, have articulated through the themes and formal structures of their work a vision of a world which could accommodate such a conception of subjectivity. Writers like Woolf, Lessing, and Christa Wolf have developed formal strategies which emphasize modes of merging or connection rather than separation and fragmentation. Nevertheless, they have also registered their awareness of the *arrest* to feminine development brought about by an economic system and a family structure which produce in women dependency, insecurity, lack of autonomy, and an incomplete sense of who they are, even at the level of bodily ego. Writers like Margaret Drabble and Grace Paley, again, produce fictions which show the centrality of the mother–infant bond not in terms of a 'natural' connection but in terms of the cultural reproduction of mothering.

Chodorow has argued that, because women retain the pre-oedipal connection to the mother at the same time that the father becomes a love object, there is no oedipal resolution or absolute 'change of object' for the girl: 'A girl never gives up her mother as an internal love object, even if she does become heterosexual' (Chodorow 1978, p. 127). Because men (psychologically and socially developed to exaggerate separateness and to deny affective connection *as the basis of identity*) cannot become adequate substitutes for this early relationship, women thus seek to perpetuate the early relational triangle (which has not been resolved) through their *own* mothering. Thus 'mothering' is invested with a mother's often conflictual, ambivalent, yet powerful need for her own mother. That women turn to children to fulfil emotional or even erotic desires unmet by other men or other women means that a mother expects from infants what only another adult should be expected to give (Chodorow 1978, p. 212). She may seek in her son those signs of sexual difference which provide possibly even *erotic* gratifications (as does Mrs Morel in Lawrence's *Sons and Lovers* (1913)) or, in her daughter, both confirmation of her own identity as a woman, and behaviour which will appear to explain to her the cultural devaluation of femininity (being 'over-emotional' or 'clingy' or 'vain', for example). Psychologists such as Luise Eichenbaum and Susie Orbach have analysed the consequences for daughters, in particular, of such an attachment. Girls often develop a deep need to please, a feeling that self-containment is selfish, and they learn to repress unmet childhood needs which, because they come to seem overwhelming and insatiable to both themselves and others, must remain hidden in the inner object world. Wider cultural reinforcements teach girls to be aware of how their actions affect *others* and thus to become cautious about self-expression. Cultural approval, they learn, is reserved not for their own self-advancement but for their expressions of concern for others ('She's a good mother and wife', 'What a helpful little girl you are'), for their thoughtfulness and nurturant behaviour. As Eichenbaum and Orbach point out, women's second-class position in patriarchy is reflected in their psychology: lack of confidence, powerlessness, overdependence, insecurity, leading to competitiveness with other women, self-condemnation, and an inability to feel whole.

What many women writers are exploring, therefore, is how human beings might be able to achieve a sense of identity which consists of accepting both connection *and* separation, so that neither is experienced as a threat. Identity would not depend on the rejection of or identification with a deeply ambivalently experienced and negatively valued figure. Women would not therefore seek to re-create the relationships of the oedipal triangle through their children. Men might be able to develop the relational, nurturant aspects of their own personalities which have been split off and devalued. Each sex would thus become less threatening to the other; men would feel less anger towards women and women less resentment towards men. Such a shift would involve changing the relations between public and private, the spheres of 'production' and 'reproduction', whose separation perpetuates the unequal evaluation of gender and the splitting of the 'emotional' from the 'rational'. If such changes were reflected in the equal sharing of functions within the family, then there would be hope for a radical reconstruction of gender and subjectivity. In the meantime we can turn to literature as one site of the expression of the desire for, and fear of, such change. The rest of this book will attempt to analyse the alternative perceptions and developments in the work of women writers who have resisted, rejected or expressed a dis-ease with both the premises of the dominant aesthetics and the cultural definitions of subjectivity in the twentieth century.

Chapter Three

FROM MODERNIST TEXTUALITY TO FEMINIST SEXUALITY; OR WHY I'M NO LONGER A-FREUD OF VIRGINIA WOOLF

WOOLF, TRADITIONAL READINGS: 'CLASSIC' MODERNIST AND LIBERAL FEMINIST

This chapter will examine the work of Virgina Woolf, whose writing, it seems to me, has consistently been misread purely in terms of an aesthetics of modernism. Such a reading prises her formal aesthetics away from their basis in a political feminist critique of the dominant patriarchal values which she saw reflected in the conventions of traditional nineteenth-century fiction. Moreover, it overlooks her commitment to the articulation of alternative modes of subjectivity which, in fact, place her close to the concerns of many contemporary women writers. This is not to argue that Woolf's writing does not share the intensely self-conscious scrutiny of form and dissatisfaction with nineteenth-century realist aesthetics foregrounded in the work of Joyce, Eliot, Pound, and Forster. I would agree with Michèlle Barrett that

> it would be wrong to argue that Virginia Woolf ever subordinated her conception of the integrity of *Art* to the overt expression of her political views, and indeed there is a real tension in her work between these two. While much of her work is explicitly political in nature, and of course *Three Guineas* is highly polemical, she frequently resisted the intrusion of any attitude which, as she wrote to Lytton Strachey, 'gets into the ink and blisters the paper' of her novels. (Barrett 1979, p. 22)

Taking a narrow *formalist* view, Woolf's technical strategies are undeniably 'modernist', involving: presentation through inter-subjective perception or a post-impressionist/Cubist dissolution of the external shape of objects through multiple perspectives and reformulation of them in an internally associative 'spatial form'; erosion of the 'solidity of the specific' or the details of the external world presented through narrative description, summary, and plot; disappearance of 'character' as the expression in action of a fixed inner 'essence'; replacement of the conventional forms of causal and temporal organization with forms of spatial structuration such as mythic analogy, symbolic association, leitmotif, the condensation and displacement of primary process logic; loss of narratorial authority and reliability; metaphorical substitution or displacement foregrounding the creative process itself as it 'transfigures the commonplace'. To analyse Woolf's writing *simply* in such terms, however, encourages a critical tendency to interpret the political, philosophical, and broader human concerns of her novels in terms of self-reflexive aesthetic artifice: the view that they are novels 'about' the artistic process itself; 'about' form or 'fact' versus 'vision'; 'about' intimations of mortality and their transcendence through the symbolic order of significant form. When Mr Ramsay's philosophical work (in *To the Lighthouse* [1927]) is presented, ironically, in the 'impressive' terms of being about 'subject and object and the nature of reality' *and* in the absurd terms of getting to letter R in the alphabet, surely there lurks here a warning to the critic to avoid the reductionism of presenting Woolf's *own* writing in such arid and schematic binary terms and series. Very often, of course, such readings of Woolf are supported with biographical evidence of her periods of insanity, her obsession with death, and her final suicide. This material is offered to confirm the image of a writer who produces internally coherent and permanent symbolist worlds, designed to assert the transcendental power of art as fixing the significance of the human imagination in the face of temporality and mortality. They offer a view of her work, in other words, in terms of the historically recurring (masculine) ideal of the unified transcendental ego.

Certainly Woolf *was* influenced by the idealist theories of G. E. Moore and Henri Bergson, by the formal aesthetics and autonomy theory of Fry and Bell, and by the dominant liberal conceptions of political and historical change. To read her fiction *exclusively* in such terms, however, is to ignore her recognition of material determinism (one cannot write without an income and a room and access to libraries), her non-fictional feminist work, and her opposition to a broadly liberal conception of 'self' with its separation of the public and the private (vehemently attacked in *Three Guineas* [1938]). A commitment to the socialist critique of the division of labour (particularly its overvaluation of the intellectual and scientific) and the inequalities of property ownership emerges in some of her writing. Powerfully expressed, also, is her resentment of her own experience of being a younger daughter in an exceptionally high-achieving, middle-class, patriarchal family (with a mother who signed Mrs Humphrey Ward's anti-suffrage petition and a father who wrote in 1907 that it was *natural law* for a wife to have no legal rights, property, money, or education). What *this* writing suggests is a very different image of Woolf from the aesthetically detached, idealist, and invalided Bloomsbury figure of much traditional literary criticism. 'All that summer she was mad' may have been true, but she was mad with rage and frustration, and for good reason. One can be 'mad' if, because of one's sex, it is considered inappropriate to offer one education or training for the mind. Her brother Toby was sent away to school while she remained at home with Vanessa to be trained for the role of wife and mother, the role of 'Angel in the House' which she was so vehemently to reject: a woman

> intensely sympathetic. She was immensely charming. She was utterly unselfish. She excelled in the difficult arts of family life. She sacrificed herself daily. ... Directly ... I took my pen in my hand to review that novel by a famous man, she slipped behind me and whispered: 'My dear, you are a young woman. You are writing about a book that has been written by a man. Be sympathetic; be tender; flatter, deceive; use all the arts and wiles of our sex. Never let anybody guess that you have a mind of your own. Above all, be pure.' ... Had I not killed her she would have killed me. ... Whenever I felt the shadow of her wing or the radiance of her halo upon my page, I took up the inkpot and flung it at her. She died hard. (Woolf [1931] in Barrett 1979, pp. 59–60)

However, even when dead, she leaves an absence. In the next paragraph Woolf implicitly reveals her impatience with the naïvety of those theories which suggest that by simply throwing off 'false' social roles we can discover the 'true' self:

> The Angel was Dead; what then remained? You may say that what remained was a simple and common object – a young woman in a bedroom with an inkpot. In other words, now that she had rid herself of falsehood, that young woman had only to be herself. Ah but what is herself? I mean, what is a woman? I assure you, I do not know. I do not believe that you know ... telling the truth about my experiences as a body, I do not think I solved. I doubt that any woman has solved it yet .... You have won rooms of your own in the house hitherto exclusively owned by men. You are able, though not without great labour and effort, to pay the rent. You are earning your five hundred pounds a year. But this freedom is only a beginning; the room is your own, but it is still bare. It has to be furnished; it has to be decorated; it has to be shared. (Woolf [1931], in Barrett 1979, pp. 60–3)

Woolf recognizes that changing the social relations between men and women at a material level is essential, but not adequate in itself to bring about a redefinition of the human subject in the terms she desires. I would argue, in fact, that her commitment to a feminist concern to deconstruct the gender distinctions which bind women's psychology to charm and dependency and men's to fact and objectivity, and her search for a formal aesthetic mode which could express an alternative, relational view of human subjectivity, has been misunderstood by both 'modernist' and many feminist critics.

What she attempts to express in her writing are the dangers of an over-masculinized culture which worships the isolated, autonomous, rational, and controlled 'ego' (the Bradshaws and Tansleys of the world), and she tries to suggest an alternative view of human relations which emphasizes provisionality but connectedness, a subjectivity defined in relationship and in specific but historically changing context.

She does, indeed, seem to perceive the world, and to seek a formal embodiment of this perception, in a classically 'feminine' relational manner. Beyond this, however, she asks for a new validation of such a perception which would involve radical social changes. She believed that women wrote differently from men:

There is the obvious and enormous difference of experience in the first place; but the essential difference lies in the fact not that men describe battles and women the birth of children, but that each sex describes itself. ... there rises for consideration the very difficult question of the difference between the man's and the woman's view of what constitutes the importance of any subject. From this spring not only marked differences of plot and incident, but infinite differences in selection, method and style. (Woolf [1918], in Barrett 1979, p. 71)

This was written early in her career. Later her sense of these differences becomes more acute and more *politically* grounded. *Three Guineas* [1938] and *Between the Acts* [1941] are haunted by her fears about the rise of fascism, and, particularly in the former, she links this with the construction of subjectivity through a social hierarchy in which men possess and control women. Even within the same class, she argues, women are basically outsiders in relation to men, and she calls on women to refuse the masculine values of militarism, hierarchy, and authoritarianism. Such values are linked not only to the patriarchal politics of fascism, but also to the so-called 'enlightened' practices of bourgeois liberalism. She calls on women both to draw strength from their marginalization, so they may express their alternative views of the world and of subjectivity, and to resist that marginalization if their voices are to be heard at all:

For all the dinners are cooked; the plates and cups washed; the children sent to school and gone out into the world. Nothing remains of it all. All has vanished. No biography or history has a word to say about it. And the novels, without meaning to, inevitably lie. (Woolf [1938], p. 89)

First, therefore, women must achieve economic independence in order to render visible their alternative political voice, for 'intellectual freedom depends upon material things. Poetry depends upon intellectual freedom. And women have always been poor, not for two hundred years merely, but from the beginning of time' (Woolf [1938], p. 106). They must become aware of their oppression through the pernicious gratifications of the 'Angel in the House' and thus view their social alienation not as the product of an essential 'femaleness' but as the product of an unequal social system. Above all, however, they must resist the temptation to fight men on their own terms and to share the dominant perception of human nature as necessarily individualistic, aggressive, and competitive. Woolf uses the devices of satire and comedy to undermine the edifices of the 'masculine' intelligence (its rituals, titles, buildings, limousines, legal, medical, and educational institutions), which reify the system at the expense of the human beings it is intended to serve. We forget that history is not built simply out of the 'admirable fabric of the masculine intelligence' (*To the Lighthouse* [1927], p. 64), a sort of iron girder, but also through the areas *between*, the links and affiliative ties left to women to maintain and to characters like Lily Briscoe artistically to express ('something she remembered in the relations of those lines cutting across, slicing down'; p. 243). The colonel in *Between the Acts* [1941] may sit back bemused at Miss La Trobe's pageant, protesting 'What's history without the Army?' (p. 115), but the novel suggests that history is not simply winning wars, it is also the 'between', the 'no man's' land largely inhabited by women.

This 'between' involves the daily domestic duties, attention to human feelings, and maintenance of connection, often expressed in Woolf's work (as in later writers such as Alice Walker) through the images of knitting, stitching, or weaving. In *A Room of One's Own* [1928], Woolf asserts that art, too, is a collective product, misconceived in aesthetic theory always in terms of 'individuality' and personal expression. Reaching down a novel by a well-regarded writer, 'Mr A', Woolf notes a shadow creeping across the page:

It was a straight dark bar, a shadow shaped something like the letter 'I'. One began dodging this way and that to catch a glimpse of the landscape behind it. Whether that was indeed a tree or a woman walking I was not quite sure. Back one was always hailed to the letter 'I'. One began to be tired of 'I'. Not but what this 'I' was a most respectable 'I', honest and logical; as hard as a nut and polished for centuries by good teaching and good feeding. I respect and admire that 'I' from the bottom of my heart. But – here I turned a page or two, looking for something or other – the worst of it is that in the shadow of the letter 'I' all is shapeless as mist. Is that a tree? No, it is a woman. (*A Room of One's Own*, p. 98)

It is through Woolf's attempt to redefine human subjectivity in terms which will *not* polarize men and women into the categories of 'rationality' and 'emotionality', or 'fact' and 'vision', that her political commitment finds expression in her 'modernist' formal strategies. Woolf is not urging a reversal of the valuation of 'vision' over 'fact', but attempting to articulate the crippling effects on the human individual of a social system which enforces such rigid gender definitions and produces pathological patterns of behaviour in actual women and men. She certainly does not identify absolutely with the articulation of femininity as 'vision'. She explores in characters like Mrs Ramsay, Clarissa Dalloway, and Rachel Vinrace the pernicious consequences of this 'vision' when it is produced out of an economic and emotional dependency on others within patriarchal institutions like conventional marriage, which stifle for women all possibility of autonomy. Such characters are revealed as caught between the suicidal desire to withdraw into a private space, the room of one's own, which, as Showalter has pointed out (Showalter 1978), is the grave, and the need to incorporate and devour others in an attempt to fill that absence of 'something central which permeated' (*Mrs Dalloway* [1925], p. 36). In object-relations terms, such a total loss of the boundaries of ego, either through dissolution outwards of one's inner objects (projection), or through assimilation inwards of external objects (introjection), produces ultimately a sense that one does not exist. Clarissa, compelled to bring people together at her parties, projects on to external objects her own need for *inner* fusion, completeness, and relationship, and thus as 'hostess' introjects an unsatisfactory substitute for the wholeness she retains only in her nostalgic memories of the 'pre-oedipal' pastoral childhood world of Bourton and Sally Seton. Septimus, meanwhile, *cannot* retain his inner objects, which dissolve out into the external world until his feelings of manic omnipotence give way to those of paranoia as he perceives Holmes and Bradshaw coming to devour him at the request of his wife.

In a society which did not overvalue separateness and rationality at the expense of the relational and affective, an ability to conceive of oneself as 'blurred at the edges' through one's connection to, and partial definition through, others would not threaten one's sense of identity and autonomy. Clarissa would not need to withdraw into a world of pre-oedipal desire which must always remain outside the dominant symbolic order. She could instead actually translate her glimpse of the possibility of connection ('a match burning in a crocus; an inner meaning almost expressed'; p. 36) into relationships with others which might persist into the world outside the party hall. Woolf thus opposes to the 'imperial ego', which is the ideal of masculine culture, a concept of subjectivity which emphasizes the collective, relational, and dispersed rather than the discrete and autonomous. In an essay called 'Street haunting', she wrote:

> Is the true self this which stands at the pavement in January, or that which bends over the balcony in June? Am I here or am I there? Or is the true self neither this nor that, neither here nor there, but something so varied and wandering that it is only when we give rein to its wishes and let it take its way unimpeded that we are, indeed, ourselves. Circumstances compel unity; for convenience sake a man must be a whole. The good citizen when he opens his door in the evening must be banker, golfer, husband, father, not a nomad wandering the desert. ... When he opens his door he must run his fingers through his hair and put his umbrella in the stand like the rest. (Woolf [1928], p. 161)

This passage is, undeniably, expressed in terms suggestive of Bergsonian conceptualizations of time and identity and of the post-impressionist aesthetics of Roger Fry and Clive Bell. It thus appears to support a reading of Woolf in purely modernist terms. It carries, however, what seem to be *post*modernist reverberations in the insistence on the illusory wholeness of the subject, a dispersed subject rather than one defined in terms of organic coherence. Woolf is clearly acutely aware of the extent to which one's sense of self is a *theory* of the self constructed out of available social practices and discourses. The 'I', in fact, is always situated in relation and relative to the 'you' of the other. Continuity is based, therefore, upon one's ability to assimilate and relate dispersed and contradictory discourses to form a 'whole'. Breaks in one's sense of self occur when contradictions erupt to remind one of the illusory or imaginary nature of this subjective wholeness. In my view, this involves a 'postmodern' awareness on Woolf's part that the discourses of the aesthetic (transcendence, integration, significant form) cannot always maintain their imaginary coherence. Her novels are centred on loss and desire: the desire for an imagined pre-oedipal wholeness which eludes aesthetic expression but which is recognized as offering not only unity but also death conceived as undifferentiation. Struggling to position herself amidst the contradictory discourses of modern aesthetics, liberalism, humanitarianism, socialism, and early feminism, and as a middle-class woman aware of the contradictions of her relationship to power and knowledge, it is not surprising that, at times, Woolf sought resolution through such an aesthetics of transcendent form. To read her novels *purely* in such terms, however, is to ignore her commitment to political change expressed through a 'postmodernist' and feminist awareness of the inauthenticity of such an aesthetic ideal.

Yet her fiction is rarely read in terms of these latter commitments. *To the Lighthouse*, for example, has been given an array of 'modernist' readings which emphasize her concern with time and identity, with multiplicity of perspective, with transcendence through art, and with 'fact' versus 'vision' as male and female universal principles. One can randomly select almost any passage in the novel to support such a reading. As the boat approaches the lighthouse near the end, for example:

'It will rain', he remembered his father saying. 'You won't be able to go to the lighthouse.' The Lighthouse was then a silvery misty-looking tower with a yellow eye that opened suddenly and softly in the evening. Now – James looked at the Lighthouse. He could see the white-washed rocks; the tower, stark and straight; he could see that it was barred with black and white; he could see windows in it; he could even see washing spread on the rocks to dry. So that was the Lighthouse was it? No the other was the Lighthouse too. It was sometimes hardly to be seen across the bay. In the evening one looked up and saw the eye opening and shutting and the light seemed to reach them in that airy sunny garden where they sat. (p. 26)

The passage begins with a blurring of the distinction between past and present which foregrounds the complexity of identity as present sensation and memory, a fragile continuity through time. The symbolic properties of the lighthouse as the unification of 'fact' (linked to Mr Ramsay) and 'vision' (linked to Mrs Ramsay) are also foregrounded. The multiple and subjective nature of reality is emphasized in James's perception of it. The ambiguous phrase, 'nothing was simply one thing', hints at the identification of unity and permanence with death, and of plurality and multiplicity with life. James's own oedipal resolution is recognized as he comes to see the lighthouse in 'masculine' as well as 'feminine' terms. The interpenetration of the human and the non-human is suggested in the references to the 'eye' of the lighthouse as it watches them in the garden watching it. The interpenetration of the physical and the metaphysical is suggested by the transition from *looking* (as perception) to *vision* (as insight). The repeated sentence which opens the paragraph circles back to the discussion of the first scene in the novel and suggests the permanence, recurrence, and eternality of the human situation.

Thus can one list the overtly 'modernist' formal and thematic aspects of the passage. More generally, one sees the loss of confidence in the nineteenth-century belief in an organic moral relationship between the form and interconnections of the novel's structure and language and the actual relations of the world outside the fiction. The realist blending of public and private experience (through the formal presentation of authorial omniscience and limited point of view to produce an impression of a commonly experienced historical world) is displaced by an emphasis on *internal* self-referring coherence and a loss of established moral connection between inner and outer. Order is not to be discovered at the level of causal chronology or historic determination, but through the play of separate consciousnesses transcending time, or at a deeper level of 'impersonality' involving a loss of self and historical significance. Such order is constructed internally through symbolic self-referentiality or 'spatial form' (see Frank 1958). In such a 'modernist' reading it is the *artist* who creates order. Here it appears to be Lily, painting her picture, who resolves the conflicting attitudes of excessive detachment from and immersion in life represented by the

97

Ramsays, and who produces something of permanence by translating her 'vision' on to canvas. In such a reading, the novel is 'about' art as transcendence; impersonality triumphing over the flux and impermanence of human history.

Some critics have, ironically, read Woolf narrowly as a modernist and then criticized her for this. Frank Gloversmith, for example, has attacked her aesthetics of impersonality, arguing that in her use of the interior monologue 'its separateness, its privacy, its radical otherness is precisely what the whole force of the writing privileges and authenticates' (Gloversmith 1984, p. 189). He sees her merging of characters' and narrators' voices through extensive use of free indirect discourse as the expression of an authoritarian desire to suppress antithesis and contradiction. Similarly her use of extensive metaphoric substitution functions to deny particularity and 'historical' existence. In his view, Woolf simply turns her back on the material world of historical change, associating it in naïve and oversimplified terms with the masculine ego because

> the aesthetic sensibility, like Lily's and Mrs Ramsay's, must preserve its identity by refusing the turbulence of acceding to emotional tensions. Lily's 'creativeness', her visionary sense, depend on stamping out her sexual response to Tansley, and on suppressing her insistently erotic awareness of Paul Rayley. The cost of individuality, emotional autonomy, is to kill off the 'masculine' order which is within. (Gloversmith 1984, p. 195).

Gloversmith first ignores the fact that Lily's ambivalence about human sexuality is a consequence of her recognition of its regulation through social institutions like marriage, which produce Mrs Ramsay's loss of autonomy and the identification of self entirely as a response to others' needs and definitions, and which also produce the imperious authoritarianism and childlike dependency of Mr Ramsay. It is not surprising that Lily is suspicious of Paul Rayley's erotic awareness! Second, it is clear that the old image of Woolf as the withdrawn, invalided aesthete of Bloomsbury lurks behind Gloversmith's assessment of her. In my view, the novel *insistently* refuses the sort of 'impersonality' which such criticism ascribes to it, and in its exploration of the psychological roots of subjectivity and gender within the context of a late Victorian marriage it reveals an *acute* awareness of the historical determinants of human behaviour.

Returning to the passage quoted earlier, this too can be read outside a simply 'modernist' interpretation. It seems to me that the central concern expressed here is not with unity, impersonality, and permanence, but with the need for human connection, the recognition of dispersal, of provisionality, and of the *sinister* attraction of a conversion of historical stereotypes (which curtail the development of human beings) into universal formal 'essences'. An entry in Woolf's diary for 1926 (as she approached completion of the novel) suggests that these were the concerns uppermost in her mind. Watching two girls walking down a dusty road, she writes:

> My instinct at once throws up a screen, which condemns them: I think them in every way angular, awkward and self-assertive. But all this is a great mistake. The screens shut me out. Have no screens, for screens are made out of our own integument; and get at the thing itself, which has nothing whatever in common with a screen. The screen-making habit, though, is so universal that probably it preserves our sanity. If we had not this desire for shutting people off from our sympathies we might perhaps dissolve utterly; separateness would be impossible. But the screens are in excess; not the sympathy. (*A Writer's Diary* [1953], p. 100).

Indeed, Woolf records earlier (20 April 1919) that the diary form itself is important to her because of its screen-breaking potential, its ability to record the 'loose, drifting material of life', in a form 'loose knit and yet not slovenly, so elastic that it will embrace anything, solemn, slight or beautiful that comes into my mind' (*A Writer's Diary*, p. 23). In *To the Lighthouse* the desire for distance and impersonality which Gloversmith ascribes to Woolf is, in fact, rendered absurd in the figure of Augustus Carmichael, the symbolist poet. Lily, struggling with her painting and her uncertainty about the value of art (which mirrors her author's enterprise), sees Mr Carmichael asleep on the lawn and thinks that he would express 'how "you" and "I" and "she" pass and vanish; nothing stays; all changes; but not words, not paint' (p. 276). Lily, meanwhile, paints with an awareness that 'it would be hung in the attics ... it would be rolled up and flung under a sofa' (p. 276). It is at this moment that she experiences acutely the direct pain of *loss*, the realization that Mrs Ramsay is gone. With it, however, comes the recognition that Mrs Ramsay is part of her, will live on in her, and that human life is worthwhile because of such connection and identification:

> For one moment she felt that if they both got up, here, now on the lawn, and demanded an explanation, why was it so short, why was it so inexplicable, said it with violence, as two fully equipped human beings from whom nothing should be hid might speak, then, beauty would roll itself up; the space would fill; these empty flourishes would form into shape; if they shouted loud enough Mrs Ramsay would return. 'Mrs Ramsay!' she said aloud, 'Mrs Ramsay!' The tears ran down her face. (p. 277)

At this moment Lily first sees Mrs Ramsay in her mind as an ordinary woman performing her daily tasks. It is the memory of the *everyday* human relationship which restores her and eases the pain of loss and not the sublime transcendence and impersonality of symbolist form.

Critical readings which interpret the novel as an assertion of how aesthetic impersonality can be the only possibility of human significance and order in a world otherwise rendered meaningless by death (in different ways those of Daiches, Bradbury, Friedman, Lodge, Empson, and Auerbach) tend to avoid confronting the novel's ambiguous presentation of 'vision', transcendence, and the character of Mrs Ramsay herself. Malcolm Bradbury offers a modified symbolist reading, for example: 'the repeated hints of a pattern which traces its mystery in the universe, the repeated suggestion that the flux is potentially a world of broken forms mirroring true forms in a world beyond, is the basis of Mrs Woolf's charged style of discourse' (Bradbury 1973, p. 129). He suggests that the 'vision' at the centre of the novel is represented by the 'unified sensibility' (Bradbury 1973, p. 131) of Mrs Ramsay, but, because she is too much tied to the human world to express the 'pattern', it is left to Lily, as artist, to translate it into Form. So the novel 'ends *as* composition, entire and of itself; while the flux may be the flux of consciousness, it moves inevitably towards a coherence, not of the human mind of the characters but of the aesthetics of composition' (1973, p. 132). Falling into the dichotomy discussed earlier, Bradbury thus argues that Woolf's work is simultaneously both 'too crystalline and complete' and too dependent on the 'particular and personal sensibility' (1973, p. 132).

Yet we have seen that Woolf fiercely opposed such a concept of impersonal form as she did the personal 'imperial' ego. Are we then simply to divorce her critical writing from her fiction and view the latter, as many critics have, as a sort of cathartic psychological exorcism of the ghosts of the beloved dead who haunted her mind and produced nervous collapse? Comparing Woolf to Joyce as central modernist writers, Michael Bell, for example, writes:

> The details of Joyce's world have a solid physical presence and he plays serenely at constructing orders out of them. For Woolf and her most typical characters, the very being of the world is more tenuous, evanescent and threatening. Hence, too, the order to be created represents a more urgent psychological investment. It is the unique stay not only against flux but against this terrifying drop into non-being. (Bell 1980, p. 73).

Mrs Ramsay is surely not, however, the focus of a simple affirmation of vision, but the focus for Woolf's very ambivalent feelings towards the socially constructed 'femininity' which she represents. Her 'vision' *could* form the basis of a better world of human relations but is ultimately expressed in the existing one in terms bordering on the pathological. For example, her moment of great triumph, her dinner party (often critically described as a tribute to her harmonizing 'vision'), can, in fact, be seen as a sacrificial offering, a rite of consumption and incorporation, whose narrative function is not to affirm the possibility of social relationship but to reveal Mrs Ramsay's need to consume others as they, ritualistically, consume her through the food she offers. In part, Mrs Ramsay clearly regards the meal as a celebration of her powers in joining Minta Doyle and Paul Rayley. They arrive late, led in by the maid and the steaming dish of food whose exquisite smell fills the room. The reader is informed, as if it were part of a tribal preparatory ritual, that the meal has taken three days to produce:

> And she must take great care, Mrs Ramsay thought, diving into the soft mass, to choose a specially tender piece for William Bankes. And she peered into the dish with its shining walls and its confusion of savoury brown and yellow meats and its bay leaves and its wine and thought, This will celebrate the occasion – a curious sense rising in her at once freakish and tender, of celebrating a festival, as if two emotions were called up in her, one profound – for what could be more serious than the love of man for woman, what more commanding, more impressive, bearing in its bosom the seeds of death; at the same time these lovers, these people entering into illusion glittering-eyed, must be danced round with mockery, decorated with garlands. (*To the Lighthouse*, pp. 155–6)

Mrs Ramsay is presented here as a high priestess, self-conscious of her power, plunging into the 'soft mass' of the meat in the pot as into the human flesh around her, kneading and moulding and rearranging. Throughout the scene, Lily, in particular, is profoundly drawn towards this power, at the same time that she struggles ferociously to resist it: 'For what happened to her, especially staying with the Ramsays, was to be made to feel violently two opposite things at the same time; that's what you feel, was one; that's what I feel was the other, and then they fought together in her mind, as now' (p. 159).

Lily is *not* simply repressing her emotions in a gesture of aesthetic withdrawal (cf. Gloversmith 1984). She is fighting for her identity, drawn by a profound desire for identification with Mrs Ramsay as archetypal mother, and simultaneously fighting against that urge to dissolve herself in the other woman which would annihilate her struggle for selfhood. Mrs Ramsay *needs* Lily's dependency, for, since she herself is identified *solely* through her familial relational position (wife, mother, hostess), she *needs* others' dependency to confirm her own sense of self. She has no subjective existence, no autonomy, no power, outside these relationships. Through her representation, Woolf suggests the value of perceiving 'self' in terms of others rather than in the objective, separatist, overrationalized terms of Mr Ramsay, but shows how such a conception of subjectivity functions at present, particularly within the institution of marriage, to *oppress* rather than to *liberate* women. That she perceived the immense potential of such a perception is evident in her attempt linguistically to transpose through her own style Mrs Ramsay's relational mode (through, for example, her mingling of voices in the extensive use of free indirect discourse; in her smooth transitions from one consciousness to another; her conflation of past and present; her highly developed use of metaphor, which proceeds through connection, perceiving similarities which link unlike objects together). Woolf desires to write as a woman and, therefore, to dissolve boundaries, break down 'screens', reject the unified rational ego, but this should not mislead the reader into ignoring the ironic narratorial distancing of Mrs Ramsay and the critique of her 'vision' articulated through Lily Briscoe.

At the dinner party, we enter, through the use of free indirect discourse, Mrs Ramsay's perception of the scene:

> Foolishly, she had set them opposite each other. That could be remedied tomorrow. If it were fine, they should go for a picnic. Everything seemed possible. Everything seemed right. Just now (but this cannot last, she thought, dissociating herself from the moment while they were all talking about boots), just now she had reached security; she hovered like a hawk suspended; like a flag floated in an element of joy which filled every nerve of her body fully and sweetly not noisily, solemnly rather, for it arose, she thought, looking around them all eating there, from husband and children and friends, all of which rising in this profound stillness (she was helping William Bankes to one very small piece more and peered into the depths of the earthenware pot) seemed now for no special reason to stay there like a smoke, like a fume rising upwards, holding them safe together. Nothing need be said; nothing could be said. There it was, all around them. It partook, she felt carefully helping Mr Bankes to a specially tender piece, of eternity; as she had already felt about something different once before that afternoon; there is a coherence in things, a stability; something, she meant, is immune from change, and shines out ... (she glanced at the window with its ripple of reflected lights) in the face of the flowing, the fleeting, the

103

spectral, like a ruby; so, that again to-night she had the feeling she had had once today already, of peace, of rest, of such moments, she thought, the thing is made that remains for ever after. This would remain. (pp. 162–3)

In support of a 'modernist' reading, the use of free indirect discourse, which makes it difficult to distinguish narrator from character, does suggest an identification of the two. The unique 'individual' world-view can be seen to find its 'objective correlative' in an impersonal aesthetic system, Mrs Ramsay becoming the idealized bearer of Woolf's desire for symbolist wholeness, vision, and integration through multiplicity (like Eliot's 'unity in diversity'; Yeats's 'mask' and 'self'; Brooks's, Empson's, and Richards's perception of the work of art as a resolution of contradictions into an organic unity at a deeper level of form). The principle of repetition and its assertion of equivalence through syntactical structures ('nothing need be said; nothing could be said') and the foregrounding of alliterative effects; the self-conscious aestheticism ('there is a coherence in things') which acts as a metalingual gloss on the condition of the novel *as art*; the spatial form constructed through the intensive use of self-reference and reverberation; the identification of human emotion with the non-human (the moment's emotional 'stillness' arises with the steam from the dish) – all seem to suggest a correspondence between the formal strategies of the novel and Mrs Ramsay's perceptual view of the world, and thus a correspondence between Mrs Ramsay's 'vision' and Woolf's own.

Such a reading, however, ignores the contextualization of the passage within the novel as a whole, and the ambiguous presentation of Mrs Ramsay herself. Are we witnessing a 'transfiguration of the commonplace', as Mrs Ramsay transforms an ordinary meal into a profound and significant ritual, or are we witnessing Mrs Ramsay's pathological need to dissolve the boundaries between self and not-self, physical and spiritual, human and object world? Surely there is some irony intended in the presentation of 'eternity' through the description of helping someone to a piece of meat, or in Mrs Ramsay's resolute detachment from the talk of boots (later associated with Mr Ramsay), or in her simple certainty that the moment will remain for ever? The moment is actually fraught with conflicts and fragmentations of which she is unaware: the class antagonism of Tansley, the ambivalence of Lily, for example. Her celebratory culinary blessing will not preserve the relationship of Minta and Paul, and, even as this section of the novel closes, the room is already in the past and 'a sort of disintegration set in' (p. 173). Lily experiences, again, the sense that Mrs Ramsay has 'forced her will on them', for 'always she got her own way', and she sees her as 'absurd', 'childish', yet at the same time 'she put a spell on them all, by wishing, so simply, so directly. Mrs Ramsay exalted that ... worshipped that, held her hand over it to warn them to protect it, and yet, having brought it all about, somehow laughed, led her victims, Lily felt, to the altar' (p. 157).

At one level, just as Mr Ramsay represents the masculine imperial ego, defined in terms of objectivity, distance, separateness, reaching the letter R, and linked to the 'blade of a knife', Mrs Ramsay represents a classically feminine mode of subjectivity, seeking connection, relationship, and contextualization. She is a subject so *totally* dependent on others for identity, however, that in moments of solitude she feels herself to be 'a wedge-shaped core of darkness', a nothingness, which is not offered as a positive visionary alternative to the imperial ego, but is viewed as a product of the same repressive and oppressive social system. Mrs Ramsay's 'vision' is as annihilating as Charles Tansley's 'facts'. Mrs Ramsay is not simply Woolf's celebration of the feminine virtues of nurturance, intuition, and responsiveness. She is also the portrait of a woman whose constitution as 'feminine' entirely within the terms of the patriarchal system threatens not only her own sense of existence but also that of others. The passage containing her sinking into the 'wedge-shaped core of darkness', her sense of herself dissolving into things outside, losing the fret and stir of personality, *can* be interpreted as a celebration of her aesthetic negative capability, the capacity to become the things she perceives. It seems to me, however (as with the character of Rhoda in *The Waves* [1931]), that the description is less one of the liberation of the transcendent artistic imagination than one of a suicidal impulse. Mrs Ramsay experiences a sense, both terrifying and exhilarating, of a central absence of identity when no one else – family, friends, children, husband – is there to offer a confirmation of self. The passage is again highly ambiguous. While it suggests the possibility of freedom through self-dispersal, the capacity to escape identification in the gaze of others, it simultaneously builds upon the novel's articulation of a sense of Mrs Ramsay as someone whose identity is simply too dependent upon others for her to be able, successfully, to develop such possibilities. Instead she appears to experience a wish for death:

> it was a relief when they went to bed. For now she need not think about anybody. She could be herself . . . and one shrunk, with a sense of solemnity, to being oneself, a wedge-shaped core of darkness, something invisible to others. . . . Beneath it is all dark, it is all spreading, it is unfathomably deep; but now and again we rise to the surface and that is what you see us by. Her horizon seemed to her limitless. Losing personality, one lost the fret, the hurry, the stir; and there rose to her lips always some exclamation of triumph over life when things came together in this peace, this rest, this eternity; and pausing there she looked out to meet that stroke of the Lighthouse, the long steady stroke, the last of the three, which was her stroke, for watching them in this mood always at this hour one could not help attaching oneself to one thing especially of the things one saw; and this thing, the long steady stroke, was her stroke. Often she found herself sitting and looking, sitting and looking, with her work in her hands until she became the thing she looked at – that light for example. And it would lift up on it some little phrase or other which had been lying in her mind like that – 'Children don't forget, children don't forget . . .' (pp. 99–101)

What functions in predominantly destructive and life-denying terms (the regressive pre-oedipal desire for merger, for death, the desire to incorporate all things into oneself and to project oneself out, losing identity as a separate self), however, could, within a different social order, function in terms which could be life-enhancing for both women and men. If Mrs Ramsay could combine her sense of the relational basis of subjectivity, the capacity to relax ego boundaries, the openness to the external world and others, with a strong sense of autonomous definition (i.e. outside the terms of others, as 'wife' and 'mother'), then her 'wedge-shaped core' might express not a wish for death but a perception of the full potential of human beings to be both separate and related. Lily would not then have to move the purple triangle off-centre and arrive at the resolute decision never to marry, never to 'give' herself to another. For Mrs Ramsay *cannot* conceive of herself outside of others, and cannot conceive of them as not needing her. She wishes always to have a *baby* in her arms, growing whole through its total dependency: 'Oh but she never wanted James to grow a day older or Cam either. ... Nothing made up for the loss' (p. 93). The power accrued through the domestic dependency of others is her compensation for the lack of any power in the world outside or, in economic terms, within the family itself. She colludes with her husband's view of the intellectual inferiority and irrationality of women, listening to his talk about square roots and cubes (intentionally abstract and slightly absurd, surely?), feeling she can 'trust herself ... utterly' to the strength of the masculine intellect. She needs to see intellectuality as masculine and 'other' because she herself has little access to the world of facts and knowledge. She experiences herself outside language, outside the dominant symbolic order, unable to tell Mr Ramsay that she loves him because, unlike Lily, she *does* believe that women 'can't write' and 'can't paint'.

The subject positions culturally available to *all* the characters are shown to be restrictive and repressive: Lily is terrified of the loss of autonomy involved in the acceptance of the Victorian wife-and-mother role, the possessive and manipulative matriarch. But, as an artist, she is denied subjectivity because of her sex, and her active ambitions are regarded by the Ramsays as both the cause and the effect of her withered, 'puckered' lack of conventional 'femininity', her 'littleness', and her unavailability for human sympathy. Alternatively, for the male characters there is the systematic, dogmatic 'masculine' detachment and denial of dependency of Mr Ramsay, or the intransigent, hyper-defensive shrillness of the unfortunate Charles Tansley, his compulsion to 'assert himself, and so it would always be with him till he got his Professorship or married his wife and so need not always be saying, "I–I–I"' (p. 165). For the Ramsay daughters, it is prettiness and marriage (and death in childbirth); for the boys, it is strength and cleverness and the military or the academy (and death in battle). A social system which produces such a binary opposition of masculine and feminine, and so rigidly structures men and women into these positions, promises only the ironic collapse of communication: misunderstanding, frustrated desire, and pathological incompleteness.

WOOLF AND THE PRE-OEDIPAL: A REREADING OF *TO THE LIGHTHOUSE*

Woolf does, indeed, express through her formal techniques the importance of a relational view of subjectivity which psychologists like Chodorow have shown to characterize the psychic formation of women. However, she sees clearly that it is both useless and dangerous for women to assert an identification wholly with such a relational, collective concept of subjectivity. Unless they also gain independence, a 'voice' in the symbolic order, a sense of autonomy, detachment, and individuality, then the relational qualities expressed through their nurturant capacities will continue to be devalued and marginalized, viewed as 'feminine' rather than profoundly *human*. 'Insight' and 'intuition' (slaves *have* to learn to 'tune' in to their masters' ways) count for little in the dominant order. If women 'can't write' and women 'can't paint', then they can't *express* their knowledge.

Woolf herself *can* express the invisible 'feminine' voice through the strategies of modernist form. She can emphasize the relatedness of subjects and their construction through objects in the world (for example, through the technique of 'triggering' subjective consciousness through communal responses to external events or descriptions). Her writing produces a sense of the loss of absolute boundaries through symbolic resonance, metaphoric substitution and linkage (Mrs Ramsay 'becomes' the things around her, *is* the Lighthouse stroke), and the denotative failure of language (she cannot 'name' her feelings for her husband, just as Lily can only paint Mrs Ramsay as a purple triangle). Loss of causal plot as the simulacrum of a teleological view of history and disappearance of the moral authority of the omniscient author are strategies common to many novels of the period, but used *specifically* in Woolf, it seems to me, as a formal articulation of a feminist politics. Unlike Joyce, Eliot, or Yeats, she does not rely upon a pre-existent public system of symbolic meanings (Christianity, Greek myth, Jungian archetypes) which reintegrate the dispersed moments at a deeper level of 'symbolic form'. In her work, meaning continuously shifts and can be referred back to no single point of origin in myth, history, or individual character. There is no explanatory core at a deeper formal or 'impersonal' level of the text. There *is* an overwhelming *desire* for such unity, but, because her novels recognize and explore the psychological roots of such desire, there is similarly a recognition of its life-threatening sterility.

The contradiction is articulated in *To the Lighthouse* both through the form of the novel and in the central thematic exploration of Lily's struggle between the desire for subjective autonomy and the desire to be at one with the mother-figure of Mrs Ramsay. Woolf herself always felt an acute lack of mothering, a loss of an idealized pre-oedipal bond with her mother Julia Stephen. Thus she sought to discover, in identifications with idealized others, and through the activity of writing (the desire to substitute words for the lost object), a wholeness which could never be. She wrote of her mother's life, divided among the needs and demands of eight or nine dependent human beings, that 'a woman who had to keep all this in being and under control must have been a general presence rather than a particular person to a child of seven or eight. Can I remember ever being alone with her for more than a few minutes? Someone was always interrupting' (Woolf [1939] p. 83).

The feeling of not having been mothered enough which creates an inability to free oneself from a pre-oedipal desire for and fear of the mother is, according to Eichenbaum and Orbach, characteristic of women and a consequence of our parenting arrangements. Recognizing herself as culturally devalued, the mother passes on to her daughter her ambivalent feelings about femininity. Experiencing her own feminine dependency needs as insatiable, uncontrollable, and inappropriate, she requires that her daughter also split off and repress such neediness in order to become a 'mature', competent woman. Object-relations theorists like Orbach and Eichenbaum have suggested that this commonly produces depression in adulthood, for the woman mourns for the split-off little girl whose needs have never been met, and longs for the ideal mother who could meet them. Moreover, the little girl, unlike the little boy, has no expectation of continued maternal nurturance from any mother-like person who might provide emotional support and understanding:

> Because of the internal psychological split between the little girl inside and the adult woman facing the world, many women suffer depression from a sense that no one will ever really see them whole. The discrepancy between the way others see them and the way they see themselves brings a sense of futility and hopelessness. (Eichenbaum and Orbach 1985, p. 150)

Mrs Ramsay, the mother of *To the Lighthouse*, strives to please, to ensure others' dependency on her, to see her own needs as utterly fulfilled in the service of her family and those connected to it. She desires a unity of structure in which she is the real, though invisible, centre. Lily is presented as a woman who both desperately desires the promise of familial wholeness which Mrs Ramsay holds out and yet recognizes, from the first, that to embrace such wholeness would involve a death of her own impulses towards non-familial achievement, independence, and creative satisfaction. The novel thus centres on the necessity for and the pain of loss in human relationships. Woolf herself, in fact, wrote in her diary:

> Father's birthday. He would have been 96, 96, yes, today; and could have been 96, like other people one has known; but wonderfully was not. His life would have entirely ended mine. What would have happened? No writing, no books – inconceivable. I used to think of him and mother daily, but writing The Lighthouse laid them in my mind – and now he comes back sometimes, but differently. (I believe this to be true – that I was obsessed by them both unhealthily and writing of them was a necessary act.) (*A Writer's Diary*, p. 137)

The novel actually begins with a struggle between desire and recognition of loss: Mrs Ramsay promises James that he can go to the lighthouse, Mr Ramsay insists that the weather will not permit. As his wife persists in arguing that the weather may improve, the narrator informs us that 'the folly of women's minds enraged him' (*To the Lighthouse*, p. 53). For Mrs Ramsay, though, to pursue truth with such astonishing lack of consideration for other people's feelings, to rend the thin veils of civilisation so wantonly, so brutally, was to her so horrible an outrage of human decency that without replying, dazed and blinded, she bent her head as if to let the pelt of jagged hail, the drench of dirty water, bespatter her unrebuked. There was nothing to be said. (p. 54)

Only a few lines later, however: 'she was quite ready to take his word for it, she said. ... He said: It won't rain; and instantly a Heaven of security opened before her' (p. 55).

The conversation introduces the reader to the play of fantasy and desire which pervades the quotidian world of this, and every, family. For James, going to the lighthouse is tied up with the illusion of infantile omnipotence, of being united with a pre-oedipal mother whom he identifies with the lighthouse itself. Thus his *violent* reaction to his father's refusal is the violence of the child towards the parental image. Mr Ramsay, in effect, attempts to deny the fulfilment of pre-oedipal desire, asserts a reality principle which insists that James enters the rational world of the symbolic order and accepts that desire can never, in fact, be satisfied. When his father says, 'It won't be fine':

Had there been an axe handy, a poker or any weapon that would have gashed a hole in his father's breast and killed him, there and then, James would have seized it. Such were the extremes of emotion that Mr Ramsay excited in his children's breasts by his mere presence; standing, as now, lean as a knife, narrow as the blade of one, grinning sarcastically, not only with the pleasure of disillusioning his son and casting ridicule upon his wife, who was ten thousand times better in every way than he was (James thought) but also with some secret conceit at his own accuracy of judgement. What he said was true. It was always true. He was incapable of untruth; never tampered with a fact. (pp. 12–13)

Throughout the novel, sexuality, though never *overtly* expressed, returns obsessively through language and metaphor. As the controversy about the weather continues and James draws closer to Mrs Ramsay, asserting a continued identification with her, Mr Ramsay too begins to seek sympathy from his wife, resenting his

111

son's displacement of himself. Mrs Ramsay, sitting with James in her arms,

> half-turning, seemed to raise herself with an effort, and at once to pour erect into the air a rain of energy, a column of spray, looking at the same time animated and alive as if all her energies were being fused into force, burning and illuminating (quietly though she sat, taking up her stocking again), and into this delicious fecundity, this fountain and spray of life, the fatal sterility of the male plunged itself, like a beak of brass, barren and bare. He wanted sympathy. (pp. 61–2)

As he stands between her knees 'very stiff, James felt all her strength flaring up to be drunk and quenched by the beak of brass' (p. 63). The father, feeling himself drawn into his wife's sympathy, at last, leaves 'like a child who drops off satisfied' (p. 64). As Mrs Ramsay settles back to read a fairy-tale to James, the whole fabric of herself 'fell in exhaustion upon itself ... while there throbbed through her, like the pulse in a spring which has expanded to its full width and now gently ceases to beat, the rapture of successful creation' (p. 64).

Mrs Ramsay is the source of both affective and erotic gratification, maternal and sexual object for both husband and son. The mingling of male and female sexual imagery reinforces her presentation as the pre-oedipal *phallic* mother. She welcomes the regressive need of her husband and the continued infancy of her children. She desires, like many women (because of their own early psychological development and economic position), to return to a pre-oedipal mode of relationship through her own mothering. She reveals an almost pathological compulsion to 'mother' both children and adults, while simultaneously seeking a sexual differentiation in James which will allow her to relate to him erotically.

In Lacanian terms, basic to all human beings is that the 'I' is alienated in the symbolic and non-existent in the sphere of the imaginary or the pre-symbolic. Desire is constituted through the search for an imaginary wholeness identified with the pre-symbolic. Men, however, do have compensatory power and definition in the symbolic – Mr Ramsay's 'masculine' posturing and access to knowledge, for example – whereas women are, according to Lacan, effectively 'written out'. In *To the Lighthouse* the desire for the recovery of an imaginary wholeness, a lost identity with the pre-oedipal mother, informs both the relations between the characters, particularly the women characters, *and* the actual language of the novel. As Lily seeks to recover Mrs Ramsay through her painting, so Woolf herself seeks, through words, a recovery of a lost imaginary wholeness. Yet, significantly, Lily can complete the painting only when she 'gives up' the desire for oneness with Mrs Ramsay, just as Woolf's novel ultimately suggests that the complete pattern of an aesthetic order can only ever be the projection of a desire whose actual realization would involve an annihilation of the self. Lily paints the purple triangle – representing the pre-oedipal dyad of mother and son (Mrs Ramsay sitting with James on her knee) – but places it *off-centre* and resists the urge to lose herself in the older woman and to identify with the feminine subject position she occupies as wife and mother.

Early on, attempting to resist Mrs Ramsay's compulsive matchmaking, Lily finds herself continually overwhelmed by the desire for unity:

> Could loving, as people called it, make her and Mrs Ramsay one? For it was not knowledge but unity that she desired, not inscriptions on tablets, nothing that could be written in *any language known to men*, but intimacy itself, which is knowledge, she had thought, leaning her head on Mrs Ramsay's knee. (p. 82; my italics)

Lily, implicitly recognizing the symbolic as an order constituted within the terms of the Law of the Father, and faced with the choice of alienation and masquerade (if she pursues her desire to paint) or acceptance and repression (of her desire in order to marry), longs to escape its terms altogether. Mrs Ramsay, as pre-oedipal mother, offers Lily a possibility of wholeness which the younger woman feels is denied her within the socially structured alternatives of marriage for women and worldly achievement for men. It is a union premised, however, on the dissolution of Lily's own sense of separate selfhood and involves an infantilist regression from the secondary social order. In part 1 of the novel, Lily's desire for such a state is uppermost, and the reader is most aware of her intense love for and idealization of Mrs

Ramsay and her resentment (like James's) of the intrusions of her husband. She desires, simply, incorporation, and such desire meets Mrs Ramsay's own need for the dependency on her of others. At the height of this feeling, Lily ponders: 'What art was there known to love or cunning, by which one pressed through into those secret chambers? What device for becoming, like waters poured into one jar, inextricably the same, one with the object one adored?' (p. 82). While Lily is caught up in such longing, however, she cannot paint, she is blocked, and it is only when she comes to accept the actual loss of the real woman that she can recognize the suicidal impulse in her wish for incorporation. Thus freed, she is able to complete her picture.

Involved in this recognition is Lily's increasing awareness of the *social* determinants of Mrs Ramsay's behaviour and her own desire to construct an identity founded on *resistance* to their coercions. Even as she lays her head on Mrs Ramsay's knee, her ambivalence flashes into consciousness, to be immediately repressed: 'Then, she remembered, she laid her head on Mrs Ramsay's lap and laughed and laughed and laughed, laughed almost hysterically at the thought of Mrs Ramsay presiding with immutable calm over destinies which she completely failed to understand' (p. 81). Such feelings of ambivalence return most insistently after Mrs Ramsay's death, as Lily attempts to complete the painting of her. Lily is forced through their intensity to return, temporarily, in her inner object world, to a pre-oedipal state of fragmentation, 'losing consciousness of outer things ..' and her name and her personality, and her appearance ... her mind kept throwing up from its depths, scenes, and names, and sayings and memories and ideas' (p. 246). This is a pre-linguistic world, the stage at which Freud posited the formation of a *bodily* ego. As she continues with her painting, she tries to fix the image of Mrs Ramsay sitting on the steps:

About life, about death, about Mrs Ramsay – no, she thought, one could say nothing to nobody. The urgency of the moment always missed its mark. Words fluttered sideways and struck the object inches too low. Then one gave it up. ... For how could one express in words these emotions of the body? express that emptiness there? ... It was one's body feeling, not one's mind. The physical sensations that went with the bare look of the steps had become suddenly extremely unpleasant. To want and not to have. . . . And then to want and not to have – to want and want – how that wrung the heart, and wrung it again and again! Oh Mrs Ramsay! She called out silently. (p. 275)

Lily's painting is both an act of reparation for her feeling of guilt that her own anger has somehow contributed to Mrs Ramsay's death, and a mark of her new-found separate identity. It becomes a symbol also of Woolf's own feminist commitment to a view of self in relationship where autonomy is not the separateness and isolation of getting to the letter R, but a way of perceiving one's connectedness to others and respecting the separateness involved in their connectedness to oneself. Mrs Ramsay will not speak her desire because she refuses the boundary between self and other imposed by language. Lily *can* 'speak', through her painting, because she sees the necessity for both separateness and relatedness, the connection of the symbolic to the realm of human emotion and the foundation of both upon loss and acceptance of its pain. Lily needs a connection to others which will reassure her of her own sense of self, but she does *not* need, as Mrs Ramsay does, to *devour* others or to 'melt out' into them. Praising Mr Ramsay's boots at the end, she can at last extend a sympathy which respects the object in itself and does not seek to incorporate or smother. (At the dinner party, of course, Mrs Ramsay had, significantly, distanced herself from a discussion of boots.) In effect, she is signalling her approval of the ability to stand on one's own feet, neither totally dependent on others nor requiring their dependency on oneself.

'SOMETHING CENTRAL WHICH PERMEATED': RECONSTRUCTING CLARISSA DALLOWAY

In effect, Lily, as well as James, perceives finally that 'nothing was simply one thing'. Unity does not exist *except* as 'nothing' and is thus a dangerous illusion in both art and life. It remains, however, a desired ideal which all of Woolf's novels confront and struggle to resist. In *To the Lighthouse* such desire is very

115

close to the surface of the text, but it is equally central, though less overt, to the structure of *Mrs Dalloway* [1925]. In this novel, the central character Clarissa intensely *fears* and *resists* what Mrs Ramsay seeks, but the very intensity of this reaction formation suggests that her *desire*, too, is equal to Mrs Ramsay's. Clarissa shares also with Mrs Ramsay the sense of the fragility of ego and the blurring of boundaries between self and other, the need to discover a sense of self in some permanent fixity of relations outside which will transcend human frailty (and, in Clarissa's case, influenza and a weak heart):

> Did it matter that she must inevitably cease completely: all this must go on without her; did she resent it; or did it not become consoling to believe that death ended absolutely? but that somehow in the streets of London, on the ebb and flow of things, here, there, she survived, Peter survived, lived in each other, she being part, she was positive, of the trees at home; of the house there, ugly, rambling all to bits and pieces as it was; part of people she had never met; being laid out like a mist between the people she knew best, who lifted her on their branches as she had seen the trees lift the mist, but it spread ever so far, her life, herself. (pp. 11–12)

Here resides the strength of Clarissa's attempt to express a subjectivity which refuses identification with that imperial ego which asserts a separateness, an 'order' and proportion, and defines itself in competition with, and through subjection of, the other. In a patriarchal society, however, such 'strength' is positioned as *weakness*, failure, the sense Clarissa has of 'what she lacked. It was not beauty. It was not mind. It was something central which permeated' (p. 36). Clarissa has refused the romantic passion offered by Peter Walsh, for, given her sense of the fragility of ego and the social position of women within marriage, she recognizes that she would have been swallowed up, incorporated:

> For in marriage, a little licence, a little independence there must be between people living together day in and day out in the same house, which Richard gave her, and she him. (Where was he this morning, for instance? Some committee, she never asked what.) But with Peter everything had to be shared;

everything gone into ... she had to break with him or they
would have been destroyed, both of them ruined, she was
convinced. (p. 10)

Instead Clarissa has married a Tory MP, Richard, a partnership
which cannot preserve her from the feeling of 'being herself
invisible; unseen; unknown ... this being Mrs Dalloway; not
even Clarissa any more; this being Mrs Richard Dalloway' (p.
13), but which allows her to withdraw when she wishes, from the
public appearance, to the monastic quiet of her room.

The 'Mrs Dalloway' which she presents to the world, arranging the rustling silk of her evening gown, is a willed composite of
parts. The struggle to assemble herself in this way is suggested in
an image which bears a striking resemblance to Lacan's
description of the mirror phase, where the individual misrecog-
nizes an illusory wholeness in the mirror which provides both
the possibility of entry into the symbolic world and entails her or
his necessary alienation from it. Alone with the memory of the
time she rejected Peter (merged in her mind with the experience
of the kiss from Sally), Clarissa looks in the mirror:

How many million times she had seen her face, and always
with the same imperceptible contraction! She pursed her lips
when she looked in the glass. It was to give her face point.
That was herself – pointed; dart-like; definite. That was
herself when some effort, some call on her to be herself, drew
the parts together, she alone knew how different, how
incompatible and composed so for the world only into one
centre, one diamond, one woman who sat in her drawing
room and made a meeting point. (p. 42)

The diamond image recurs later in the novel in association
with the complacent, uncaring, and almost sinister Lady Bruton.
Her egotistical obsessions have hardened into a 'core' of self,
'this object around which the essence of her soul is daily secreted
becomes inevitably prismatic, lustrous, half looking-glass, half
precious stone; now carefully hidden in case people should
sneer at it; now proudly displayed' (p. 121). Clarissa fears that
her own emotional withdrawal, her terror of merging, has
produced in her, too, a coldness, a hardness, a sense of herself as
bird-like, little, unavailable for sympathy. Despite her capacity

for relationship, therefore, Clarissa's feeling of not having
boundaries, of the struggle to will a 'self' which remains
precarious and threatened ('it was very, very dangerous to live
even one day' (p. 11)), her sense of 'invisibility' as Mrs Dalloway,
and her fears of incorporation by others, lead to a contradictory
pull in her between desire for intimacy and attachment and a
fear of its consequences which leads her to withdraw and
separate.

Peter Walsh, in fact, is thus perceived as a 'liberal' version of
those forces of patriarchy which are revealed so monstrously
and paradigmatically in the characters of Holmes and Bradshaw.
Like Mr Ramsay, but more insistently, he is identified with the
image of a knife ['an extraordinary habit that was, Clarissa
thought; always playing with a knife' p. (49)], and he too is a
figure who thrusts into and disrupts a pre-oedipal dyad,
demanding sympathy and attention. Like Lily and Mrs Ramsay,
Clarissa is haunted by a sense of loss, a longing for a wholeness
which she associates with Bourton and with the kiss of Sally
Seton, pure, untainted, outside the constraints and repressions
of the world of sexual codes and morals:

> The strange thing, on looking back, was the purity, the
> integrity of her feeling for Sally. It was not like one's feeling
> for a man. It was completely disinterested, and besides it had a
> quality which could only exist between women, between
> women just grown up. It was protective, on her side, sprung
> from a sense of being in league together, a presentiment of
> something that was bound to part them (they spoke of
> marriage always as a catastrophe). (p. 39)

She recognizes that to 'give' herself in such a fashion in the
symbolic world, in her relations particularly with men, is to offer
the self for consumption or to be seen oneself as attempting to
consume. Thus she robes herself in the attire of the society
hostess, arranges flowers, and retires periodically to her narrow
bed before emerging to arrange another social event, seeking
(but through the safe distance of social convention) the spurious
merging of herself with others, the *temporary* intimacy of the
party. Peter Walsh reflects upon Clarissa's compulsive party
organizing, on her need to maintain affiliative relations in this
way:

118

And behind it all was that network of writing, leaving cards, being kind to people; running about with bunches of flowers, little presents; So-and-so was going to France – must have an air cushion; a real drain on her strength; all that interminable traffic that women of her sort keep up; but she did it genuinely, from a natural instinct. (p. 86)

Yet, in the strange passage where he fantasizes a vision of the solitary traveller, Peter reveals the extent of his own ambivalence towards Clarissa's behaviour. He both desires women to be maternal, nurturant figures and simultaneously fears the loss of ego which sexual intimacy seems to threaten. Clarissa pulls him back into the past, into memory, and he sees this as characteristically feminine, 'for women live much more in the past than we do, he thought' (p. 62). She is conflated in his mind with the nurse/mother figure, apron blowing, who waits for the traveller: 'let me walk straight on to this great figure, who will, with a toss of her head, mount me on her streamers and let me blow to nothingness with the rest' (p. 65). Classically, Peter projects on to Clarissa his *own* fear of and desire for regression to the pre-oedipal. Woolf shows in *Mrs Dalloway* the extent to which Edwardian society as a whole has projected on to women its fear of intimacy and developed a structure of values in which 'propriety' becomes all, whereas intimacy and affection are seen as threatening and in need of control. Miss Kilman, with her passionate desire for conversion, her greed as she frustratedly consumes the chocolate éclairs (having been denied the 'pink cake' clearly associated with Clarissa's daughter, Elizabeth), is a projection of one aspect of this fear and a representation of its social consequences. The closed cars, mental institutions, military strategy, and the titles of patriarchal authority are another. The alternatives seem to be either an over-identification which 'consumes' others (and which is, on the whole, associated with the feminine) or a 'screening' which similarly destroys the subjectivity of the other by converting her or him to the condition of an object (an activity associated with the masculine). Clarissa is half aware that such restrictive polarizations curtail human potential and individual happiness, but, given her lack of power, it is only through her parties that she can express her desire for a different mode of relationship.

Thus is she connected throughout the novel to Septimus, another 'outsider' who feels alienated from the accepted polarization of gender roles. Unable during the war to suppress his need for emotional connection and thus to be 'manly', Septimus has been forced into the extreme psychological defence of total ego disintegration in order to protect his vulnerable sense of subjectivity. Clarissa's ego boundaries may be diffuse, necessitating her emotional protectiveness, but Septimus's have melted out entirely into the external object world so that he believes the trees have taken root in his body and he can communicate with God and animals. This manic defence against the fear of dissolution is continually threatened, however, by Holmes and Bradshaw: 'Human nature, in short, was on him – the repulsive brute, with the blood-red nostrils' (p. 102). Bradshaw diagnoses that Septimus has lost 'his sense of proportion', and, if the social institutions of family, status, and 'honour', cannot restore it, then 'he had to support him the police and the good society, which, he remarked very quietly, would take care, down in Surrey, that these unsocial impulses, bred more than anything by the lack of good blood, were held in control' (p. 113).

Clarissa shares Septimus's perception of Bradshaw, recognizing his power as the institutionalization of a masculine defence: the obsession with screens, reason, proportion, boundaries, the obliteration of others' subjectivity – 'they make life intolerable men like that ... there was in the depths of her heart an awful fear ... She had escaped. But that young man had killed himself' (p. 204). She recognizes in Septimus's suicide a sacrifice intended to preserve autonomy. She recognizes that he, like herself, has been unable satisfactorily to resolve the need for attachment and separateness, given the social positions and gender roles available to each of them. As Clarissa alternately withdraws and bursts forth like a flower, so Septimus, failing to maintain such balance, seeks the only unity available to him: death. Clarissa, mingling with her titled and powerful party guests, recognizes that Septimus has spoken for her; he 'had done it' (p. 206):

A thing there was that mattered; a thing wreathed about in her own life, let drop every day in corruption, lies, chatter.

This he had preserved. Death was defiance. Death was an attempt to communicate, people feeling the impossibility of reaching the centre which, mystically, evaded them; closeness drew apart; rapture faded; one was alone. There was an embrace in death. (p. 204)

Clarissa will not commit suicide but will have to continue to accept the masquerade of being Mrs Dalloway, seeking periodically the release of her narrow room, for, as the novel ends, 'there she was' (p. 215). This is not, in my opinion, an example of Woolf's recommendation of a feminine retreat into 'inner space', but an indication of her recognition of the *extreme* difficulty of killing the 'Angel in the House'. Elaine Showalter has argued that 'Woolf's female aesthetic is an extension of her view of women's social role: receptivity to the point of self-destruction, creative synthesis to the point of exhaustion and sterility. The ultimate room of one's own is the grave' (Showalter 1978, p. 297). This verdict seems to me to ignore Woolf's profound insight into the social and contradictory nature of desire at an unconscious level and her commitment to a vision of subjectivity which, though opposed to the unified, 'imperial' ego, would involve a recognition of both the self's relational connection to others and its separateness and autonomy.

VISION AND 'RE-VISION': THE LATER NOVELS

In her later novels this vision becomes more urgent and the expressed need for the dissolution of rigid ego boundaries, for receptivity and connection, even more central. *The Waves* [1931], in particular, focuses on the insight which Bernard expresses near the end of the novel:

But it is a mistake this extreme precision, this orderly and military progress; a convenience, a lie. There is always deep below it, even when we arrive punctually at the appointed time with our white waistcoats and polite formalities, a rushing stream of broken dreams, nursery rhymes, street cries, half-finished sentences and sights. (p. 219)

Here, the attempt to crystallize a diamond, to mould an 'inner core', the feeling that we must be 'very private, very explicit', because 'outside the undifferentiated forces roar', is seen explicitly as the product of a society which has split the public from the private so that the world of inner object relations has become disconnected from the world of external social relationships. Woolf perceives that this 'inner world' has become the domain of the female and that men and women find themselves positioned on either side of an ever-widening gulf. Bernard, above all, recognizes the necessity for a relational conception of self which would break down such distinctions between public and private, self and other, man and woman. He recognizes, too, the difficulty of achieving such a position. When he asks: 'Who am I? I have been talking of Bernard, Neville, Jinny, Susan, Rhoda and Louis. Am I all of them?' (*The Waves*, p. 248), he knows that to experience oneself as indistinguishable from a collective subjectivity may, however, be dangerous. Such a desire carries with it not only a disregard for the distinction between life and death, but also the possibility of annihilating one's own sense of selfhood. Early on, Bernard recognizes the cultural constitution of subjectivity through language and thus the *illusoriness* of the self-determining, unified subject: 'we melt into each other with phrases. We are edged with mist. We make an insubstantial territory' (p. 12). He accepts that the best we can do is to make up stories about people, aware always of their provisionality, refusing the lure of fixity. But he needs an audience for these stories, a response to his words which will allow for the placing of himself in relation to them: 'To be myself ... I need the illumination of other people's eyes, and therefore cannot be entirely sure what is myself' (p. 99). To admit his relational needs, however, does not involve him in the annihilation of his identity as it does for Rhoda, nor in the utter dependency on the sexual approval of others as it does for Jinny. When Rhoda looks into the mirror, seeking a unified image of self, she sees nothing, 'for I am not here. I have no face. Other people have faces; Susan and Jinny have faces; they are here'. (pp. 35–6). Like Septimus, Rhoda cannot distinguish a self at all, whereas Jinny seeks distinction only through the eyes of male approval. Sitting on a train, she 'puts forth a frill under his gaze', as a man surveys her. She experiences her body as an object, watching herself through the eyes of a man watching a woman, seeing her body as an artefact which produces pleasure in others. Meanwhile, Louis, the class and cultural outsider, finds security behind his mahogany executive desk, issuing commands that produce effects around the globe, compulsively asserting a will to dominate, a desire for achievement, substituting the alienation of the culturally marginal with the isolation of the 'man at the top': 'I luxuriate in gold and purple vestments. Yet I prefer a view over chimney-pots, cats scraping their mangy sides upon blistered chimney-stacks; broken windows; and the hoarse clangour of bells from the steeple of some brick chapel' (p. 188).

From *The Waves* onwards, Woolf experiments increasingly with the articulation of a more radically 'collective' concept of subjectivity, shifting the 'I' to 'we' and completing her rejection of the quest or romance plot. In *The Years* [1937] and *Between the Acts* [1941], she expresses the possibility of a new society based on a shifting, dispersed, multiple subjectivity which moves even further away from the dispositions of the familial constellation and the romance plot. Towards the end of *Between the Acts*, for example, Isa sits with Giles in the library, and surveying the dark uniform, the mark of masculine power, she expresses her longing for the 'time someone invented a new plot, or that the author came out from the bushes' (p. 150). Miss La Trobe's pageant expresses a pastoral desire for a new order, but the remnants of the old one – the military, the priest, the rituals of eating, the conflicts of family – weigh on the proceedings and impede the vision. One is reminded of Freud's admission in *Civilization and its Discontents* (1930) that, despite its unsatisfactory nature, he could not imagine how sexual relations would develop if the traditional family structure were to disappear. In this novel, too, the glimpse is only partial and extremely tentative.

The Years, in fact, with its abandonment of focused narrative and the romance plot, its loosely connected collection of friends, relatives, marginalized people, is more optimistic about the possibility of significant change. More characters articulate and share this vision. In the earlier novels only isolated characters, and then fleetingly, express the possibility of social change. In *The Voyage Out* [1915], Rachel Vinrace has to *die*, in order to escape the plot of marriage and romance, in the desperate manner of nineteenth-century heroines who are offered no other choice. Lily achieves some insight, but her 'expression' of this, her painting, will be hung in the attics. Clarissa hears Septimus's message, but, powerless, cannot translate it into social action. The social isolation of these women prevents their private vision connecting with that of others who also experience marginalization and oppression. They can only give parties, organize social gatherings, produce pageants, generate artistic symbols which are unlikely to be interpreted in the desired radical terms.

The Years begins in 1880 with the delineation of an oppressive, traditional, conflict-ridden patriarchal family where resentment and ambivalence pervade the everyday activities as mother lingers between life and death, and father pursues his mistress and middle-class respectability. Even in this early section of the novel, however, Woolf's formal techniques (the inconsequential interludes, the conversations left unfinished, the repetition of the same phrase by different characters) undermine the concept of fixed subjectivity and suggest a more fluid, social, relational view of identity. This is developed in the middle section of the novel where the family circle widens to include more distant members and friends, and at the end the family actually disintegrates to be replaced by the transient, informal groups of people who meet, disperse, and reassemble. The interior setting of the beginning also shifts on to the streets, into space, in and out of different houses. As Martin thinks back to the early days, he recognizes: 'It was an abominable system, he thought, family life, Abercrom Terrace. No wonder the house would not let ... there all those different people have lived, boxed up together, telling lies' (*The Years*, p. 169).

Again, parties are used to express the possibility of a shift in human relationships, but in this novel the reader is made continuously aware of the *social* pressures which bring people together and drive them apart. Woolf still does not underestimate the obstacles to social change, however. Near the end, conversing with a man at a party, Peggy recognizes that she has been cast in the traditional feminine role of sympathetic listener, mirror to egotism:

> She had heard it all before, I, I, I, – he went on. It was like a vulture's beak pecking, or a vacuum cleaner sucking, or a telephone bell ringing. I, I, I. But he can't help it, not with that

nerve-drawn egotist's face, she thought, glancing at him ... ,
He noted her lack of sympathy. He thought her stupid, she
supposed.

'I'm tired,' she apologised. 'I've been up all night,' she
explained. 'I'm a doctor –'

The fire went out of his face when she said 'I'. That's done it
– now he'll go, she thought. He can't be 'you' – he must be 'I'.
She smiled. For up he got and off he went. (*The Years*, pp.
272–3)

'He' must be 'I' because 'she' must be 'you'. 'He' cannot accept
the assertion of a feminine subjectivity, for he seeks in women
simply a sympathetic ear for his own obsessions and worries.
Lily, in *To the Lighthouse*, also attempts to resist the male demand
for sympathy (Charles Tansley's and Mr Ramsay's) but, knowing
her work will be hung in the attics, compromises with both of
them. Peggy, less dependent upon the approval reserved for
women exclusively in their capacity as domestic carers, can begin
to articulate her own subjective needs – she is tired and
therefore will not take on the burden of his concerns.

Change is only glimpsed in the novel, however, expressed
through the fragile images of haphazard connection. Woolf
visualizes a future society based on a different conception of the
relations between women and men, but it will be up to women to
bring about such change and it will not be easy to initiate:

We, daughters of educated men, are between the devil and
the deep sea. Behind us lies the patriarchal system, the private
house, with its nullity, its immorality, its hypocrisy, its servility.
Before us lies the public world, the professional system, with
its possessiveness, its jealousy, its pugnacity, its greed. The one
shuts us up like slaves in a harem; the other forces us to circle
like caterpillars head to tail, round and round the mulberry
tree, the sacred tree of property. (*Three Guineas*, p. 74)

Chapter Four

POST-WAR WOMEN WRITERS: CHALLENGING THE 'LIBERAL TRADITION'

This chapter will consider the work of five post-1945 British and North American women writers whose work has generally been received in terms of an orthodox 'liberal' critical reading. Certainly the work of Margaret Drabble, Anita Brookner, Sylvia Plath, and Ann Tyler has been read as formally unadventurous, eschewing the narrative experiment of postmodernist fiction and espousing a broadly realist aesthetic. (The work of Grace Paley has been either ignored or assimilated to a 'liberal' reading.) In my view, this reading has ignored their significant, though often unobtrusive, formal innovations (no fabulatory fireworks here), and their contribution to a political and psychoanalytic understanding of gender and subjectivity. They are, by no means, all declared feminists. Brookner has explicitly distanced herself from feminist politics and declared that her aesthetic ideal is one of Enlightenment rationalism, yet her work is similar to Woolf's in its perception of the relational basis of identity and its portrayal of her women characters' obsessive need for and fear of connection. Woolf observed that 'women have seemed all the centuries as looking glasses possessing the magic and delicious power of reflecting the figure of man at twice its normal size' (*A Room of One's Own*, p. 35). Brookner's women function very much as looking-glasses, while longing, at the same time, to cry out, passionately and unrestrainedly: 'Look at me!' Their moral strengths function as weakness in the patriarchal, consumerist, and acquisitive world of the post-1960s, and they themselves internalize this disparaging view of their qualities, resulting in a perpetually low self-esteem. As Jean Baker Miller argues: 'Dominants are usually convinced that the

126

way things are is right and good, not only for them but especially for the subordinates. All morality confirms this view, and all social structure sustains it' (J.B. Miller 1983, p. 9). Like Mrs Ramsay and Clarissa Dalloway, Brookner's characters are compelled to resolve their ego boundary confusion through repressive or self-destructive patterns of behaviour. Similarly also, their actions often imitate the aesthetic options open to their author, as art and literature are explored as possible routes to imaginary wholeness. Unlike Woolf, however, Brookner seems to imply that their fate, like their identity, is sealed and fixed, and only resignation or neurosis are offered as ways of dealing with this 'truth'.

MARGARET DRABBLE

Drabble's work is more optimistic. She presents a similarly dispersed, relational conception of subjectivity, but shows a greater *political* awareness of the social (and therefore provisional) and historical determinants of the construction of gender and identity. Again, she is acutely aware of the continuing effects of pre-oedipal relations on the construction of subjectivity, revealing the extent to which the traditional family infantilizes human beings and prevents them from ever achieving adulthood. Her women characters often struggle to deny dominant conceptions of femininity which have structured their own subjectivity in terms of emotionality and sexuality, and often express a deep ambivalence towards their mothers (see *The Millstone* [1965], *The Waterfall* [1969], *Jerusalem the Golden* [1967], *The Ice Age* [1977]).

The earlier fiction often centres on a struggle for wholeness which involves either 'the flight from womanhood' (see Horney 1974) or the lapsing into extreme passivity. In her first novel, *A Summer Birdcage* [1963], for example, despite her academic excellence, Sarah feels it is simply not possible to be both an Oxford don and a woman:

I used to fancy myself as one. But I'll tell you what's wrong with that. It's sex. You can't be a sexy don. It's alright for men being learned and attractive, but for a woman it's a mistake. It detracts from the essential seriousness of the business. You'd

soon find yourself having to play it down instead of up if you
wanted to get to the top and when you've only got one life that
seems a pity. (p. 128)

In the later novels, however, her characters seem to accept the
impossibility of being 'whole' and, recognizing the ideological
purpose of such wholeness, begin to develop a more 'postmodernist' awareness of the imaginary identity of the self-
determining ego. Jane Grey, the narrator of *The Waterfall*, for
example, though pursuing an image of wholeness through her
reflection in the absolute 'other' of romance, also recognizes
the inauthenticity of such an account and provides an accom-
panying critique which reveals the psychological roots of such
desire:

> It's obvious that I haven't told the truth about myself and
> James. How could I?... And yet I haven't lied. I've merely
> omitted: merely, professionally, edited. This is dishonest, but
> not as dishonest as deliberate falsehood. I have often thought
> – and it's a dull reflection, but then there's no virtue in novelty
> – that the ways of regarding an event, so different, don't add
> up to a whole; they are mutually exclusive: the social view, the
> sexual view, the circumstantial view, the moral view, these
> visions contradict each other; they do not supplement one
> another, they cancel one another, they destroy one another.
> They cannot co-exist. And so, because I so wanted James,
> because I wanted him so obsessively, I have omitted
> everything, almost everything except the sequence of
> discovery and recognition that I have called love. (*The
> Waterfall*, p. 46)

Drabble's women tend either to seek connection, 'drowning'
their subjective identity in another's (as in *The Waterfall* or
Jerusalem the Golden) and seeking a loss of self, or they may move
from a position of over-defensive separateness and repression of
the need for human connection to a recognition that their
identity is at least partly bound up with loved others (Rosamund
in *The Millstone*, for example, or Frances in *The Realms of Gold*
[1975]).

Early in her writing career, Drabble did not seem to promise
very much beyond limited survival. In *The Millstone* [1965],

however, she presents a heroine who does, *partially*, resolve her defensive need to erect boundaries and is able to acknowledge her repressed desire for connection without fear of subjective dissolution or loss of self in other. The resolution is confined, though, to her relationship with her infant daughter. She remains at the end fixated in what is essentially a pre-oedipal union which offers only the as yet unrealized *potential* for a satisfactory adult relationship. Rosamund, in fact, is an excellent fictional example of Chodorow's analysis of the psychological basis for the reproduction of mothering. At the beginning of the novel, she presents herself through the first-person narrative as an independent, articulate, and highly rational woman about to embark upon an academic career. She is, however, still situated both physically and spiritually in a binding relationship to her family, living in her parents' flat with its 'grand parental atmosphere which never quite left the place', and morally positioned within the terms of their liberal Protestant ethic of individualist self-reliance.

Rosamund fiercely desires not to *need* anyone. In fact, her over-defensive obsession with independence and separateness suggests that she has come to terms neither with her dependency needs nor with her ambivalent feelings in general towards her parents and, in particular, her mother as a woman. She idealizes rationality as an essentially male mode and is at great pains to dissociate herself from what she perceives to be a weaker, female emotionality. Recognizing her deep desire not to need others, Rosamund believes it to be the legacy of her parents' values which she has internalized 'so thoroughly that I believed dependence to be a fatal sin' (p. 9). She is over-scrupulous in her need to rationalize and justify all human relations. She metes out praise and blame to herself, for example, when she conceives from her first sexual encounter: 'Being at heart a Victorian, I paid the Victorian penalty' (p. 18). Her judicial weighing of social relationships reads like a double-entry cash account:

> It took me some time to work out what, from others, I needed most, and finally I decided, after some sad experiments, that the one thing I could not dispense with was company. After much trial and error, I managed to construct an excellent system, which combined, I considered, fairness to others, with the maximum possible benefit to myself. (pp. 18–19)

Intimacy and human relationship are curtailed in order to protect a fragile identity founded on the rejection of the 'emotional' (conceived as female) and an identification with the 'rational' (conceived as male). She views her pregnancy as a *punishment* for 'having been born a woman in the first place. I couldn't pretend that I wasn't a woman could I, however much I might try from day to day to avoid the issue? I might as well pay, mightn't I?' (p. 16). Her account of it reveals almost nothing of the *bodily* processes, the *physical* aspect of childbearing. Rosamund is delighted when her stomach inhumanly 'snaps' back into place after the birth (p. 109) (of which we are given none of the painful and messy details), for it confirms her apparent control over the feared and potentially overwhelming femininity from which she is 'in flight'.

The term is Karen Horney's. In response to Freud's theory of penis envy, Horney argued that, whereas the male's separation from the mother involved an emphasis on renouncing her but on identifying with the father (because of castration fears), girls 'not only renounce the father as sexual object but simultaneously recoil from the feminine role altogether' (Horney 1967, p. 64). This is, in part, because 'a girl is exposed from birth onward to the suggestion – inevitable, whether conveyed brutally or delicately – of her inferiority, an experience that constantly stimulates her masculinity complex' (p. 69). Later analysts have emphasized how the mother's own ambivalence about her femininity is introjected by her daughter. Since she experiences herself as devalued because of her sex, and shares to some extent the male fear of femaleness as absorption and regression, it is not surprising that the daughter's maternal legacy is likely to be conflict-ridden. Often such conflicts become fixated to the body as the sign of difference, for, as de Beauvoir pointed out, in a culture where subjectivity is, implicitly, male, women function primarily as objects or bodies. The female body thus becomes the vehicle for a complex of conflicting and ambivalent feelings towards the mother, about human mortality, limitation, dependency, and powerlessness.

Such is the manner in which Rosamund experiences the changes in her body of pregnancy. It forces her to recognize human limitation as she sits next to the weary and impoverished women in the antenatal clinic with their burden of anaemia, swollen legs, sagging bodies, and varicose veins. She has to admit:

> And there we all were, and it struck me that I felt nothing in common with any of these people, that I disliked the look of them, that I felt a stranger and a foreigner there, and yet I was one of them. I was like that too. I was trapped in a human limit for the first time in my life, and I was going to have to learn how to live inside it. (*The Millstone*, p. 58)

Dorothy Dinnerstein has argued (see chapter two) that the infant's utter dependency on the mother at the start of life results in the female body becoming the focus of our fears about mortality, the flesh, the uncontrollable and irrational perceived as *female*. The need to control the feminine, though clearly stronger in the male, is nevertheless also present in women. Just as the pre-oedipal mother was experienced as boundless, so too feminine sexuality is perceived as threatening and potentially annihilating. It may be that the woman can allow herself to experience sexual feelings only if they are rendered non-threatening – through the displacements of popular romance, for example, or through the distantiation produced by perceiving herself purely as an object for the male's sexual desire.

Thus Rosamund likes men and knows that she does, but fears intimacy, and does *not* know why. Her 'crime' was

> my suspicion, my fear, my apprehensive terror of the very idea of sex. I liked men, and was forever in and out of love for years, but the thought of sex frightened the life out of me and the more I didn't do it and the more I read and heard about how I ought to do it, the more frightened I became. It must have been the physical thing itself that frightened me, for I did not at all object to the social implications, to my name on hotel registers, my name bandied about at parties, nor to the emotional upheavals which I imagined to be its companions: but the act itself I could neither make nor contemplate. ... I have thought of all kinds of possible causes for this curious characteristic of mine – the over-healthy, business-like attitude of my family, my isolation (through superiority of intellect) as a child, my selfish, self-preserving hatred of being pushed around – but none of these imagined causes came anywhere near to explaining the massive obduracy of the effect. (p. 18)

Similarly, she struggles to emphasize her difference from other women. Her PhD thesis, although a study of poetry essentially about love and sexuality (Elizabethan verse imagery), is conducted entirely in the terms of a scientific investigation: scholarly, precise, 'objective', and, she says, 'wholly uncreative'. Rosamund repeatedly connects 'creativity' with femininity in the negative terms of irrationality, uncontrollability, excess. Her flatmate Lydia, a 'creative writer' who clearly shares none of Rosamund's inhibitions about sexuality, is perceived by the latter in terms of messiness, dirtiness, slatternliness: 'Lydia never looked clean. ... Lydia did wash from time to time, for I had seen and heard her do so; she washed her clothes too, but perhaps not quite often enough' (p. 153).

This association of femininity with emotional and physical uncontrollability leads to Rosamund's suppression of her own dependency needs. Such behaviour appears to be common in women because of the social construction of their gender identity, and again contributes to their need to turn to children to feel 'complete'. Rosamund cannot risk intimacy with another adult, particularly a *male* adult (because of the sexual threat), but with her baby Octavia can feel needed and loved, can experience herself simultaneously as a mother and *as a little girl*. Rosamund's identity is thus delicately balanced on the contradiction of a denial of identification with the mother (as a female) and a desire actually *to be* a mother to both a child and to the neglected child in herself. In her mothering, it is significant that she desires, above all, exclusivity. She wishes to reproduce the pre-oedipal dyad where she is both mother *and* father to Octavia. George is not informed of his part in the conception, and she assiduously avoids the 'parental' advice of friends and relatives. Like Rosamund's thesis, Octavia herself seems almost to be a *cerebral* creation of her mother, involving little of the messiness and emotional entanglement of sexual and reproductive processes. It is only when Octavia becomes ill and may die, so that Rosamund has to face the close relationship of sex, birth, and death, the *physical* fragility of human life, that her rational control relaxes and she emits the incredible, 'hysterical', overwhelming scream that stuns the hospital waiting-room. As she screams, Rosamund can, momentarily, integrate her masculine-identified rationality with her repressed 'feminine' emotional need:

Inside my head it was red and black and very hot, I
remember, and I remember also the clearness of my
consciousness and the ferocity of my emotion and myself
enduring them, myself neither one, nor the other, but
enduring them and not breaking in two. (p. 134)

As a result of the scream, her overwhelming – *human* – need to
see her child is recognized (despite the *inhumanity* of the hospital
system), and she is taken to Octavia. Rosamund does not manage
permanently to resolve the contradiction of her regressive need
for pre-oedipal connection and her obsessive need for rational
control and separation, but, in this image of human *need*,
Drabble does suggest that recognition of our human connection
to others may allow us to begin to heal our own destructive
internal divisions.

Jane Grey, the central character and part-narrator of Drabble's
The Waterfall [1969], is not content with the mother-infant dyad
and seeks to re-create, through inclusion of her lover James,
a familial triangle which forms the basis of a regressive
Romanticism symbolized in the title of the novel. Jane, too, like
Rosamund, experiences deeply ambivalent feelings towards her
parents and, in particular, her mother, emphasizing from the
first their hypocrisy and vanity: 'My mother was thought,
generally, to be a charming woman: she was pretty, flattering,
gracious, and yet I knew the profound depths of her insincerity,
or I would hear her in private savage, relentlessly, the ante-
cedents of those very people she took such pains to charm' (p.
55). Later, she reveals her preoccupation with feelings of
rejection and her obsession with the preferential treatment
received by her sister, who thus 'remained a whole person', while
'I split myself. I went underground' (p. 114). Infantile anger at
this treatment was projected out on to the 'bad mother', who
then appeared to threaten the annihilation of her own sense of
self. In attempting to destroy this mother, she would destroy
herself: 'I felt all the time afraid that any word of mine, any
movement, my mere existence, might shatter them all into
fragments' (pp. 50–1). Jane feels, therefore, both an absence of
parental love and an absence of self. The desire for wholeness,
for 'full' possession, was experienced even in her childhood
games with her cousin Lucy. She collected marbles, for example,

but 'I felt there was always something left undone, some final joyful possession of them, some way to my having of them more completely' (p. 119). Playing shopping, also, she felt at the outset of each game the promise of 'bliss beyond belief – some violent orgasmic moment, perhaps, where we would *become* adults, where we would *be* our mothers; but the moment never happened' (p. 119).

Later she feels that this moment has happened with James her lover. *He* has become 'her mother', and she his, as they lie together in the bed where she has just given birth to her departed husband's child. In a later section of the alternating third-person narrative, a telling image reveals the psychological needs which structure their relationship:

> He could not choose but want her: he had been as desperate to make her as she to be made. And he had done it: he had made her, in his own image. The throes, the cries, the pains were his; and he could no more dissociate himself from them than from his own flesh. She was his, but by having her he made himself hers . . . . He wanted her, he too had sweated for this deliverance, he had thought it worth the risk: for her, for himself, he had done it. Indistinguishable needs. Her own voice, in that strange sobbing cry of rebirth. A woman delivered. She was his offspring, as he, lying there between her legs, had been hers. (p. 151)

James is here seen as both God and all-powerful phallic mother who 'makes' Jane in his image and is thus 'made' himself as God/ mother (both 'makers') as he gives birth to her.

In a society where the mother provides almost exclusive care of infants so that identity is formed in relation to her, this relationship is 'the foundation upon which all future relations with love objects are based' (Fairbairn, quoted in Chodorow 1978, p. 79). Jane, feeling her needs never to have been recognized, experiences the relationship as profoundly unsatis-factory and grows up defining herself as someone whose needs drive others, and love, away. She thus remains preoccupied with negative internal object relations which have never been resolved. Chodorow argues:

Because this situation is unresolvable, and interferes with the ongoing need for love, the infant represses its preoccupation. Part of its definition of self and its affective energy thus splits off experientially from its central self, drawing to an internal object energy and commitment which would otherwise be available for ongoing external relationships. The growing child's psychic structure and sense of self thus comes to consist of unconscious, quasi-independent, divided experiences of self in affective (libidinal-attached, aggressive, angry, ambivalent, helpless-dependent) relation with an inner object-world, made up originally of aspects of the relationship to its mother. (Chodorow 1978, p. 78)

Jane experiences her own fragmentary sense of self in this way. She has blamed herself for the breakdown of the relationship with her husband Malcolm, accepting his projection on to her of guilt and sexual ambivalence and his view of her as accusatory, rejecting, frigid. When James lies suspended between life and death after the accident, she puts on his bloodstained shirt, describing it as a shroud, and again sees herself as someone whose negative emotions *destroy others*. The sight of the holly tree outside the hospital weighs painfully upon her. The energy which Jane could have used in external, social relationships is thus drawn inwards, creating an internal need for an impossible wholeness which she projects outwards through regressive romantic desire. In the sections of first-person narrative, and increasingly through her third-person voice, Jane glimpses the psychological compulsions behind the affair, at times viewing it cynically as 'some ridiculous imitation of a fictitious passion, some shoddy childish mock-up of what for others might have been reality – but for what others? For no others, as non-existent an image they had pursued as God, as Santa Claus, as mermaids, as angels, as that non-existent image of eternity' (*The Waterfall*, p. 202). Similarly, she is capable of detached analysis of James. After the accident, she rejects her previous idealization of his close relationship with his mother, recognizing in it the same psychological dynamics as in her own family. James's mother, 'that figure whom she had capriciously elected to redeem the maternal role' (p. 202), has, Jane realizes, in her precocious masculinization of her little boy, her 'little man', pushed James into the role of being 'a sexual object at the age of three' (p. 203). Thus he, too, is later compelled to seek passion in a maternal bed (literally, for Jane has just given birth) and succour at Jane's nursing breast. Yet he ensures the continuity of his own marriage, a wasteland of resentment and sexual failure, for together with his obsession for fast cars this guarantees his access to a separate world outside the pre-oedipal relation with Jane.

She herself attempts to secure a measure of distance through the play with language, subjectivity, and narrative voice facilitated by the choices available to her as author. A first-person voice presents the affair through a critical perspective, while a third-person narrative presents it in the classic terms of romance. Lacan identified the mirror phase as that moment where the child, having conceived an image of itself in alienation as the reflection of the other, thus proceeds to enter the symbolic order through a similarly alienated relationship to language (struggling to articulate as 'I' that which is perceived as 'he' or 'she'). For the reasons discussed earlier, the process is doubly alienating for women, and Jane struggles, through language, to integrate a sense of self as 'other', as 'object', with the need to experience herself as a subject. She seeks in literary 'reflections' (Austen, Brontë, Eliot) and in actual mirrors (which abound in the novel) an image of wholeness which she seems only to experience materially through a loss of self, a dissolution of boundaries and merging with others. She has sought desperately to identify with, to 'become', Lucy her cousin (to the point of sleeping with her husband) and to 'become' James through their passion. Even her children are experienced, for the most part, as extensions of herself. Seeking dissolution and ultimately self-destruction in the affair with James, she feels somehow cheated of its final revelation, the ultimate realization of desire as death, when he recovers from the accident. Earlier, when he returns from a family holiday, she cannot believe that he is there, whole, separate, not destroyed by her fearful hallucinations of his death: 'She had feared that she might have destroyed him by too much love. But he had survived her attachment: he stood there, quite whole, not yet maimed or blinded by her need' (p. 165). There is surely an implicit identification with another Jane here, Jane Eyre, and the identification is based on a perception of *this* heroine as one who destroys the male with her tragic passion and overwhelming female needs. Drabble's Jane, however, signifies her need for distance and autonomy, her awareness of the regressive pathology of romance, through her play with narrative form. Later, she refers *explicitly* to Brontë's Jane, metafictionally foregrounding the illusory and fictional nature of both her own desire and the structure of romance:

> Perhaps I should have killed James in the car, and that would have made a neat, a possible ending. ... Or, I could have maimed James so badly, in this narrative, that I would have been allowed to have him, as Jane Eyre had her blinded Rochester. But I hadn't the heart to do it, I loved him too much, and anyway it wouldn't have been the truth because the truth is that he recovered. (pp. 230–1)

James, however, returns bathetically with a 'boring tendency' (p. 231) to recount the details of his accident, and Jane recovers from a thrombosis, 'the price that modern women must pay for love' (p. 238). There are no tragic drownings, suicides, departures, or ruptures. There is no magical 'wholeness' to be discovered, but Jane does, partially, awake from the slumber of the Sleeping Beauty, and through her own efforts rather than simply through her dependency on James. At the beginning of the novel she clearly seeks, romantically, that exclusive possession of the One who will give birth to her, nurture her, and thus satisfy those emotional needs which have remained starved since infancy. As Phyllis Chesler argues:

> Female children are quite literally starved for matrimony: not for marriage, but for physical nurturance, and a legacy of power and humanity from adults of their own sex ('mothers'). Most mothers prefer sons to daughters and are more physically and domestically nurturant to them. Within modern society, women's 'dependent' and 'incestuous' personality probably stems from not being experienced as 'divine' by the mother (and father). Most women are glassed into infancy, and perhaps into some forms of madness, by an unmet need for maternal nurturance. (Chesler 1972, p. 18)

Jane both experiences James as divine and feels herself reborn into divinity in her union with him: 'He stroked her hair, not seeming to mind that it was dirty and smelled of humanity' (p. 33). He becomes the adoring mother who will 'complete' her, and she, reciprocally feeding him with her body, can also become the all-giving mother to herself. However, through the displacements of narrative voice, and an almost 'postmodern' recognition of the contradictory construction of subjectivity through desire and language, Jane begins ultimately to recognize that her desire for connection must involve also an awareness of the need for separateness and a sense of her own effective agency in the world. By the end of the novel she has, I believe, begun to renounce the attractions of feminine passivity and the role of being 'victim'.

Drabble's novels after *The Waterfall*, in fact, narrate the development of heroines who can more successfully integrate their relational needs with a subjective sense of their own autonomy. In *The Realms of Gold* [1975], for example, Frances Wingate, an archaeologist, is able to give up her search for an illusory romantic 'golden world' which promises transcendence and salvation, recognizing that she has sought 'golden worlds from which we are banished, they recede infinitely, for there never was a golden world' (p. 124). She perceives that her idealism about human communities has, ironically, as effectively banished the actual needs, limitations and desires of human beings as the obsessive cataloguing of the natural world meticulously conducted by her geologist cousin David. Both are defences against the recognition of human limitation and the contradictory basis of human connection. Increasingly reminded of her own physical deterioration – toothache, a breast tumour – she recognizes the isolationism of her idealist fantasy and, through her discovery of the relationships within her own living family rather than those of the ancient dead, achieves an identity which reconciles her to the human lot. Drabble again reveals the limitations of defining identity in terms either of a western liberal rationalism or of a romantic transcendence, just as she perceives the exclusion of women from such definitions (because of their maternal function) to be detrimental to the human race as a whole. Like Woolf, she seeks, through formal experiment and thematic exploration, ways of deconstructing the stereotypes of gender which are produced out of the destructive relations within the traditional family. Her novels offer glimpses of the psychological and social changes required for a more equal society, viewing *all* human beings as 'part of a long inheritance, a human community in which we must play our proper part' (Drabble 1975, p. 36).

ANITA BROOKNER

Anita Brookner, like Drabble, rejects easy solutions to social inequality, but unlike Drabble has explicitly distanced herself from feminism. She has argued that her best-known novel, *Hotel du Lac* [1984], was meant 'as a love story pure and simple: love triumphed over temptation. The *ideal* of love. Basically I don't like adversarial positions. I see no need for them, since life is too complicated and is rarely just' (in Haffendon 1985, p. 73). Yet her novel persistently, though implicitly, undermines the romantic ideal in spite of its author's intentions, revealing the profoundly conflicting needs both catered for and reinforced by romance. Edith Hope, the central character, is herself a writer of romances which are a plea for the acceptance of traditional courtship and marriage, but in her own life she reveals that these institutions cannot ultimately satisfy her own emotional and intellectual needs. Edith tends to blame herself, however, seeing her 'innate disposition' as the source of her exclusion from wedded bliss. She feels unable, therefore, to identify with those women who seek to change the institutional basis of romance, and her writing seeks to *contain* protest, to protect her liberal view of the fatalistic working out of human character. Brookner's novel as a whole, however, fails to suppress the contradictions inherent in this position.

Janice A. Radway has suggested the following reasons for the popularity of romance:

Romance reading supplements the avenues traditionally open to women for emotional gratification by supplying them vicariously with the attention and nurturance they do not get enough of in the round of day-to-day existence. It counter-valuates because the story opposes the female values of love and personal interaction to the male values of competition and public achievement and, at least in ideal romances, demonstrates the triumph of the former over the latter.

Romance reading and writing might be seen, therefore, as a collectively elaborated female ritual through which women explore the consequences of their common social condition as the appendages of men and attempt to imagine a more perfect state where all the needs they so intensely feel and accept as given could be adequately addressed. (Radway 1984, p. 212)

Edith is herself aware of such reasons, though she views them as part of the *innate* disposition of women. As she reminisces at the hotel on her failure to go through with the marriage to Geoffrey, we are given a flashback to an earlier episode where she had lunched with her publisher and discussed the psychological dynamics of romance reading. He has suggested to Edith that her market is changing: 'It's sex for the young woman executive now, the Cosmopolitan reader, the girl with the executive briefcase' (*Hotel du Lac*, p. 26). Edith, however, disagrees, claiming that women still prefer the 'old myths', that romance is a form of consolatory gratification, and that her readers 'want to believe that they are going to be discovered, looking their best, behind closed doors, just when they thought that all was lost, by a man who has battled across continents, abandoning whatever he may have had in his in-tray, to reclaim them' (p. 27). Edith writes out of her own psychological compulsions, finding her identity dependent upon the 'daily task of fantasy and obfuscation' (p. 58), and yet, in a letter to David at the end of the novel, asserting what is for her both the truth and a romantic fiction: 'I believed every word I wrote. And I still do' (p. 181).

Edith's writing is produced out of her own ambivalent feelings about femininity and an implicit though repressed recognition that what society offers to women in the form of marriage cannot satisfy both their need for autonomy and their need for connection. She is fascinated at the Hotel du Lac by the spectacle of pre-oedipal regression and 'ultra-femininity' paraded to the world in the figures of Mrs Pusey and her daughter Jennifer, whose main concern in life is shopping for 'pretty things' ('A woman owes it to herself to have pretty things. And if she feels good she looks good. That's what I tell Jennifer. I always see to it that she's fitted out like a queen. ... She loves her silly mother, don't you darling?'; p. 43). Edith is both mesmerized and repelled by what she sees as this female 'will to repletion and to triumph' (p. 29), their 'avidity, grossness, ardour' (p. 39), and the implicit threat to the gratification of her own desires which their voracious appetites carry. She responds similarly to the seductive lingerie bought for herself by the 80-year-old Mrs Pusey and to the vaguely obscene 'gamine' attire of the fleshly and voluptuous 40-year-old Jennifer. Yet Edith regards Mrs Pusey as an 'enchantress' (p. 39) and is haunted by the image of the embrace of mother and daughter, 'a physical closeness ... that surpassed anything Edith had ever known' (p. 39). Jennifer, she perceives, is simply an extension of the monstrous needs and desires of her mother,

> so much a reflection of her mother that although she occupied quite a large space and had a curiously insistent physical presence, she did not have too much to say for herself, and indeed Edith had once or twice had the impression that behind the large smiling face Jennifer was somewhere else. (pp. 38–9).

Edith's memories of her own mother are set against this spectacle: a woman, rejecting, slatternly, so utterly defeated and frustrated by life that eventually she had taken to her bed in disgust – as her sexual attractiveness dwindled – and required Edith to serve her as if she were an invalid. Compared to the soft, frilly, perfumed effusiveness of Mrs Pusey, her own East European mother is remembered as 'punishingly corseted, with badly pencilled eyebrows, and large, hard bosoms' (p. 49), railing against her fate and projecting her anger against the female lot on to her 'pale, silent daughter' (p. 48). Edith, pondering this, wonders what has brought her to the Hotel du Lac, out of season, with its oppressive grey skies and respectability, and its mainly hopeless and lonely clientele. She recognizes that her writing of romances has functioned as a means of displacing repressed desires and memories too painful and complex to acknowledge. She remembers the childhood feeling after her father died of being 'vividly unsafe' (p. 117), and admits the possibility that her romance stories are acts of reparation to the mother who comforted herself with tales of love and whose 'fantasies ... taught me about reality' (p. 104).

Thus Edith starts to accept that her legacy from the mother is a deeply ambivalent attitude towards other women and her own femininity, a confusion as to what constitutes 'a proper woman': 'I am harsh because I remember Mother and her unkindnesses and because I am continually on the alert for more. But women are not all like Mother, and it is really stupid of me to imagine that they are' (p. 83).

Edith sees so far. What she fails to grasp, however, is the extent to which her ideal of love and her relations with men are determined by her unresolved need and fear of connection, as well as the extent to which her view of women as voracious and gross in their appetites is a consequence of her own obsession with denial and control of emotional need. Repeatedly, she refers to herself as someone who has not grown up, experiencing with pleasure the image in her mirror as she twists her hair up before the wedding: 'She looked elegant, controlled. Grown up, she thought. At last' (p. 126). Obsessively, she seeks an acceptable image of 'grown-up' femininity, viewing Mr Neville's calculating and rationalized marriage plan as offering one such possibility. She imagines, as his wife, an identity based upon social position, rather than one based on what she perceives as the compulsive displacement of regressive fantasies in her vocation as writer. Thus she writes to David (her married lover), to inform him of the offer of marriage and her acceptance and intention to be a 'good wife': 'I will very soon, under his guidance, develop into the sort of acceptable woman whose confidence and stamina and indeed presumption I have always envied. Rather like your wife, in fact' (p. 180). That she will have, continuously, to repress her great emotional need for love, connection, intimacy, in such a 'business' partnership, seems preferable to Edith to what she sees as an inevitable decline into the uncontrollable, insatiable neediness of the ageing woman, displayed so differently in both her own mother and in Mrs Pusey. The Puseys fascinate and repel Edith because she sees in them a reflection, monstrous and overwhelming, of her own desire for possession and love.

Femininity is again perceived in the Puseys in the negative terms of fleshliness: Mrs Pusey in her appetite for possession, her compulsive need to shop, and consumption of objects, food, people, and Jennifer with her plump body squeezed into fashionable 'gamine' clothes and expressing, above all, latency, 'uninformed voluptuousness', despite her 40 years. What both suggest, in fact, is a caricature of femininity which is close to the infant's view of the mother as an all-encompassing physicality which must later be controlled and denied. Edith herself experiences femininity as uncontrollability and seeks in a man, through the partnership of marriage, some measure of control and social rationalization of feeling. Marriage to Mr Neville thus presents itself as an escape both from loneliness and from the terror of identification with the inchoate and the insatiable.

That Edith experiences herself in terms of diffuseness and lack of autonomy is emphasized throughout the novel. She has politely removed herself to the Hotel du Lac to please others, because she was not 'herself', just as she had allowed her 'friend' Penelope to choose the colour scheme for the marital bedroom, bowing to her greater experience with men and her assurance – 'You have to recognize his needs' (p. 122). Edith writes in order to separate inner from outer: 'the main purpose of [writing] ... was to distance those all too real circumstances over which she could exert no control' (p. 66). As the novel opens, the understated tone refers to Edith's 'unfortunate lapse', the almost eighteenth-century measured sentences promise order and containment, and yet the weather remains 'distressingly beyond control' (p. 8). In fact, Edith experiences the greyness of the Hotel du Lac as an objective correlative for her own state of mind, and, though she asserts throughout the need for distance, in fact the novel reveals her inability to separate inner and outer. When the uproar arises from the Puseys' room (on the night when presumably Mrs Pusey has caught 'little' Jennifer *in flagrante delicto*), Edith feels responsible for the external chaos because she has spent the night in a state of *inner* turmoil: 'she felt as if her grief and terror had been unleashed by her long night of introspection and that she must now be called to account whenever and wherever damage might be done and atonement might be made' (p. 137).

Edith fears she has released the 'uncontrollable' contents of her own mind upon the external world, and now she must make reparation. Significantly, the only other woman in the hotel with whom she feels comfortable is Monica, who, inhumanly thin and disgusted by the Puseys' vulgar consumption, suffers from an 'eating disorder'. She too, like Edith, has been removed to the hotel as an 'incomplete' woman, one who has failed to please, for Monica has not provided her husband with the required sons and heirs. Her refusal to eat and her violent feelings towards the Puseys suggest that she, like Edith, experiences a deep ambivalence towards femininity itself, her refusal to eat signifying, unconsciously, a protest at the impossible alternatives offered to women.

Monica's experience of marriage as a vehicle through which her husband can ensure the continuity of his lineage is little removed, in fact, from what is offered to Edith in the two proposals she receives. She will, in return for a social position with a 'name', provide for the particular needs of men from whom an admission of even the existence of such needs would deeply threaten their sense of male identity. For Geoffrey, she will simply substitute for the recently deceased mother as provider of nurturance and emotional stability, and for Mr Neville she will provide 'respectability' while he pursues his sexual pleasures elsewhere. For this she will give up her freedom of choice, her garden, her writing, and even her own bedspread. Geoffrey will install her in 'the marital bed in Montagu Square, where [he] had formerly lived with his mother' (p. 122), and Mr Neville will hand over to her the cleaning of his expensive china while he seeks sexual pleasure presumably with non-threatening, 'adolescent' girl-women like Jennifer. Edith, Mr Neville feels, will be an excellent business proposition, a 'sleeping partner' (in effect) who will not undermine his masculinity by eloping, as his wife did, with a younger man. Edith will be another possession; she will 'gratify the original monolithic infant wish for ownership of a woman' (Dinnerstein 1976, pp. 49–50), but she will remain safely under control along with Mr Neville's feelings.

Ironically, Mr Neville shares many of Edith's unconscious feelings that women are emotionally insatiable, narcissistic, requiring continuous flattery and devotion. He informs Edith that he has had enough of the emotional drain of battling for ownership under these conditions, 'knocking other men down ... one gets no work done' (p. 166). Edith is partially attracted to the 'control' offered by marriage to Mr Neville, though his desire for control is clearly sadistic and misogynistic. She feels that by marrying she will become 'a proper woman', will gain self-control and 'grow up', but the price of this is the *loss* of autonomy, of precisely that selfhood over which she seeks control. Both states therefore involve a sense of infantilization: it is simply not possible within the available social terms and practices to 'grow up' and be a 'proper woman' at the same time. Brookner never offers any *explicit* feminist critique of marriage, but the social and psychological contradictions which determine Edith's choice are made manifestly clear throughout the novel, even if its author *does* dismiss it as simply a 'love story'.

In fact, all of Brookner's novels explore the infantilizing effects of family life on women. In her first novel, *A Start in Life* [1981], Ruth Weiss, 'greedy for books' (p. 28) yet like Edith recognizing that her 'life had been ruined by literature' (p. 7), seeks through words the comfort she never received as a child. Her parents, volatile, narcissistic, and irresponsible, 'play' at being adults, expecting support and nurturance from the child they have failed to nurture themselves. Looking into her mother's face, Ruth recognizes that 'lost and petulant air that [she] remembered from her childhood and which seemed to turn the mother into the child and the child into the mother' (p. 81). Fearful of growing old, and by profession an actress, Ruth's mother masquerades in the perpetual role of 'little girl', requiring a continuous narcissistic confirmation of her attractiveness from those around her whom she regards as her 'audience'. When summoned to the school because of concern about Ruth, she brushes anxieties aside: '"She can do whatever she likes, of course. But don't turn my baby into a blue-stocking." She smiled the enchanting smile. "You know how it puts men off"' (p. 25). Ruth, however, has never been a 'baby', and this is one of the reasons why she becomes what her mother considers a 'blue-stocking', seeking in the consolatory plots of literary tradition 'the sound of the most beautiful words a girl could hear: "Cinderella *shall* go to the ball"' (p. 8). School dinners replace maternal nurturance, providing comfort in 'the form of baked beans and sausages, stewed prunes and custard' (p. 22), just as later she greedily 'consumes' books, feeling in the college library 'as close to a sense of belonging as she was ever likely to encounter' (pp. 28–9).

Ruth, too, discovers that cultural acceptability will entail either a repression of the needy little girl beneath the role of maternal servant or a regression into the refuge of permanent adolescence like her mother's: positions which, in their splitting of dependency and their control of the feminine, will ensure masculine security. Her father, for example, tiring of his little girl wife as her petulance sits ever more incongruously with her increasing age, turns to the 'maternal' Mrs Jacobs for comfort and succour: 'He particularly liked the way Sally took his plate away the moment he had set it down, how she ran to the kitchen and washed it up' (p. 61). To 'cheer her up' and with boyish enthusiasm, he fills her kitchen with expensive gadgetry, unconsciously desiring to import a 'masculine' control and efficiency into her fussy world of lace doilies and tiny embroidered napkins.

Ruth's repressed emotional needs, unsatisfactorily displaced on to the study of 'Balzac's women', seek expression not through 'little girl' behaviour like her mother's, but through activities similar to those of Mrs Jacobs. Ruth seeks to *earn* love and attention through serving, seeking to please. When Richard arrives hours late to her laboriously prepared cordon bleu meal and proceeds, without apology, to discuss his difficulties with another woman, Harriet, Ruth feels only shame at her tiredness, accepting his criticism, 'Sometimes, Ruth ... I wonder if you're really a caring person' (p. 59), and offering a hundred pounds to help Harriet over her financial worries. Similarly, feeling that she cannot be the 'ideal mother' required by her parents because of her own lack of mothering, Ruth senses herself continuously bound to them through anxiety and guilt. Like Edith, she becomes partially aware of her psychological compulsions, wondering, 'Would she always react in the same way to those who did not want her, trying ever more hopelessly to please?' (p. 131). Near the end of the novel, however, her fears and despair overwhelm her. Turning to the back of the taxi, she realizes that her mother is slipping down under her blue eyeshadow and jaunty denim cap – that she is, in fact, dying: 'Ruth screamed. "Take me home. Take me home. Take me home." Tears spurted from her eyes and her mouth opened like a child's. "Take me home," she chanted. "Take me home"' (p. 164).

Her fear is that of the lost child who believes no one will find her and that she will disintegrate. By the time they reach 'home', Ruth's mother is, indeed, dead. Ruth, unable to maintain any longer her precarious boundaries through the discipline of work, marries Mrs Jacobs's son, 'an amiable but childish character' who seeks in Ruth 'maternal protection' and in return allows her to cling to him in the night 'when she wakened so inexplicably in terror' (p. 173). All of the characters, in fact, remain imprisoned in a state of neurotic dependency and infantilization. As Jane Flax has argued, for the little girl, 'the rift between identifying with the mother and being oneself can only be closed within a relationship in which one is nurtured for being one's autonomous self' (Flax 1978, p. 179). As in all of Brookner's novels, it is virtually impossible for her women characters to achieve this sort of autonomy and self-esteem because of their identification with a maternal figure or a feminine cultural stereotype which involves continuous denial and repression of their own needs. They seek, in literature or in romance, an ideal union and a satisfaction of need and desire which reveals, as Flax argues, that 'women's unresolved wishes for the mother is the truth behind Freud's claim that what women wish for in a husband is their mother' (1978, p. 179).

Brookner's heroines, however, equally fear success. To be 'successful' in the 'public' world involves emulating and embracing what the culture perceives to be 'male' values – independence, efficiency, ambition – and repressing what it regards as 'female': nurturance, dependency, self-effacement. To masquerade as successful thus involves an implicit denial of the connection to the mother and, therefore, a repression of the wish that the woman's needs will ultimately be met through the mother's nurturance.[8] Flax has argued:

The wish to fail is buried deep and is hard to retrieve from the unconscious. It does not cease to exist when women are able to identify the social forces that also pressure them towards failure or compromise. One may have a very sophisticated analysis of patriarchy and female socialization and still engage in self-defeating acts at work or in relations with others. The wish to fail may take more disguised forms, for instance, in a profound ambivalence towards work. A woman's desire to succeed may be undercut by a sense of being a 'fake' – of being much less competent than people think, of not really belonging in this world, of marking time until her real fate

147

arrives. It may be difficult for her to think of her work as a career, to work as single-mindedly as a man would. She may be profoundly troubled by questions about the ultimate worth and meaning of her efforts. (Flax 1978, p. 181)

Not only Brookner's but also Woolf's and Drabble's novels are full of women characters who cope with their ambivalent feelings in this way. Lily Briscoe finds it difficult to take her painting seriously, while Drabble's Frances Wingate, a well-known archaeologist, dismisses her life's work as the pursuit of an illusion. Edith Hope makes 'no claim for my particular sort of writing' (p. 9) and sees her success as neurotic substitution rather than talent. Brookner's academic women, Ruth Weiss and Kitty Maule (*Providence* [1983]), similarly, if unconsciously, regard their work 'as a sort of hobby', as Kitty says in *Providence* (p. 34), and see it as a betrayal of their mother's desires for them to be 'proper women'.

Fanny Hinton, in Brookner's *Look at Me* [1982], similarly obsessed by the image of the absent mother, also sees her writing as a form of substitute gratification. She, too, is terrified of being seen as needy and hence idealizes those who appear to be powerful and beautiful, who appear *not* to need. Nick is admired above all because he is 'devoid of that element of need that makes some men, and rather a lot of women, unattractive in their desires; he was, in fact, desire in its pure state' (p. 38). Yet Nick is clearly not devoid of need. He requires the gaze of others to confirm his sense of perfection and, with Alix his wife, he indulges in a mutual masturbatory fascination which requires the presence always of a third person to consolidate their image of perfect unity. Fanny in fact senses:

> they found my company necessary. ... I felt lonely and excited. I was there because some element in that perfect marriage was deficient, because ritual demonstrations were needed to maintain a level of arousal which they were too complacent, perhaps too spoilt, even too lazy, to supply for themselves, out of their own imaginations. (p. 57)

Fanny does not wish to be cast in the role of voyeur, however, seeking vicarious satisfaction from the sexual intimacies of others. She wants to be looked at herself, to be the focus of their gaze, to be received as a 'gift'. Again, like Kitty, she feels herself to be deficient, lacking some essence of femininity which she cannot define. Indeed, Kaja Silverman has suggested that the female 'body is charted, zoned and made to bear ... a meaning which proceeds entirely from external relations, but which is always subsequently apprehended as an internal condition or essence' (in Lauretis 1984, p. 183).

Fanny obsessively seeks such an essence, poring over the 'charted' and 'zoned' images of women in the library where her job is to catalogue facts about mental disorder. She wonders why melancholy, traditionally female, 'is very frightening, but the person she frightens most is herself. She is her own disease' (*Look at Me*, p. 6). As with other Brookner female characters, Fanny experiences her own sense of loss and neediness as an illness, a disease. Like Edith Hope, she views her writing as a pathological displacement of such need – 'It is an attempt to reach others and to make them love you' – and Fanny would give her entire writerly output 'for permission to state "I hurt" or "I hate" or "I want". Or indeed, "Look at me"' (p. 84). Her relationship with James fails largely because of his own inability to relate to women without splitting the intimate from the erotic. Fanny, however, blames herself, feeling that her pleasure in his company had 'seemed to dwindle into the occupations of a child, or an invalid' (p. 129). She is caught between the fear that 'femininity' is itself a form of regression, an illness, a neediness, and the fear that she herself is ill, 'an invalid', or 'childlike', precisely because she lacks a feminine 'essence'. Nick, she believes, can bestow this upon her, for 'his greatest gift to us was that intermittent, speculative gaze' (p. 40). Such a gift, however, will only fall, she believes, if she can cultivate the same moral insouciance and erotic carelessness as Alix with her 'aura of power', rapacious teeth, and 'immense reserves of appetite and pleasure' (p. 47). Fanny's self-hatred is thus directed at what she sees as her infantile neediness, her craving for love, her inability to give up the memory of her invalid mother whose house she preserves like a shrine and whose loss she mourns daily in her writing. She feels herself *psychologically* to be in the same state of invalidism which manifested itself *physically* in her mother. In both instances, the consequences are dependency and neediness. Thus, in order to be loved, Fanny believes that *she* must care for and please others and on no account reveal the child within herself which needs care. Repeatedly, Alix and Nick are referred to as 'glamorous parent' figures whom she seeks, like a good girl, to please, accepting their exploitative and egotistical behaviour 'because I was a child and I was waiting for the adults to come back from what was so mysteriously keeping them and to allow me once again into their company' (p. 131).

In her short relationship with James, Fanny experiences, she believes, being 'looked at', growing whole and complete, con-stituted as a person through his gaze. His attention to her leads her to believe that she has at last achieved the mysterious state of 'essential femininity', has grown up, become a woman. But as Catherine McKinnon argues:

> Socially, femaleness means femininity, which means attractiveness, which means sexual availability on male terms. What defines woman as such is what turns man on. Good girls are 'attractive', bad girls 'provocative'. Gender socialization is the process through which women come to identify themselves as sexual beings, as beings that exist for men. It is that process through which women internalize (make their own) a male image of their sexuality *as* their identity as women. It is not just an illusion. (MacKinnon 1982, pp. 530–1)

Just as Fanny in fact begins to experience a sense of purpose, having 'James, my life's work to study' (p. 93), he, unable to combine erotic attachment with affectional intimacy, is pursuing one of Alix's protégées, Maria, whose femininity he does, indeed, perceive as 'sexual availability on male terms'. As she compares herself with Alix, 'powerful, in her tight black dress', Fanny, 'blameless in my grey dress', urges silently 'Look at me'. As she recognizes James's betrayal, her sense of illusory wholeness and identity fragments, and she sees it is 'so damaged that it was simply a question of safety, of survival, to protect the ruins' (p. 135). She flees at the end, pursued, it seems, by a possible sexual attacker until, terrified, she arrives at her flat and immerses herself in water, feeling herself seep out into its elemental comfort. For the first time she puts on her mother's nightdress and climbs also into her bed. She sinks into a 'dense' sleep, 'hungry for it, as for some gross food' (p. 178), seeing her face 'questing, in my pig-like search for unknowingness' (p.

150

178), and feeling her body, thin and flat, pleased that 'I should dwindle, that I should shed my biological characteristics' (p. 179). Unable to accept an impossible, socially defined femininity, Fanny prefers the annihilation and regression of withdrawal to a pre-oedipal world suggested through the oral images and the deliberate taking on of the dead mother's garments. Here she fantasizes herself as biologically neutral, neither male nor female, in possession of, because at one with, the phallic mother. She has sought in James the 'good mother' who will assure her of her own 'goodness', a mutual nurturance which produces in both, however, an incapacity for erotic expression. Sexually inhibited, therefore, Fanny feels herself to lack that so-called 'feminine essence' constituted through male desire. Yet though she desires to be looked at erotically, to *be* desired, the terror of potential sexual violence conveyed through the pursuit at the end is an objective correlative for Fanny's own sense that such an incorporative gaze would, in fact, annihilate her altogether. She escapes – but only to immerse herself in the maternal bed, to shut out the world and regress.

→ SYLVIA PLATH ←

In both Drabble's and Brookner's novels, romance, marriage, and motherhood (as socially institutionalized) offer an irreconcilable loss and discovery of possible identity for women. Like Woolf's, their heroines are compelled to cope with these contradictions in ways that deny their human potential. In Plath's novel *The Bell Jar* [1963], *death* is actively embraced and sought as a state in which opposing demands can coexist and where the need for resolution no longer makes its conflicting claims on body and mind. Esther's madness is represented as the individual human extension of a social alienation which, through her experience as a female growing up in the United States in the 1950s, both constitutes her identity and determines its subsequent disintegration. The protective 'flip' style in which she narrates her experiences persistently dehumanizes, constructs a defensive barrier between inner and outer worlds. Her schizoid failure of affective response, her fragmentary sense of self, and her moral neutrality articulate a 'postmodern' subjectivity. They reveal, too, a deeply ambivalent attitude to that socially constructed femininity with which she is compelled to identify. The 'screen' which Esther erects is a rigidly defensive set of ego boundaries designed to protect her inner world from external threat, but the 'screen' shuts down so completely that she is finally unable to make any connection between inner and outer. Lacking a secure inner object world, Esther has split off her own 'bad' inner objects and projected them on to a world which thus appears to be overwhelmingly threatening. She thereby achieves, however, an inner state of numbness inside the bell jar, where she need no longer feel. In W. R. Bion's account of schizophrenia:

> The patient feels imprisoned in a state of mind he has achieved and unable to escape from it because he feels he lacks the apparatus of awareness of reality, which is both the key to escape and the freedom itself to which he would escape. This sense of imprisonment is intensified by the menacing presence of the expelled fragments within whose phantasy movements he is contained. (Bion 1960, p. 39)

Esther experiences herself imprisoned in *glass*: she can see but cannot feel; the barriers are strong but fragile. Two central symbols in the novel are the bell jar and the image of another dome: the uterus, containing the suspended foetus. Esther experiences her inner object-relational world as an infantile 'self' which cannot be born, whose emotional vulnerability and 'newness' must be protected from the rapacities and annihilating threats of the world outside. She sees an actual foetus in a jar when she is taken by Buddy to see a woman giving birth in a teaching hospital. The birth itself is described through the dehumanized language of mechanics and technology: functions, parts, anaesthesia, the birth bed 'like some awful torture table, with those metal stirrups sticking up in mid-air at one end and all sorts of instruments and wires and tubes I couldn't make out properly at the other' (*The Bell Jar*, p. 67). The mother-to-be is simply a synechdochic 'ugly spider-fat stomach', the place between her legs 'lurid with disinfectant' (p. 68). Birth, for Esther, is a place where her own perception of femininity as monstrous struggles with her recognition that monstrosity is a creation of the male and of technology. Just as birth has become a place of disinfectant, metal stirrups, drugs, and surgical masks, so too the other alternatives offered to Esther as a woman are equally dehumanizing: images of cosmeticizing, cleaning, cooking, pushing prams, making rugs, making faces, serving men.

Images of female victimization abound in the novel: the execution of the Rosenburgs at the beginning is linked to Esther's own experience of electro-convulsive therapy, the pregnant or sick woman becomes an image of the violation of self by machines, of a *rape* by technology and male power. (After the visit to the birth ward, Esther is given her first glimpse of the male genitalia, and not surprisingly experiences disgust at their appearance of *not being human*.) Esther's own feelings of alienation begin with her initiation into the glossy world of the woman's magazine, where female visibility is dependent upon the adoption of the cosmetic mask, projecting an acceptable 'self' for consumption. Her state of alienation is recorded linguistically in the disparity between the flippancy and slickness of her narrative prose and the profound social implications of the experiences it describes. Significantly, this stylistic dissociation is first relaxed, and emotional nuances allowed to creep in, as Esther describes what is, in effect, her first suicide attempt on the ski-slope. Here it is the feeling of cessation of being, loss of boundaries, dissolution, which is presented as invigorating and exhilarating in the way that the pursuit of the American dream of success pretends to be but actually never is. The passage begins with the description of the relaxation of boundaries between the human and non-human world, as Esther feels the 'great, grey eye of the sky' upon her as she pauses at the top of the ski-run and looks down at Buddy, arms folded, 'of a piece with the split-rail fence behind him – numb, brown and inconsequential' (p. 101). Esther plummets down the slope and 'into my own past' (p. 102), hurtling on to 'the pebble at the bottom of the well, the white sweet baby cradled in its mother's belly' (p. 102). She experiences herself as struggling towards a new birth, a new 'self' which will be whole, unified, resistant, transcendent, separate, invulnerable: 'A dispassionate white sun shone at the summit of the sky. I wanted to hone myself on it 'till I grew saintly and thin and essential as the blade of a knife' (p. 103). But, as Esther crashes into gravel, she receives not maternal succour but a birth into iced water and crunchy rock and the 'queer satisfied expression' on Buddy's face as he tells her that the leg is broken and 'You'll be stuck in a cast for months' (p. 103).

Throughout, Esther represents her 'self' through figures of absence: holes, shadows, nothingness, something which has been swallowed or consumed. Images of mingling and consuming convey the desire for a 'rebirth' into wholeness which is inseparable from the fear of reincorporation. Life and death are inextricably bound together: food nourishes and poisons; water gives life and drowns; sexuality promises new life and nearly kills Esther as she haemorrhages. 'I never feel so much myself as when I'm in a hot bath' (p. 21) connects the imagery of birth, of the foetus in the amniotic sac, to the images of purification, denial, and transcendence of the human state. The bath is both a womb and a coffin, just as the bell jar is the uterus with its potential for life and thus, inevitably, death. As Esther bathes, she feels herself 'growing pure again. ... The longer I lay there in the clear hot water the purer I felt, and when I stepped out at last and wrapped myself in one of the big, soft, white, hotel bath-towels I felt pure and sweet as a new baby' (p. 22). The bell-jar as the womb is both the symbol of Esther's hope for rebirth as a new woman and her perception of femininity as an imprisoning and suffocating and deathly globe. Esther shares her culture's perception of the feminine as 'nature', inchoateness, and physicality, which must be controlled and given form, precisely, put 'in a cast'. She clearly identifies nature with the maternal and thus seeks an 'elemental' rebirth through a deathly reunion, but simultaneously, therefore, perceives the 'feminine' as a non-human force threatening identity and requiring control and resistance. As Dinnerstein argues:

> When the active project of selfhood feels too strenuous or too dangerously lonely the temptation is strong in all of us to melt back into that from which we have carved ourselves out. The mother supports the active project, but she is also on hand to be melted into when it is abandoned. She may, indeed, even encourage the child's lapses from selfhood, for she as well as the child has mixed feelings about its increasing separateness from her. (Dinnerstein 1976, p. 111)

Femininity may thus be perceived as *dangerous*. The mother is the person in whom one's subjectivity appears to be mirrored, and, if she fails to confirm one's significance, then she may be seen as annihilating and monstrous. When Esther looks into the mirror, she sees either nothingness or a garish caricature of femininity, a 'mask' which is a projection of the cultural perception of the feminine as monstrous. What she seeks is a rebirth through a union with a 'natural' which both incorporates the feminine and impossibly transcends its cultural forms and representations so that she will emerge whole, clean, thin, honed: *fleshless*, in other words.

The physical body is the focus of much of Esther's ambivalence towards her femininity. She longs to transcend the restrictions of physical being, experiencing her suicide attempts as a process of outwitting her body. She fears 'growing up', developing a 'mature' body, becoming the potential *carrier* of the baby in the jar rather than being the baby itself. She sees Dodo pushing the pram as the ultimate image of imprisonment and the blank O of her contraceptive device signifies, above all, freedom. At a magazine dinner she is fascinated by Hilda's expensive-looking scarf, 'furry tails fastened on one side by a dangling gilt chain' (p. 29): imprisonment in luxury and dead skin. Later in the photography session she breaks down and cries, feeling like a skin discarded by an animal. When she attempts to slit her wrists, she fails because 'it was as if what I wanted to kill wasn't in the skin or the thin blue pulse that jumped under my thumb, but somewhere else, deeper, more secret, and a whole lot harder to get at' (p. 155). Feminine identity is symbolized through images of softness encased in the hard and unyielding: a baby in a jar; her leg in a plaster; the cervix inside the contraceptive dome. She seeks encasement as a way of controlling the inchoateness of the soft, inevitably sharing a patriarchal culture's obsession with control of 'the feminine': of emotionality, physicality, sexuality. The only other woman with whom she positively identifies is the Russian interpreter at the UN building, rattling off 'idiom after idiom' like a machine-gun fire, and 'I wished with all my heart I could crawl into her and spend the rest of my life barking out one idiom after another ... one more little pebble of efficiency among all other pebbles' (p. 78). This woman is described as muscular, with scrubbed bare face and double-breasted grey suit: she is everything which for Esther 'the feminine' is not. Yet Esther feels *herself* to be *not feminine* as she adds up her failings:

155

that she cannot cook, dance, ride a horse, serve men, write shorthand. Femininity is simultaneously desired as a state of transcendence and feared as deadly and annihilating. When Esther returns home to the suburbs, she feels the 'motherly breath' upon her 'like death' and experiences her mother's house as a 'large but escape-proof cage' (p. 120). Shortly after she is taken to see Dr Gordon, the psychiatrist, and again describes her emotional state through the imagery of the uterus: feeling as 'if I were being stuffed further and further into *a black airless sack* with no way out' (my italics).

Such images culminate in the description of her suicide attempt as she crawls into a womb-like cavern under the house, and of her recovery, as she regains consciousness in the hospital. This experience is described, in effect, as a passage down the birth canal:

A cool wind rushed by. I was being transported at enormous speed down a tunnel into the earth. ... A chisel cracked down on my eye, and a slit of light opened, like a mouth or a wound, till the darkness clamped shut on it again. I tried to roll away from the direction of the light, but hands wrapped around my limbs like mummy bands, and I couldn't move. ... Then the chisel struck again and the light leaped into my eye through the thick, warm, furry dark, a voice cried, 'Mother!' (pp. 180–1)

When her mother appears, Esther cannot bear to see her, and shortly afterwards she sees in the mirror the horrible caricature of her 'reborn' femininity – and smashes it to the floor.

Throughout, the mother has appeared as the most significant source of her victimization, colluding with the system which inflicts drugs, ECT treatments, and lobotomies, with her row of hairpins described as sticking up like a line of little bayonets. Esther both wants and does not want a mother, just as she both seeks and fears that 'essential' femininity which forever eludes her. She desires the bell jar to lift but cannot survive without it; because her desire for connection is so intense and so unresolved, she needs the protection of separation, dissociation, distance. At the end, as the snow settles over everything, recalling the end of Joyce's story 'The Dead', Esther knows that nothing has changed, nothing *can* change, and that 'To the person in the bell jar, blank and stopped as a dead baby, the world itself is a bad dream' (p. 250).

ANN TYLER

The narcissistic dependency exhibited by Esther and by Brookner's female characters is revealed to be the product of a social system which engenders a deeply ambivalent attitude towards femininity and leads to an inadequate level of self-esteem in women. These concerns are central, too, in the work of Ann Tyler, a writer who, again, eschews *radical* formal experiment, preferring to draw on traditional forms of 'women's writing' (the family saga and gothic, for example) but to deploy their conventions in new ways. In *A Slipping Down Life* [1969], for example, the gothic motifs of entrapment, violent threat, kidnapping, and escape are the vehicles for an exploration of the relations between feminine narcissism and the power relationship between men and women. Evie, the central character, is an overweight and physically unprepossessing 17-year-old who longs to chisel out a shape for herself, to become distinct, to feel that she is no longer a grey inchoate mass which merges with the drab environment outside. She seeks these outlines in an imaginary identification with the 'ideal' sexually seductive femininity reproduced through the popular romances and radio music she avidly consumes. Evie becomes obsessed first with the disembodied voice and then with the physical presence of 'Drumstrings' Casey, a small-time teenage pop-singer who himself inhabits a fantasy world of stardom and fame more real to him than the actuality of working as a garage mechanic in his father's shoestring business. Evie, like Brookner's Fanny, silently screams 'Look at me!' Unlike Fanny, however, she has no access to the world of books and dinner parties and money and, unable, therefore, *verbally* to articulate her needs, expresses a socially produced and pathological masochism in the sensational act of carving the letters CASEY on her forehead during one of Drumstrings's concerts. As the authorities register horror and incomprehension at the extremity of her conduct, Evie feels only a sense of contentment:

'I believe this might be the best thing I've ever done,' said Evie. 'Something out of character. Definite . . . '. While I was walking through that crowd with the policeman, I kept thinking of my name: Evie Decker, *me*. Taking something into my own hands for once. I thought, if I had started acting like this a long time ago, my whole *life* might've been different. (p. 31)

The letters read backwards, for Evie has gouged them while contemplating her reflection in a mirror. Later they heal into a startling white scar which Evie bears as a badge of identity. They were cut, she says at the end, for the 'purposes of identification' (p. 156). As she stares at the new-formed letters in the mirror, a sense of 'I' crystallizes for the first time in her life, but it is an identity gained through the dissolution of her own physical boundaries. As the letters, Casey's name, become *more* distinct, Evie feels her own physical body becoming almost invisible:

Her forehead was an angry doll's, crisscrossed with black stitches. The word 'Casey' reflected right side around, formed itself only after several seconds, during which she stood stunned and motionless with her mouth barely open. Later, maybe, it would be immediately legible. But today the threads turned her forehead first into a jagged design, a greyish-white crazy-quilt covering the space between her hairline and her straight brown eyebrows, which were flaked with dried blood. All her other features seemed to have drained away. Her lips were pale, and her eyes had lightened. Her nose looked flatter. For years she had cherished the few surprises hidden away in her shapelessness: a narrow nose, slender wrists, and perfect oval fingernails. Now, still looking into the mirror, she held up both wrists and turned the blue-veined, glistening insides of them towards the glass. Then she backed away, very slowly. But when she was as far as she could get, pressed against the wall behind her, the letters still stood out ragged and black. 'Casey'. A voice inside her read the name out, coolly: 'Casey'. (p. 34)

Evie thus flaunts her bizarre but 'normal' discovery of identity through another, and advertises also the incipient sado-masochism of the pop culture's romantic couple. Significantly, when her father comes to visit in the hospital, bringing the gift of a bedjacket, Evie recognizes that it 'must have been what he brought her when Evie was born – something he had been told was expected of him, along with flowers and a bottle of cologne. Evie's mother had been the last woman in Pulqua County to die of childbed fever' (p. 32). The bedjacket reminds Evie that she has survived at her mother's expense, an inadequate substitute partner for her father. But, having now discovered and given birth to a new 'self', having christened her forehead with the name of Casey, she can accept the gift and take up the maternal position.

'Drumstrings' Casey initially responds to Evie's act with repugnance, but, prompted by his 'manager' David, begins to appreciate the promotional possibilities offered in her face. She thus becomes a grotesque caricature of the glamorous 'starlet' who, through her body, advertises the 'star'. Sensing the possibility of thus creating in Casey a dependency on her, she colludes with their conversion of her into a 'bait and switch ad' (p. 66), believing 'publicity was everything. She felt that more and more. She thought of publicity as the small, neat click that set into motion machines that had previously been disengaged' (p. 129). She thus displays, also, a caricature of that feminine narcissism produced by a culture which offers self-esteem to women only through the physical gratification and service of others. As with all adolescents, particularly girls, Evie seeks in friendships a replacement for the lost idealized parent, and, because in Evie's case the loss has been absolute, Drumstrings becomes, in her eyes, a god. As she watches him perform, thinking that 'the audience must have noticed the separate, motionless circle of air he moved in' (p. 20), she is perturbed to discover that he has an actual father and mother: 'Did he wind his watch every morning, check its accuracy, try to be places on time like ordinary people?' (p. 51).

When they marry, Evie seeks identification with the image of 'wife' offered to her in the popular women's magazines, striving to gratify Casey's desires by 'mixing orange juice: saying no to a vacuum cleaner salesman' (p. 97). As the fantasy of his transcendence and stardom begins to falter against the evidence of the mundane and the ordinary failure, however, Casey experiences Evie's body with its CASEY sign as a reproach, a mockery of his desires. He tells her that he's tired of 'having to face that nagging forehead of yours. I don't know why you don't wear bangs anymore' (p. 138). As his dependency on her wanes, Evie begins to construct another identity for herself through the use of her body. She becomes pregnant and with the new life inside her leaves Casey, determined to make a fresh start. She appears to be asserting her own needs, acting independently and decisively for the first time. Again, however, her behaviour is presented ambiguously, and the reader is left with a sense of the overwhelming force of cultural determination in the construction of gender and identity:

> She went to the bedroom and pulled out a suitcase, which she opened on the bed. Then she began folding the blouses that hung in her closet. Hundreds of times, in movies and on television, she had watched this scene being rehearsed for her. Wives had laid blouses neatly in overnight bags and had given them a brisk little pat, then crossed on clicking heels to collect an armload of dresses still on their hangers. There was no way she could make a mistake. Her motions were prescribed for her, right down to the tucking of rolled stockings into empty corners and the thoughtful look she gave the empty closet. (p. 155)

If she cannot facilitate the translation of Drumstrings's dreams of stardom into reality, then she will translate desire from one medium into another (song to film), trade one culturally prescribed feminine role for another, in a potentially endless series of displacements and transformations around an impossible, absent, 'unified' subjectivity.

GRACE PALEY

Grace Paley's refusal of 'totalization', of 'ultimate' human significance, and of 'organic form', and her fragmented, mercurial, comic, and often violent stories, do, indeed, seem to call for a 'postmodern' reading in a much more overt manner than the other writers in this chapter. Yet her stories, like theirs, are deeply rooted in the everyday, the ongoing, the tiny disturbances which flicker, often unobserved, across human lives and relationships. Her fictions do, indeed, offer more hope for women than those of Plath, Brookner, or Tyler, revealing the communal and relational basis of feminine identity as a source of great potential, and often gently ridiculing the grand schemes and idealisms with which men seek to defend themselves against a substantiality and cheerfulness they cannot comprehend or attain.

Yet Paley's refusal to offer us human identity, either through the traditional literary structures (plots, rounded characters, formal patterns of significance) or through the dehumanization of postmodernist rupture, has led, in my view, to her critical neglect. Her work cannot be categorized within the terms of the dominant contemporary aesthetic. Her own awareness of this is recorded in a story in her second book *Enormous Changes at the Last Minute* [1975], entitled 'A Conversation with my Father'. In this, a woman writer attempts to please her dying father by writing for him a 'plain' story, like those of Turgenev and Chekhov, with 'full' characters, plot, and realistic description. The father is clearly, also, her superego, chastising her in the name of 'literary tradition' to give up her inconsequential stories about 'people sitting endlessly in trees talking senselessly, voices from who knows where' (p. 162). The woman, however, refuses to write transcendental tragedies which insert the individual human life into the grand order of things and which view people's 'meaning' in terms of an impersonal determinism. For this reason, she cannot write plots: 'the absolute line between two points which I've always despised. Not for literary reasons, but because it takes all hope away. Everyone, real or invented, deserves the open destiny of life' (p. 162). The traditional plot joins an arbitrary starting-point in history with an equally arbitrary point of ending and attempts to create a retrospective human significance out of the space between. But, for this woman writer, there are no patterns of ultimate significance: 'it's a funny world nowadays and the best one can do is to be optimistic in the face of the unpredictable and the uncertain' (p. 167).

Paley's women characters view 'life' in relation to their experience of it: the routines of housework and childcare, the interruptibility, fragmentariness, and unendingness of domestic work. To create 'order' is not to impose a grand 'tragic' vision, but to have a clean house and enough money for the day's food – the next day may bring disorder and hunger again. The

161

woman writer in this story speaks for Paley herself: there will be no oedipal resolution, no closure, no symbolic significance. Instead, the reader is offered the shifts and manœuvres, the temporary focusing of identity, which has become the formal mode of the postmodern text, but which has *always* been the experiential mode of most women's daily lives. She cannot afford the distance of tragedy despite her father's reproach – 'When will you look it in the face' (p. 167) – nor can she accept his tragic essentialist view of human character. For him, her story can only end with its central woman character alone: 'Yes ... what a tragedy. The end of a person' (p. 166), he says. His daughter, however, knows that the woman will stoically carry on despite her abandonment and the great misfortunes of her life:

> Of course her son never came home again. But right now, she's the receptionist in a storefront community clinic in the East village. Most of the customers are young people, some old friends. The head doctor has said to her, 'if we only had three people in this clinic with your experiences'. (p. 167)

There is always an identity 'to be going on with', constructed and reconstructed through one's relationship with others in the temporal and mundane world.

None of Paley's women characters sets her sights on grand achievements – the woman in the story 'Wants' [1975], for example, had 'promised my children to end the war before they grew up' (p. 5), but she settles resignedly with the consolatory thought that she *has* at last taken her library books back. They are eighteen years overdue! Without sustained psychological analysis, Paley manages to suggest, nevertheless, how the perceptions of her men and women characters are rooted in different social and historical experiences and expectations. In 'Enormous Changes at the Last Minute' [1975], her central character Alexandra struggles with the day-to-day responsibility for a dying father, eleven young methadone addicts, and her own desire for the pleasure which has disappeared from her life of duty and service. She tries to identify, therefore, with the idealism of the communard cab-driver/poet Dennis who becomes her lover and who promises that the young will achieve 'enormous changes at the last minute' (p. 126). Alexandra, however, thinks of the desperate youngsters in her care: 'She

162

had always had a progressive if sometimes reformist disposition, but at that moment, listening to him talk, she could see straight ahead over the hot road of love to solitary age and lonesome death' (p. 126). The story ends with Dennis 'splitting' to write songs about fatherhood and responsibility, as Alexandra prepares for the birth of a baby and sets up a home for pregnant teenagers, thus establishing 'a precedent in social work which would not be followed or even mentioned in state journals for about five years' (p. 134). Dennis's songs become popular – and result in an increase in visitors to 'old-age homes'. Thus each of them, working out of a different vision and experience of the world, and despite their final inability to communicate across cultural and gender differences, act in ways to improve the world for the human beings who live in it. Ironically, of course, Alexandra (with her acceptance of the inevitability of mortality) works for the next generation, and Dennis (with his hopes in the young) tries to improve life for the old and dying.

Paley's stories reveal that, while men are given opportunities to extend their idealism and poeticizing, women are generally required, because of their familial positioning, to be pragmatists: limited, 'realistic' optimists. In 'The Immigrant Story' [1975], the emphasis is on the *limitations* of the woman's pragmatic approach to Jack's sense of the personal tragedy of his life. He tells the woman how his father was forced by his mother to sleep in the baby's crib. She, impatient with what she assumes to be the prelude to a neat Freudian interpretation of her partner's personality, tells him: 'The reason your father was sleeping in the crib was that your sister who usually slept in the crib had scarlet fever and needed decent beds and more room to sweat and come to a fever crisis, and either get well or die' (p. 173). Jack, however, is given the last words of the story, to explain how his parents fled as refugees from Poland to America but not before the famine had claimed all their children. He ends the story with an image which has persisted from childhood of his father reading to his mother under an old light bulb, and 'Just beyond the table and their heads, there is the darkness of the kitchen, the bedroom, the dining room, the shadowy darkness where as a child I ate my supper, did my homework and went to bed' (p. 175). Neither the story nor Jack reveals any more information or analysis, but the implication is that the mother has turned to the father who must substitute for the lost babies in an attempt to make reparation for her own survival. Jack, the later-born child, is excluded from the intensity of this relationship based on loss, grief, and guilt.

The woman narrator's practical and brisk explanation is rendered deeply inadequate by the fuller knowledge of Jack's history, but Paley does not condemn her as unimaginative or short-sighted. Her stories, instead, reveal the pressure on women to make the most of things, to appear contented, cheerful, optimistic. Jack tells the narrator, 'you have gotten a rotten rosy temperament' (p. 173), whereas all he can feel and express is 'misery, misery, misery. Grayness. I see it all very gray' (p. 172). Yet her cheerful exterior is not, as the man believes, simply a consequence of her less tragic childhood, nor the projection of an 'innate' self. Women are required to be cheerful as an aspect of their compulsion to please (see chapter two). W.R.D. Fairbairn, for example, has argued that, if the caretaker regularly fails to meet the needs of the infant (highly likely in the present socially situated mother-daughter relationship), the infant will not view the mother's responses as inappropriate but will see its own needs as bad and driving the loved object away. These 'negative' needs must therefore be repressed, and more acceptable, more 'pleasing' and biddable characteristics must be offered to the world, if care and approval are to be found in it (Fairbairn 1952). Thus the little girl (later the woman) is not allowed to express *her* sadness, misery, and need, but must learn to be cheerful, optimistic, and supportive to the men and children who will bring their sorrows to her. In Paley's stories the women make the most of their constrained situations, accept the necessity for optimism, and find consolation in each other's company, in children, in neighbourly deeds, expressing their inner frustration only through occasional and often bizarre and violent outbursts. The tragic view of life or the idealism of grand optimistic schemes they leave to the men, preferring to make their connections and identify themselves through their everyday cares and duties.

The old woman in 'Anxiety' in *Later the Same Day* [1985], for example, leans out of her window to chastise a father who has punished a little girl. The man, politically progressive, is angry with his daughter for pretending he is a pig. The old woman is angry with his lack of empathy with the child, for, though in his mind pig signifies police, the word, clearly, does not have the same connotations for the child. She tells him that children are to be treasured as the hope for the future, for despite his progressive ideals he fails to see that it is through the acts and the imaginations of the young that a new world will be built. The man gallops away with the little girl pretending to her that he is a horse (signifying freedom), but the old woman does not smile indulgently upon his idealist symbolism. Instead, she reflects that they are

> galloping towards one of the most dangerous street corners in the world. And they may live beyond that trisection across other dangerous corners. ... I wish I could see just how they sit down at their kitchen tables for a healthy snack (orange juice or milk and cookies) before going out into the new spring afternoon to play. (p. 103)

Paley often records the relations between men and women as a sort of serious but mockingly enacted contest. Faith (who appears in several stories) is forced to accept that she can 'rarely express my opinion on any serious matter but only live out my destiny, which is to be, until my expiration date, laughingly the servant of man' (*The Little Disturbances of Man* [1970], p. 132). She protests with occasional violent eruptions, but remains, essentially, silent. The men require such mute service, but fear and shun the commitment which must accompany it. In 'The Pale Pink Roast' [1970], Peter (Anna's former lover, who speedily departed on the birth of his daughter) arrives for a short stay of pleasure and enters parading his body, his male boundaries, his 'difference', lecturing Anna on his new-found philosophy of the body as the dwelling-place of the soul. He tells her, 'Don't mix me up with biology. Look at me, what do you see?' (p. 47), but as she stares at this 'dwelling-place of the soul' all she can recall is that 'cannibals, tasting man, saw him thereafter as the great pig, the pale pink roast' (p. 148). He continues with an account of his new philosophy, his body-building sessions, his vitamin supplements; she asks him if he's working. Peter ignores her questions, desiring only the pleasure of the moment, the sexual intimacy for which he has returned, and fearing conversion into a 'meal ticket' – a roast, a salary – he hurriedly dresses and prepares to depart (having satisfied the dwelling-place of the soul). Anna chooses this moment to tell him that she has a new – and rich – husband, and he looks at her 'coldly'; for it seems that she has used him, Peter, also, for the pleasure of the moment. Anna, however, cannot escape her conditioning and has to tell him: 'I really mean it, Peter, I did it for love' (p. 51). The sentence is ambiguous, possibly referring to her recent marriage or the even more recent sexual intimacy with Peter. He, however, remains free because, centred so completely in himself, all ambiguity is resolved. He smiles and cartwheels off eastward, free and satiated, happy in the knowledge that Anna is still 'his'. He has 'established tenancy' (p. 50) again.

In 'The Contest' [1970] the male narrator's fears of the voracity of women and his determination not to be 'trapped' are conveyed again through a blending of the poetic and the grotesque, the inconsequential and the sublime, that suggests the continuous dislocations and chance connections of contemporary human life. The story opens, typically for Paley, with a stylistic shift from the 'eternal' and poetic to the historical and mundane: 'Up early or late, it never matters, the day gets away from me. Summer or Winter, the shade of trees or their hard shadow, I never get into my Rice Krispies till noon' (p. 67). The insouciant style conveys the narrator's need to remain detached, free-floating, independent of the connections which he sees women attempting to force on him (first his mother, who 'died with a sizeable chunk of me in her gullet' (p. 73) and then Dot). He can appreciate Dot's need for security, her requirement of a steady income and an engagement ring, but 'my impression of women is that they mean well but are driven to an obsessive end by greedy tradition' (p. 69). Dot, however, is clearly driven to an obsessive end not by 'greedy tradition' but by her realistic expectation that passion will be declared and abandonment will shortly follow. Her fear of abandonment is as deep as his of commitment. When she fails to trick him into marriage through 'the contest' (they win first prize: a holiday for a *married* couple), she cuts her losses and departs for the holiday without him but with the prize money. Neither character is castigated, but the behaviour of each is revealed as determined by a social structure where women's economic dependency on men and their exclusive parenting produces an emotional fear of women in men, and in women it produces the substitution of material acquisitions for both emotional security and the expectation of being cared for and loved. Dot is, in effect, the twentieth-century version of the eighteenth-century theatrical 'clever servant', using her wiles to survive in a world where *her* power is limited to the observation of the weaknesses and follies of those who have material power.

Deriving consolation from a communal network which they construct through their own relational and pragmatic skills, Paley's women characters, however, do not allow the bell jar to descend. Occasionally they rattle the bars of the cage to make small, but significant changes, sometimes they erupt into violence. Faith, in 'A Subject of Childhood' [1970], tears off Clifford's earlobe as he dares to tell her she has been a 'faulty' mother. Nursing her guilt and anger, she looks down at the youngest child, whose behaviour has triggered the row and who now looks up at her and says, 'I love you, Mama.' Faith finishes her story:

> I held him so and rocked him. I cradled him. I closed my eyes and leaned on his dark head. But the sun on its course emerged from among the water towers of downstairs office buildings and suddenly shone white and bright on me. Then through the short fat fingers of my son, interred forever, like a black and white barred king in Alcatraz, my heart lit up in stripes. (p. 145)

This final image is of the paradox at the heart of women's lives: that which brings most joy and intense pleasure is, under our present social arrangements, often that which is the source of imprisonment and pain.

For the most part, the six writers examined in this chapter offer different forms of understanding of this state of affairs, but only a cautious hope for the possibility of change. The writers in the next chapter, more overtly 'postmodernist' and experimental in style, are often more optimistic about the potential for drawing on women's relational strengths to forge a new human community. None of them, however, underestimates the pain, difficulty, and frustration involved in such a struggle.

Chapter Five

CONTEMPORARY WOMEN WRITERS: CHALLENGING POSTMODERNIST AESTHETICS

FANTASY, UTOPIA, AND SUBVERSION

Although generally not thought of as 'postmodernist', the work of writers such as Margaret Atwood, Fay Weldon, Doris Lessing, Joanna Russ, Marge Piercy, Muriel Spark, Angela Carter, Toni Morrison, and Alice Walker reveals fictional structures in which the forms of desire, only superficially if at all modified by a realist consensus and a liberal ethos, are closer to the surface of the text than in the fictions discussed in previous chapters. Often this process is entirely self-conscious. Writers like Spark and Atwood, for example, flout the reader's expectations of tradi- tional non-realist forms like gothic or romance. Both Russ and Piercy work self-consciously in utopian modes, asserting the necessity and inevitability of fantasy in our lives, not as regressive or escapist, but as part of a drive for relationship and connection to others. Fantasy functions in the work of the writers in chapter four predominantly in terms of regressive withdrawal or compensation, but in the writers mentioned above there is also a more positive articulation of the possibility of connecting our desires to a potential world outside them. Freud, of course, argued that 'a happy person never fantasizes, only an unsatisfied one. The motive forces of fantasies are unsatisfied wishes, and every single fantasy is the fulfilment of a wish, a correction of unsatisfying reality' (Freud 1908, p. 146). Clearly, the ideological pressures of the dominant social formation may lead us to doubt the validity of our fantasies, labelling them as 'infantile', 'hysterical', or 'neurotic', but writers like Lessing and Piercy attempt to counteract this view through asserting the *political*, utopian potential of fantasy. Like other writers mentioned above, they seek ways of integrating the worlds of fantastic desire with the world of material reality, of envisioning a society where, indeed, difference would not be separation, but connection which does not threaten autonomy – a collectivism that preserves the individual self. Such writing constructs a new subject, one who is necessarily 'dispersed' but who is also an effective agent, neither the old liberal subject nor the contemporary post-structuralist site of the play of signification. This subject is positioned in a fictional world, too, where morality has neither been relativized out of the window nor been seen simply as the reflection of an 'essential' human condition.

The use of fantastic forms by the writers mentioned earlier, whether 'alternative worlds' or the paradigmatic structures of human desire which erupt in genres like gothic signals an overt departure from mimetic or expressive realist conceptions of the fictional text. Many of these texts are aesthetically self-reflexive in an axiomatically 'postmodern' way, but I would argue that all articulate the processes of fictionality as functions of human desire and imagination rather than as an impersonal, intertextual play of signification. They express an optimism about the possibility of human relationship and human agency which is rarely articulated in the 'classic' postmodern texts of writers such as Barth, Pynchon, Barthelme, or Sukenick.

Rosemary Jackson, discussing the subversive potential of fantasy, has argued that it 'characteristically attempts to compensate for a lack resulting from cultural constraints: it is a literature of desire, which seeks that which is experienced as absence and loss' (Jackson 1981, p. 3). In 'fantastic' texts by writers such as Carter, Russ, Atwood, and Weldon, the feminine subject is fragmented, dispersed, in an attempt to rupture or deconstruct the 'fixed' ego formed doubly in alienation. These writers push their representations to the limits of the signifying order, attempting to reverse the development from the imaginary to the symbolic and to envision an alternative subjectivity formed out of the dissolution of the unequal boundaries of gender. Images of mirroring, reflection, rebirth, and noncorporeal or non-material forms of connection (telepathy, 'plugging in' to others' minds) express an impulse to re-enter and reformulate the mirror stage.

What is particularly prominent in such texts is the extent to which dissatisfaction with the bodily ego and the female body itself becomes the impetus behind the desire for utopian change. In the work of Atwood and Weldon, the fantastic disintegration of the body as the locus of femininity within the present culture takes on a gothic character. Novels such as *The Edible Woman* [1969] and *The Life and Loves of a She-Devil* [1983] explore the displaced desires which must be freed from the taboos and repressions of patriarchal society if a utopian alternative is to be imagined. In these works, the 'uncanny' (in Freudian terms) recovery of that which has been denied is experienced through a shift in the relationship of ideal to bodily ego. Such a shift releases repressed desires and involves regression to a state of infantile dissolution which holds the possibility of reconstructing the bodily ego in alternative terms. Such texts are essentially *gothic* in structure, exhibiting the features of the genre specified by David Punter in his definition:

> most of its manifestations are closely related to perceptions of the failure of accounts of the world and the mind predicated on the supremacy of subjectivity. The Gothic world is one in which health, strength and moral wellbeing will not serve to get one by; on the contrary, they will prevent one from seeing the real sources of power and control, and thus make one's demise the more fitting an object for irony. (Punter 1980, p. 400)

The effect of this, as he goes on to discuss, is that gothic 'demonstrates the potential of revolution by daring to speak the socially unspeakable; but the very act of speaking it is an ambiguous gesture' (Punter 1980, p. 417).

In the work of 'utopian' writers like Lessing, Russ, and Piercy, the impulse to connect, to dissolve the boundaries of the corporeal, is intentionally projected on to the material world itself in the image of a new and better society. The alienation and estrangement from their bodies experienced by the female protagonists as a consequence of their gender positioning releases a desire for transformation not simply of the body as an individual corporeal unit, but of the whole social structure. As Tom Moylan argues:

Thus the romance or the fantastic, including utopia, focusses on a quest for what has been repressed or denied, for Heimat, as Ernst Bloch puts it – that sense of *home* which includes happiness and fulfillment and which the human collectivity has never known ... The operation of the uncanny, of estrangement, in the fantastic genres opens readers up to what Freud calls 'unfulfilled but possible futures to which we still like to cling in fantasy, all the strivings of the ego which adverse circumstances have crushed, and all our suppressed acts of volition which nourish in us the illusion of Free Will'. (Moylan 1986, pp. 34–5)

Moylan's view is that such 'critical' utopias are metaphorical displacements of contradictions within the political unconscious itself. Given the acute contradictoriness of women's lives and sense of subjectivity, it is not surprising that many contemporary women writers have sought to 'displace' their desires, seeking articulation not through the rational and metonymic structures of realism but through the associative and metaphorical modes of fantasy: romance, science fiction, gothic, utopia, horror. This chapter will examine the social and psychological roots of this narrative impulse and its transformation in the work of Atwood, Weldon, and Lessing, and briefly in Piercy, Russ, Carter, Spark, Morrison, and Walker.

THE LIMITS OF MY BODY ARE THE LIMITS OF MY WORLD: FANTASY AND FEMININITY

Discussing *L'Histoire d'O*, Kaja Silverman has argued:

There is ultimately an alarming consensus as to what woman is and wants, and that consensus has been produced through shared assumptions about the female body. This discursive 'surplus' assures the stability of traditional definitions of the female subject. It also exerts intense pressure upon what might be called the 'brute materiality' of real bodies. (Silverman 1982, p. 346)

Freud observed that the ego is first a *bodily* ego, and Klein's work extends our understanding of the construction of a sense of self through increasing differentiation of one's corporeal surfaces

171

from what is 'other'. Clearly, boys and girls experience this process in different ways, and their perception of and relationship to their own bodies will also be the focal point of a complex interrelationship of different symbolic meanings. It may thus also become the focal point for the desire for and the possibility of *change* in the relationships between men and women, and in the construction of subjectivity and gender.

The 'body' is not simply a natural 'given'. Foucault's work, in particular, has drawn attention to the discursive construction of the body through the social practices and discourses which regulate sexuality. In *The History of Sexuality* (1984), he questions the simple traditional historical view of sexuality as controlled simply through *repression* and posits a more complex view which links sexuality inextricably with knowledge and power relations which regulate the meanings of the human body. Discussing the historical origins of sexuality, for example, he emphasizes the significance of events like the reform of the religious practice of confession which do not appear, ostensibly, to exert pressures in the sphere of the sexual. He points out that in the reformed confession after the Council of Trent, for example, one can observe the beginnings of the transformation of desire: from the need simply to *confess* to sin, through a description of one's sexual acts, to a need to *probe* the reasons for one's behaviour, offer motivations, discuss, tell, talk about sexuality:

> the nearly infinite task of telling – telling oneself and another, as often as possible, everything that might concern the interplay of innumerable pleasures, sensations, and thoughts which through the body and the soul had some affinity with sex ... an imperative was established: Not only will you confess to acts contravening the law, but you will seek to transform your desire, your every desire, into discourse. (Foucault 1984, p. 20)

As sex thus ceases to be a 'private' matter, opaque to the probing of public authority in the *religious* sphere, so in those of science, medicine, administration, and welfare similar changes are taking place. From the eighteenth century onwards, there is an increasing trend towards the publicization and thus the regularization of sexuality. This is evidenced, for example, in the concern with population growth, the development of psychological medicine, the increasing fear of the 'masses' as threatening political stability with their untamed 'energies', and, above all, the hysterization of women's bodies, identifying them, in particular, with a sexuality in need of surveillance and control. According to Foucault, therefore, any attempt to alter sexual relations cannot begin until sexuality is perceived as a historically constructed imaginary unity rather than as a 'natural energy' or a set of drives which have been repressed:

> Sexuality must not be thought of as a kind of natural given which power holds in check ... it is the name that can be given to a historical construct: not a furtive reality that is difficult to grasp but a great surface network in which the stimulation of bodies, the intensification of pleasures, the incitement to discourse, the formation of special knowledges, the strengthening of controls and resistances, are linked to one another, in accordance with a few major strategies of knowledge and power. (Foucault 1984, pp. 105–6)

Furthermore, our apparent 'freedom' in being able to 'tell all', to discuss, confess, and analyse sexuality, is a spurious one, simply the way in which power disguises itself:

> The obligation to confess is now relayed through so many different points, is so deeply ingrained in us, that we no longer perceive it as the effect of a power that constrains us. . . . The confession is a ritual of discourse in which the speaking subject is also the subject of the statement; it is also a ritual that unfolds within a power relation, for one does not confess without the presence (or virtual presence) of a partner who is not simply the interlocutor but the authority who requires the confession, prescribes and appreciates it, and intervenes in order to judge, punish, forgive, console, and reconcile. (Foucault 1984, pp. 61–2)

Sex is thus 'an especially dense transfer point for relations of power' (p. 103). In particular, women's position as tokens of economic exchange is reinforced in the modern state by the intervention of welfare control to ensure a healthy and numerically regulated population. Ironically, of course, though this posits women as 'objects' in an exchange economy, it also, unintentionally, draws attention to their potential *power* in the reproduction of this system of exchange, a power which can be transformed, perhaps, through changing the social meanings attached to their bodies.

The 'hysterization' of women's bodies for the purpose of social control and the regularization of the production of modern state power begins, according to Foucault, in the eighteenth century as part of a group of strategies which centre knowledge and power on sexuality. It was

> a threefold process whereby the feminine body was analysed – qualified and disqualified – as being thoroughly saturated with sexuality; whereby it was integrated into the sphere of medical practices, by reason of a pathology intrinsic to it; whereby, finally, it was placed in organic communication with the social body (whose regulated fecundity it was supposed to ensure), the family space (of which it had to be a substantial and functional element), and the life of children (which it produced and had to guarantee, by virtue of a biologico-moral responsibility lasting through the entire period of the children's education); the mother, with her negative image of 'nervous woman', constituted the most visible form of this hysterization. (Foucault 1984, p. 104)

Thus is women's sexuality *produced*: it is *not* a 'natural given' which must then be held in check by power, or probed and investigated by knowledge. To the extent that femininity is thus historically positioned and defined in terms of the *body*, however, any attempt to reconstitute its terms will necessarily involve a return, in one form or another, to the female body itself as the site of a complex focus of social meanings.

Traditionally, women themselves have always known this, using their bodies as instruments of *protest* against their 'feminine' positioning and identification. For Freud's female hysterics, the bodily symptom – paralysis, tics, phobias, coughs, ritual behaviour like hand-washing – 'speaks' or signifies the conflict produced within the psyche as a consequence of the organization of sexuality and the acquisition of gender. Hysteria can thus be seen as both a 'symptom' of powerlessness and a form of *resistance* to power. Recently, the growing number of 'illnesses' which express struggle for control of the female body testifies to the continuity of the bodily symptom as a form of resistance. Most commentators, however, see only the *negative* implications of such symptoms. Discussing eating disorders (predominantly a female problem), for example, Kim Chernin argues that the radical dissatisfaction that women feel with their cultural position is turned back in rage against their own bodies because they masochistically perceive this site of 'femininity' to be itself, in its imperfections, the source of their frustration and depression:

> The radical protest she might utter if she correctly understood the source of her despair and depression, has been directed against herself and away from her culture and society. Now, she will not seek to change her culture so that it might accept her body; instead, she will spend the rest of her life in anguished failure at the effort to change her body so that it will be acceptable to her culture. (Chernin 1981, p. 106)

Chernin fails, however, to emphasize that the body is not the ultimately 'natural' to be opposed to a culture which negates and represses it. The body is, itself, a cultural construction, and the psychological 'illnesses' which she describes in her book are a 'voicing' of cultural contradictions. Women do, however, turn their rage, frustration, and ambivalence about femininity on to their own bodies, carrying the culture's contradictory feelings towards the flesh and its ambivalence about the mother. The female body is an area where struggle for control is likely to be enacted because it has come to signify the threat of incorporation and loss of identity (see chapter two). Women do, indeed, have difficulties with oral behaviour such as eating, kissing, speaking, smoking, and biting and discover that the acceptable 'feminine' forms of such behaviour are highly regulated. Medicine, psychology, fashion, welfare guidelines (rules of hygiene, for example), religious practices – all regulate, *control*, and construct the female body in various ways. Women's bodies are almost literally burdened down with social meanings, proscriptions, and contradictions, and as a consequence:

> If men are cruel to women, or unyielding, or rape us, and make pictures of us in which we are being tortured and abused, and become sadistic to women as an expression of rage against the mother, we as women are spared the

temptation to inflict this torment upon another human being. Our own bodies will serve to receive the rage we would like to direct against our mothers.

And so we create a hell for the body, in which it can be afflicted with all the torments pornography inflicts upon the body of woman, the same sufferings our mythology reserves for sinners in the underworld. Thus, the female body is starved, emaciated, bound, driven, tortured with cold, shaken by rubber belts. (Chernin 1981, p. 153)

Many eating disorders, however, express not simply *rage* against the female body, but also the woman's desire for control over her own needs. Thus the illness may constitute an attempt to resist her objectification within the social relations of patriarchy. The attempt to 'reduce', the obsession with making the body smaller, *appears* to conform to the dominant culture's requirements of 'femininity', that it be placed under reproductive and sexual control so that women take up less space. It seems to reflect, also, the cultural fear of the inchoateness and voracious desire of female maturity which must be controlled through, for example, medicine, the pop culture, or welfare, ensuring that women remain in appearance and behaviour like *little girls*: that they carry neither the reminder of ageing, death, and mortality (keep slim, dye your hair, have a facelift) nor the reminder of the all-powerful mother of infancy with her imagined threat to self-identity and independent agency. To keep the body small also expresses the feminine desire to please, not to be 'needy', to be a person who, while serving and feeding others, appears herself to have transcended the importunate gnawings of need, hunger, and desire. Such a person thus appears to have brought that area of the human perceived as dark, irrational, animal, and threatening under *rational* control. Thinness is perceived as freedom:

Hence the implied directive to conceal the physically maternal side of oneself. Slimness is opposed to fertility. In this regard, Twiggy's pre-pubescent thinness sets up the association of the ideal of femininity as being separate from woman as fecund and childbearing. A pre-pubescent body cannot reproduce. Thus Twiggy's size and cuteness played a supporting role in the contemporary version of women's bodies being made into objects. (Orbach 1986, p. 75)

An obsession with 'reducing' the body, however, also expresses real *dissatisfaction* with current human relationships and is not simply the exaggeration of a cultural stereotype but also a resistance to it. Women are forced to seek an acceptance through their bodies in order to reinforce an inadequate corporeal sense of self produced by their early individuation and socialization. Just as the 'slim' woman seems to conform to and accept the cultural expectations discussed above, the self-inflictedly *emaciated* woman is a horrible parody. She is both an exaggeration and an *implicit* denial of these cultural norms, just as the fat women *explicitly* denies them. To be emaciated is both to be the fashionable height of 'femininity' as represented in western culture and also to embody a rejection of such femininity. It is both to appear to escape surveillance and definition as a commodity, an object for (controlled) sexual consumption, and yet to encourage spectatorship, morbid observation of oneself as 'unique', a 'super'-being who has transcended the weaknesses and repulsiveness of the flesh. As Orbach argues:

> Rather than making such a woman more 'attractive', anorectic thinness keeps her in retreat, but in a way that magnetizes others. She is now looked at, not as someone who is appealing, but as somebody one cannot take one's eyes off. The attention attracted is of a vaguely morbid nature. The thinness becomes disagreeably fascinating and intriguing. Thus the anorectic woman gains attention of an altogether different nature than that to which she originally aspired. Now it is her invisibility that makes her remarkable. Now she has a presence larger than her size. A presence which demands a response rather than a reflex. (Orbach 1986, p. 87)

In other words (in Brookner's words), 'Look at me!'

Such behaviour expresses the deep cultural ambivalence towards femininity, both the urge to rage against and control the female body (experienced by men and women) and the desire for possession of or identification with a quintessential 'femininity'. Moreover, within the context of a late capitalist consumer society, these contradictions are rendered even more acute through the alienating effects of commodification. As women's bodies, increasingly, are used to 'sell' products, the body itself is made non-threatening through its identification with an inert

consumer good, and the goods item itself is spuriously anthropomorphized to increase its desirability: the sleek, seductive
'good looks' of the latest saloon car, for example, or the maternal
and homely comforts of a slice of Hovis with fresh butter. Susie
Orbach, in fact, argues that 'The receptivity that women show
(across class, ethnicity and through the generations) to the idea
that their bodies are like gardens – arenas for constant
improvement and resculpting – is rooted in a recognition of
their bodies as commodities' (Orbach 1986, p. 36). Thus
feminine 'narcissism' can be seen to be a consequence of a
socially and psychologically overdetermined insecurity about
identity which is rooted in women's unsatisfactory cultural
formation of a bodily ego and their ensuing low self-esteem.

As a consequence of their social alienation, women experience
their bodies as parts, 'objects', rather than integrated wholes.
However, their dissatisfaction with and desire for a 'better' body
can form the basis of a genuinely subversive fantasy of social
change. Such feelings are not necessarily simply turned back in
masochistic rage against the existing body. The experience of
fragmentation and disintegration can become the starting-point
for a reconstruction of the bodily ego. Rosemary Jackson has
noted the characteristic fragmentation of 'character' in fantasy
and has argued:

> fantastic texts which try to negate or dissolve dominant
> signifying practices, especially 'character' representation,
> become, from this perspective, radically disturbing. Their
> partial and dismembered selves break a 'realistic' signifying
> practice which represents the ego as an indivisible unit.
> Fantasies try to *reverse* or *rupture* the process of ego formation
> which took place during the mirror stage, i.e., they attempt to
> re-enter the imaginary. Dualism and dismemberment are
> symptoms of this desire for the imaginary. (Jackson 1981, p.
> 90)

It seems to me that this fantastic tendency is very strong
in the work of many contemporary writers who draw on that
highly fragmented and contradictory sense of bodily ego as
the basis of subjectivity which is acutely felt by many
women.

MARGARET ATWOOD

Food, nourishment, first given by the mother, is the most profound expression of relationship – the symbol for entry into the world. It *is* the world for the first few months of life – the mode of communication between mother and child – and it prepares one for the assumption of life outside the dyad. (Orbach 1986, p. 144)

In Margaret Atwood's *The Edible Woman* [1969], the contradictions in feminine identity and the potential for change are explored almost exclusively through the relationship of the central character Marian to the act of consuming. Increasingly *unable* to consume as the novel progresses, she can, finally, through her symbolic baking of a cake-woman offered to Peter (her erstwhile fiancé), ritualistically mark the end of a rite of passage which has led her to the knowledge of the possibility of refusing self-sacrifice. Peter may now eat the cake-woman, but he may no longer cannibalize Marian's own body, and Marian can break her own identification with the consumable, the confection; she can refuse the signifying processes which endlessly substitute 'sweetie pie', 'honey', 'sugar', 'tart' for her own sense of corporeal identity. As Rosalind Coward argues, 'ritual meals are designed to signify the ability of men to provide and the duty of women to prepare and service' (Coward 1984, p. 112). Although Marian serves Peter the cake, however, it is in order to signify her new-found recognition that it is *she* that he has been consuming, *her* hungers and needs he has attempted to destroy, *her* female body he has felt compelled to devour before it should devour him. The structural features of romance which organize the novel – the pursuit, descent into the underworld, the founding of new relationships – do suggest, indeed, that Atwood intends the reader to perceive the concluding 'feast' as a rite of passage. Food has, of course, traditionally functioned not only as a symbol for entry into the world but also as a marker of significant points of transition in human lives and culture (for example, the Christmas feast and Mrs Ramsay's dinner party). Chernin points out that 'in earlier, tribal cultures food was always an essential part of those transformative, collective ceremonies through which individuals were brought step by step, to separate from one phase of

179

their development and enter the collective' (Chernin 1986, p. 168).

Once Marian perceives the symbolic relationship between women and food, she can reassert her own hunger, resume the first-person narrative voice (abandoned in the middle section of the novel for an 'objective' third-person voice), and shift from the passive 'vocalization' of protest through her body as instrument of resistance to an articulation of protest through effective action in the world. She bakes, subversively, a cake, an act which *undermines* the role of women as servers and women as consumables, just as it appears to *confirm* it. Afterwards, she begins to chew, swallow, bite, relish the texture of food. The passage echoes an earlier one where she presents Peter with a Valentine's Day gift of a heart-shaped cake in return for his dozen roses. However, when Marian herself attempts to eat a piece of this cake, 'it felt spongy and cellular against her tongue, like the bursting of thousands of tiny lungs. She shuddered and spat the cake out into her napkin and scraped her plate into the garbage' (*The Edible Woman*, p. 207). At the end, as Marian offers the cake-woman to Peter, and laughs at her flatmate Ainsley's assertion that she is rejecting her femininity, she looks back at her platter: 'The woman lay there, still smiling glassily, her legs gone. "Nonsense," she said. "It's only a cake." She plunged her fork into the carcass, neatly severing the body from the head' (p. 273). Marian can eat the cake because she no longer identifies with the spurious 'wholeness' which has been offered to her as 'essential' femininity in a culture where women are in fact continuously anatomized for consumption.

Marian's 'feast' is both a rejection and a parody of the wedding feast which in conventional romance would have symbolized her union with Peter. The novel as a whole, in fact, inverts the structure of nineteenth-century romantic fiction, where the heroine is educated into self-control and socially appropriate behaviour so that she may be delivered to a man whose public voice and role is to keep her safe and protected within a domestic world of moral virtue. Female protest can only be through the body itself, for, like Freud's hysterics, the central women characters of romantic fiction 'speak out' through psychosomatic illnesses, fevers, 'wasting' diseases or sexual transgression (for example, Emma Bovary, Anna Karenina,

Katherine Earnshaw, Maggie Tulliver, Dorothea Brooke, Tess of the D'Urbervilles, Lucy Snowe, Caroline Helstone). Having no public voice, they can 'speak' only through their *visual* appearance.

Marian's body, in fact, enacts a twentieth-century existential rebellion against the cultural requirements which place her as a woman at the end of a continuum of nineteenth-century heroines. By the end of the novel she has begun, indeed, to find a voice. As a traditional woman's skill, the baking of the cake is her mute and 'feminine' act of protest which also bears the seeds of potential liberation: she will, henceforth, refuse to be consumed. Although she speaks only through the 'marginal' art of culinary decoration, rather than through the culturally approved channels of 'high art', and although her protest is ambiguous (Peter and Ainsley interpret the act in different ways), she has registered a *voluntary* and *intentional* protest which releases her body from its *involuntary* rejection of food. For although Marian has felt herself to be an independent agent in the world, college-educated and economically self-providing, psychologically she manifests all the dependency traits of the 'classic' image of femininity whose contradictoriness is finally 'voiced', involuntarily, through her female body.

The novel opens with an image of woman as consumer (conveyed through Marian's own narrative) which immediately establishes her deeply ambivalent feelings towards femininity. Her image of the female is basically that of a monster whose 'natural' body must be adorned and disguised through the products and skills of a consumer society. Indeed, Marian's job in her exclusively female office is in market research, testing the consumer desires of the housewife with the technical knowledge provided by her college degree. Yet, despite her BA, Marian is unaware of the extent to which her own body is constituted through the economic requirements of the consumer world. She has to learn that there can be no 'pure' relationship with a 'natural' body because in contemporary western society her body will *inevitably* function as a consumer good. Susie Orbach, in fact, points out:

Increasingly because of automation on the one hand and the export of labour-intensive industry to S.E. Asia on the other, a generation of American and British youth is growing up fundamentally divorced from seeing their bodies as contributors to physical production, and beginning to regard them rather as instruments for active consumption. In other words, Westerners are experiencing an increasingly less physical relation to the wealth of the society in which they live. This alienation increases a general mystification as to how the available goods are actually produced. Quixotically, the avenue offered out of this particular alienation is the involvement in further or more intense consumption. (Orbach 1986, p. 34)

Marian tries to find out how people like their products packaged, for consumer desire is satisfied through the safe boundaries of the polystyrene box or the pink icing around the spongy, formless cake. In such a society, reification replaces process, so that human beings, particularly women, must also be safely wrapped and 'contained' for consumption. Once they are 'cooked', 'dressed', and tied up in ribbon, then they may safely be bought, owned, and married. An 'unpackaged' femininity is perceived as *dangerous*. When the office air-conditioning system breaks down, for example, the place takes on the attributes of a swamp or jungle in Marian's perceptual field. She 'wades' to her desk, noting the immense bulk and stasis of her female co-workers, the way in which they 'squatted at their desks, toadlike and sluggish, blinking and opening and closing their mouths'. Images of incorporation, ingestion, and orality are from the first associated with women. She is seen as the archetypal consumer, helplessly pursuing the material accoutrements of modern style as a substitute for or supplement to the acquisition of a man and the protective security of marriage. Peter chooses Marian in the belief that she will neatly fit into the dehumanized design of his labour-saving apartment and thus increase its labour efficiency with invisible service. He repeatedly bemoans the fate of various friends who have been 'sucked' into marriage and nods sympathetically with a fellow sufferer who agrees, 'you've got to watch these women when they start pursuing you. They're always after you to *marry* them' (*The Edible Woman*, p. 64). Marian, too, nods in agreement, collaborating in the myth of male independence, unconsciously aware of the necessity for protection of the masculine fear of exposing emotional need or dependency on women.

In her reading of western philosophy in *Speculum de l'autre femme* (1974), Luce Irigaray extends de Beauvoir's argument that women are outside representation. Western (male) thinkers present their philosophical speculations in terms of the 'universal' and the 'essential', but in fact reflect only their own (masculine) being. Thus femininity is that which cannot be represented, and which cannot, therefore, be thought. Woman can only be perceived as the 'other', the negative of the male philosopher's own reflection. In Freud, for example, she is 'lack'; she is 'seen' as castrated. Marian can only see herself 'held' in Peter's gaze (when he proposes all she can see is her self 'small and oval, mirrored in his eyes'; *The Edible Woman*, p. 82). A reflection, she must remain silent or must mimic or masquerade and accept her representation as a lesser male. Irigaray offers no alternative except, possibly, the *self-conscious* mimicry or parody – the imitation of an imitation – which may negate the system by rendering it absurd. Marian, in fact, in adopting what is essentially the parodic strategy of the anorectic, refuses silence and uses her body to articulate a caricature of patriarchal culture's image of femininity which involves both rejection and subversion of its requirements. Gayatri Spivak, discussing the Derridean critique of phallocentrism on which Irigaray draws, has argued for the importance of such strategies in explicitly political terms. Women, she argues, must avoid the seduction of the 'hysterocentric' (which is simply the mirror image of the 'phallocentric') discourse, and should instead work from within her position of double displacement to produce a parodic discourse which will undo the 'presence' of the phallocentric order. Marian's act of offering an imitation (the cake) of an imitation (her 'feminine' body) reveals not her capitulation to consumerist capitalism nor an assertion of her discovery of the 'natural' body (see Davidson and Davidson 1981), but a postmodernist refusal of the 'speculative' terms of representation available to her within a patriarchal society.

Marian's alienation from her body begins with the 'hunting' episode during which she notices that a 'large drop of something wet had materialized on the table near my hand' (p. 70) and is horrified to discover that she is in tears. Leaving the bar, the group return to Peter's apartment and Marian finds her body propelling her to lie under the bed – parodically enacting the sexual subjugation of which her conscious mind is unaware. Throughout, Marian's relationship to her body is one of voyeuristic distance. She surveys herself through the eyes of Peter and sees her female body as something to be inspected, improved, picked over, and packaged like quality-tested, processed food. As Rosalind Coward has argued:

> Men defend their scrutiny of women in terms of the aesthetic appeal of women. But this so-called aesthetic appreciation of women is nothing less than a decided preference for a 'distanced' view of the female body. The aesthetic appeal of women disguises a preference for *looking* at women's bodies, for keeping women separate, at a distance, and the ability to do this. Perhaps this sex-at-a-distance is the only complete secure relationship which men can have with women. Perhaps other forms of contact are too unsettling. (Coward 1984, p. 76)

Certainly Marian colludes in the presentation of her body as an aesthetic object, a gourmet dish. She must be dressed for consumption in order to allay masculine fears that she will herself consume. In fact, Marian's collusion extends to an inability finally to consume anything. It is a collusion, however, which allows for the development of a reverse discourse. Marian cannot eat because she identifies with the food and comes gradually to the conscious awareness that though women are presented as voraciously pursuing the male, consuming him, in fact men silently consume women, soak up their energies, take away their names, and deny them a public voice or definition which is not dependent on their own.

Emotional and psychological states are described throughout in the imagery of food. The company for which Marian works is 'layered like an ice-cream sandwich', and Marian and the other women constitute 'the gooey layer in the middle' (p. 19) from her perspective. Feeling ill, she experiences the sensation that someone has 'scooped the inside of my skull like a cantaloupe' (p. 183), and at the hairdresser's she feels like a cake being iced. Food is increasingly perceived by her as alive, so that to eat is to murder. An egg is experienced as 'sending out a white

184

semi-congealed feeler like an exploring oyster' (p. 84), men and women are seen devouring each other like exotic fish, and Peter is described by Lucy in the office as a 'catch'. Ultimately, Marian experiences even the consumption of an ultra-synthetic rice pudding which she tests for the company as an act of cannibalism. Her sense of the boundaries between different species and varieties of life breaks down as her body identifies with all organic substances, anything 'fit for consumption'. Once engaged to Peter, her passivity (and unconscious resistance) increases, for 'now that she had been ringed he took pride in displaying her' (p. 176). The 'dressing' of the female body (the office women in the WC mirror, the visit to the hair and beauty parlour, the 'baiting' red dress Marian wears for the party) is viewed as a ritualistic preparation for a cannibalistic feast. Thus, when Peter attempts to photograph Marian, hysteria erupts, for the cold, scientific gaze of the lens threatens to consume her entirely.

Marian's ambivalence, not only towards her own body, but towards the female body in general, is made most explicit at the office party, where she perceives the 'mature' women as ripe fruits 'in various stages of growth and decay' (p. 167). She surveys them at first as 'peculiar creatures' caught, in Kleinian fashion, in a continuous flux of taking in and giving out so that inner and outer endlessly merge: 'chewing, words, potato chips, burps, grease, hair, babies, milk, excrement, cookies, vomit, coffee, tomato juice, blood, tea, sweat, liquor, tears and garbage' (p. 167). Horrified, she resists identification with them, feels suffocated by such a 'thick sargasso sea of femininity', desires 'something solid, clear, a man', and focuses her eyes on hard, metal surfaces, seeking 'a fixed barrier between herself and that liquid amorphous other' (p. 167). Femininity is perceived as the utmost threat to identify, despite the fact that she is a woman: flesh, inchoateness, dissolution, a merging with matter, and a loss of form. It must be carefully packaged, therefore, girdled, reduced, painted. Hunger must be denied, consumption controlled, and the flesh contained. She regards with horrified fascination her friend Clara's fertility and the engendering of babies. The image of the pregnant woman is, for Marian, the image of the monstrosity of the female. Once Clara has given birth, Marian experiences some relief:

She was thinking that now Clara was deflating towards her normal size again she would be able to talk with her more freely: she would no longer feel as though she was addressing a swollen mass of flesh with a tiny pinhead, a shape that had made her think of a queen ant, bulging with the burden of an entire society, a semi-person – or sometimes, she thought, several people, a cluster of hidden personalities that she didn't know at all. (p. 115)

The post-parturitional Clara is no longer simply a vessel but, Marian naïvely believes, again 'in uncontended possession of her own frail body' (p. 115). She believes that her own orderliness and neatness, so approved by Peter, will keep her safely distanced from such messy dissolution. But her body continues to sabotage such attempts to erect absolute boundaries between self and world, expressing its protest through disordered perception, confusion of species, hysterical conversion. Unable finally to summon the energy to clean and order her domestic world, Marian finds strange moulds invading its previously disinfected surfaces. The novel, in fact, has worked through Marx's four basic types of alienation – people's alienation from their labour, from their species, from nature, and from their own selves – but has concentrated on the fundamental site of alienation for women; their bodies. *The Edible Woman* offers little hope for radical social change, but it does suggest that the possibility of change for women must lie, in part, in their need to recognize the relationship between the female body and the construction of femininity.

This suggestion is reinforced in Atwood's other novels. Joan, the central character of *Lady Oracle* [1976], also believes that she can change her 'self' by changing her body. Deeply ashamed of her bulky appearance, the name Joan is suffered as a constant reproach, for she was named after Joan Crawford, who 'was thin' (p. 42). Even when she sheds her layers of fat, however, Joan finds herself still caught up in the image of herself as large, unable to shed mentally that insulation laid down in childhood to protect her against a denying and repressive mother. She imagines people watching her as she walks down the street:

What did they see, the eyes behind those stone-wall windows? A female monster, larger than life, larger than most life around here anyway, striding down the hill, her hair standing on end with electrical force, volts of malevolent energy shooting from her fingers, her green eyes behind her dark tourist's glasses, her dark mafia glasses, lit up and glowing like a cat's. (p. 336)

'Fat' Joan, the buffoon, a structure of defences against the fear of nothingness within, cannot, psychologically, be 'reduced'. Her body has always been her weapon in the struggle with a mother who both overidentifies with her daughter and sees her as an embodiment of the failure of her own 'essential femininity'. As Orbach argues:

Compulsive eating becomes a way of expressing either side of this conflict. In overfeeding herself, the daughter may be trying to reject her mother's role while at the same time reproaching the mother for inadequate nurturing; or she may be attempting to retain a sense of identity with her mother. (Orbach 1979, p. 32)

Food and feeding always carry the marks of the early relationship with the mother, and, as the medium through which the outside is first taken in, the self differentiated from other, they are likely to remain caught up with issues of identity. Food, to this extent, personifies the early mother. Before Joan comes to experience herself as 'monstrous', she perceives her mother as 'a monster' and also as her 'manager, the creator, the agent; I was to be the product' (*Lady Oracle*, p. 67). Joan's body is the commodity through which her mother desires to renegotiate her position in the world, for to bear a 'pretty' daughter is to reinforce one's own sense of femininity. As Joan's body expands, however, defying the limits of cultural packaging and control, her mother comes to see it as 'a reproach to her, the embodiment of her own failure and depression, a huge edgeless cloud of inchoate matter which refused to be shaped into anything for which she could get a prize' (p. 67). For Joan, her fat body is both a refusal of the chic, controlled, *denying* femininity which her mother desires and also a protective armour against the fear that she is *essentially* unfeminine and will therefore never please anyone. Classically, Joan wishes to be both like and unlike her mother, viewing the latter's carefully cosmeticized face and neat body with extreme ambivalence. The mother's 'femininity' represents for Joan both sexual attractiveness *and* powerlessness and denial of need. Her own enormous body, meanwhile, is experienced as both a triumph over and rejection of her mother's desire to be 'feminine' and as a horrible unleashing of an uncontrollable *monstrous* femininity associated with the flesh. Joan wakes up one morning:

> I happened to glance down at my body. ... I didn't usually look at my body, in a mirror or in any other way; I snuck a glance at parts of it now and then, but the whole thing was too overwhelming. There, staring me in the face, was my thigh. It was enormous, it was gross, it was like a diseased limb, the kind you see in pictures of jungle natives; it spread on forever, like a prairie photographed from a plane, the flesh not green but bluish-white, with veins meandering across it like rivers. (pp. 120–1)

Even this 'speculative' distance from her body cannot 'contain' it, and Joan experiences herself as spreading and dissolving uncontrollably. As her thigh metaphorically becomes part of tropical and savannah landscapes, Joan recognizes that the 'identity' derived from her layers of flesh has not, in fact, provided a boundary of self, a bodily ego which can differentiate the me from the not-me, but has increased her feelings of mergence and inchoateness. Thus she decides to reduce and so begins the torture of exercise, laxatives, pills, self-inflicted headaches, and stomach cramps which she views as her penance for being female. Significantly, as Joan struggles to define herself through corporeal surfaces, she finds that she is increasingly drawn into identification with the heroines in the gothic fictions which she writes under the pseudonym of Louisa K. Delacourt. Tania Modleski has argued that gothic essentially deals with the paranoia generated in women as a consequence of their frail ego boundaries and their cultural devaluation. Often confined within the social isolation of the modern nuclear family, women experience estrangement and disorientation, are vulnerable to feelings of being hunted, pursued, and trapped. If women need a relational network to provide a sense of identity, then in the absence of such a community they may project a pseudo-community of persecutors which takes the place of 'real' object relations. To be persecuted is to be noticed and is, therefore, to exist.

Joan's fantasies of male pursuers (which intersect with the plots of her gothic stories) can thus be seen as another aspect of her search for the boundaries of self and her desire to be *unlike* her mother. Like her heroines, she too is haunted and feels suffocated by the past and the connection to the mother. If she sheds the layers and becomes a 'sexual object', she may then project her aggressive feelings on to male pursuers who are *allowed*, culturally, to express anger and aggression. *Fat* Joan does not attract sexual pursuit: 'it would have been like molesting a giant basketball. . . . I knew I would be able to squash any potential molester against a wall merely by breathing out' (p. 140). Yet without her fat she feels 'naked, pruned, as though some essential covering was missing' (p. 141). Though imprisoned in the gothic structures of her own psyche (and fiction), what Joan actually desires is romance, with its promise of full presence and self-fulfilment. The novel's events, however, come full circle. Joan returns from the dead (she has unsuccessfully faked suicide in an attempt to 'start again'), and the reader recognizes that there can be no resolution, no miraculous discovery of identity, that, however many layers Joan sheds, there is no inner, honed, 'essential' self. Joan will, necessarily, remain constituted in and through social relations of power and socially determined structures of desire. The only hope offered of liberation is again, therefore, through *self-conscious* masquerade, parody, the flaunting of one's postmodern condition. For

there is no question of the freeing of representations ('reality') from the determinations of fantasy. There is, however, a considerable benefit to be achieved from an *awareness* of the agency of unconscious fantasy in representation: the representation of women by men; the representation of blacks by whites; the representation of 'homosexuals' by 'heterosexuals', and so on. (Burgin 1986, p. 106)

FAY WELDON: CONTEMPORARY FEMINIST GOTHIC

In Fay Weldon's novel *The Life and Loves of a She-Devil* [1983], the structures of gothic fantasy also displace those of conventional realism as Ruth sets about creating herself anew – in a feminist recapitulation of the Frankenstein story – in order to avenge her sexual betrayal by her husband Bobbo. Although Ruth gathers together her tremendous transformative powers in the service, still, of an enchainment to the myth of romantic love, the novel does reveal the subversive potential of fantasy and gothic for decentring liberal concepts of gender and identity. A useful definition of fantasy is offered by Kathryn Hume:

> A departure from consensus reality, an impulse native to literature and manifested in innumerable variations, from monster to metaphor. It includes transgressions of what one generally takes to be physical facts such as human immortality, travel faster than light, telekinesis, and the like. ... I would include as a departure from consensus reality some technical or social innovations which have not yet taken place, even though they may well happen in the future: cloning on humans and utopian societies are both examples of this sort of fantasy. I would include alternative worlds and universes, for although other forms of life probably exist elsewhere in the cosmos, any current literary portrayal is the embodiment of our desires, a metaphor and subcreation from matter we know in our own world, not an intuition of another world. (Hume 1984, p. 17)

In this novel, Weldon presents a heroine who believes she has broken free from the dominant economic and social structures of power, yet who uses her freedom in the pursuit of a romantic myth which continues to oppress her as effectively as purely economic constraints.

In their discussion of primal fantasy, Laplanche and Pontalis argue that infantile fantasies centre around the question of origins: 'the primal scene pictures the origin of the individual; fantasies of seduction, the origin and upsurge of sexuality; fantasies of castration, the origin of difference between the sexes' (Laplanche and Pontalis 1976, p. 19). Gothic texts are organized, paradigmatically, around such fantasies. In the libidinal economy of Weldon's gothic text, the unleashing of Ruth's desires (which are the fury of a woman scorned) challenges the dominant western myths of origins. Ruth *creates herself* in her hellish fury in order to assert a new sexual power over Bobbo.

190

Ruth is another heroine who believes that, given the impossibility of changing her culture, she may gain acceptance within it only through changing herself. This means, specifically, changing her body. Thus she embarks upon the masochistic torture of diets, excruciating pain, extreme self-denial, surgery, and technological bombardment of her body, in order to effect the necessary transformation. Ruth, however, literally transforms her *whole body*, limb for limb, driven by a desire to 'look up to men ... that's what I want' (*The Life and Loves of a She-Devil*, p. 174), to resemble the petite and 'feminine' Mary Fisher (romantic novelist and Bobbo's lover), for she is 'a lady of six feet two, who had tucks taken in her legs. A comic turn, turned serious' (p. 240). She remains enslaved to the myth of romantic love (despite attempts to reveal to others its danger), but seeks to reverse its sado-masochistic power relations once she becomes the ideal object of male desire: 'I cause Bobbo as much misery as he ever caused me, and more. I try not to, but somehow it is not a matter of male or female after all; it never was, merely of power. I have all, and he has none' (p. 240). Ruth transforms herself into the original lost object of Bobbo's desire, the phallic mother who, offering the hero the promise of full identity, thus renders him absolutely dependent upon her. Ruth wants Bobbo to suffer the hellish torments of desire for *her*, those desires which, as a housewife in Eden Grove, she was forced (through economic and emotional dependency) to suffer for him.

Socialized into the role of slave, Ruth has in fact become adept at economic and emotional survival, for as she knows:

> those on the right side of everything take care to know as little as possible about those on the wrong side. The poor, exploited and oppressed, however, love to know about their masters, to gaze at their faces in the paper, to marvel at their love affairs. ... So Ruth would recognize Bobbo, lover and accountant; Bobbo would not recognize Ruth, former hospital orderly and abandoned mother. (p. 116)

Ruth does not have Bobbo's formal knowledge of accountancy, but she still manages to defraud him of millions of pounds of clients' money. Once operating from a secure economic base, powerful in the invisibility of her marginal position, Ruth begins her *own* creation and her destruction of Bobbo. Just as she manipulates the power relations between the sexes, Weldon manipulates the dominant cultural myths which produce and maintain such relations. She draws, for example, on the potential offered by the Frankenstein myth for parody of the ideology of feminine monstrosity and for subversion of liberal culture's belief in an 'essential self'.

Ruth recognizes that 'largeness' is experienced as effrontery. Even her mother could not love her because 'ugly and discordant things revolted her: she couldn't help it' (p. 11), and Ruth sees her own daughter's future dismally determined by the fact that she is 'big and lumpy as I am, voicing a vindictiveness that masks the despair of too much feeling' (p. 14). She realizes the signifying power of the body in which she feels trapped: its reminder to the world of its human fears of uncontrollability, inchoateness, neediness, hunger, potential engulfment, and the boundlessness of the feminine. As Dinnerstein has argued: 'women can be defined as quasi-persons, quasi-humans; and unqualified human personhood can be sealed off from the contaminating atmosphere of infant fantasy and defined as male' (Dinnerstein 1976, p. 93). As the original non-self, providing they do not seek subjective definition or power, providing they remain contained and marginalized, women can thus become the carriers of the human species' conflicting attitudes towards existence itself. Ruth's body refuses such containment, so she decides, literally, to become the female 'monster' of primal fantasy, beyond moral boundaries, beyond good and evil: the She-Devil. Paradoxically, her 'monstrous' desires are pursued most effectively by her later transforming this body so that it signifies the required contained and controlled femininity. Underneath, however:

> I want, I crave, I die to be part of that other erotic world, of choice and desire and lust. It isn't love that I want; it is nothing so simple. What I want is to take everything and return nothing. What I want is power over the hearts and pockets of men. It is all the power we can have ... and even that is denied me. (*The Life and Loves of a She-Devil*, p. 24)

The anthropologist Sherry Ortner has argued that in every society the psychic mode associated with women is situated at the two extreme ends of the scale of human forms of relationship.

She is thus associated either with the 'subversive feminine symbols (witches, evil eye, menstrual pollution, castrating mothers)' or with the 'feminine symbols of transcendence (mother goddesses, merciful dispensers of salvation, female symbols of justice)' (Ortner 1974, p. 86). Both positions are regarded as outside the sphere of cultural hegemony, occupying a realm of marginalization and 'otherness'. Repeatedly in Weldon's novels, her women characters seek to construct a subjectivity through these marginal representations, and, as witches, herbalists, monsters, and she-devils, to subvert the moral complacencies of liberal-humanist and patriarchal society. Gilbert and Gubar's study of nineteenth-century fiction has shown the extent to which the image of the woman as monster functions as the subversive 'other' of the 'Angel in the House'. They explicitly connect this to the representation of the female body:

> The sexual nausea associated with all these monster women helps explain why so many real women have for so long expressed loathing of (or at least anxiety about) their own, inexorably female bodies. The 'killing' of oneself into an art object – the pruning and preening, the mirror madness, and concern with odours and ageing, with hair which is invariably too curly or too lank, with bodies too thin or too thick – all this testifies to the efforts women have expended not just trying to be angels but trying *not* to become female monsters. (Gilbert and Gubar 1979, p. 34).

Ruth 'kills' her monstrous body and submissive psyche in order to 'give birth' to a new 'ultra-feminine' corporeal shape and an assertive, sadistic, 'monstrous' psyche. The process of creation is explicitly connected to the Frankenstein myth at several points in the novel. At the most dangerous point of the operation to decrease her size, and as Ruth lies drugged and semi-conscious:

> There was an earthquake, a nasty rumble, the crust of the earth yearning to split along the line of its weakness, the San Andreas fault ... life support systems had to be switched over to the emergency generator. ... Ruth observed their pallor, their distraction. When she could speak, she said, 'You needn't have worried. An act of God won't kill me.' (*The Life and Loves of a She-Devil*, p. 232)

193

For Mary Shelley, the monster is created not out of a void but out of chaos (see 1831 preface), his evil is not innate but the product of social determinations. Similarly, just as Ruth's 'monstrosity' is socially constructed, her new body, which she regards as the creation of her own desire, is the product of modern science and medicine. Her claim to be 'beyond nature' is in this sense true, but her belief that she-devils 'create themselves out of nothing' is founded on an illusion of her own omnipotence, betrayed by the novel's revelation of her submission to the ideological power of both romance and science. The modern-day medical men, like Frankenstein, defying God and attempting to create life, seek the accolade of scientific success and the realization of their own fantasies and womb envy. As the surgeon Mr Genghis observes the 'new' Ruth (Miss Hunter): 'He loved her. She would never be grateful. He did not expect gratitude any more. He had made her as a mother makes a child: to be its own self, not hers. And as in any child successfully reared, it is indifferent to the parent' (p. 225).

Imagining herself to be 'free' after the transformative surgery, Ruth has in fact exchanged one form of submission for another. Weldon's novel echoes here the Pygmalion myth, for Ruth becomes the artistic object whose apparent creation through the male artist's skill allows him to suppress his knowledge that it is the female body which has created *him*. Ruth does, however, challenge the myth, for the woman whom Pygmalion creates is the projection of his own desire: she is submissive, silent, and responsive. Ruth's body may appear to signify such containment, but it has become an instrument of her new subjectivity, her monstrous assertiveness and will-to-power which is equal to both Bobbo's and the surgeon's. Ruth is not 'free', but she has traded the dependency of the slave for that of the master and the marginalization of the subhuman and monstrous for the transcendence of the superhuman and angelic. Such a reversal of the normal relations of power may be the first step towards deconstructing the sado-masochistic ties which bind men and women unhappily together. As 'the second coming, this time in female form', Ruth proposes to do for women 'as Jesus did in his day for men. ... He offered the stony path to heaven: I offer the motorway to hell. I bring suffering and self-knowledge' (p. 164). Not salvation – yet.

The same preoccupation with the subversive potential of feminine desire as expressed through the female body runs through Weldon's novel *The Fat Woman's Joke* [1967]. Esther, like Ruth, begins with her identity circumscribed by the daily round of domestic duty and provision of food, which 'set the pattern of our days ... all day at home I would plan food and buy food and cook food, and serve food, and nibble and taste and stir and experiment and make sweeties and goodies and tasties for Alan to try out when he came home' (p. 17). The struggle to deny herself (in order to be slim) while providing for others becomes increasingly difficult, however, but 'one should be able to control one's size, if one is going to control one's life' (p. 36), she reflects. Gradually, Esther recognizes that her wish to be small and insubstantial is simply a reflection of the cultural requirement that women be contained, for 'her lack of flesh negates her' (p. 50). She welcomes a regression, therefore, to the orality of infancy: gobbling, gorging, taking in, revelling in the uncontroll-ability of being a 'very dirty little girl' (p. 53) who refuses any longer to repress her needs and hungers.

Liffey, the central character of *Puffball* [1980] and another child-bride, contained and responsive with her small neat hips and 'boyish' figure, similarly discovers a new power as her belly swells with pregnancy: 'She would never easily look like a little boy, feel like a little girl, ever again. It was a loss: she knew it: she was at her best when very young. All charm, no sense. The days of charm were gone. Now she was real and alive' (p. 212). Early in the pregnancy, while her stomach is still flat, Liffey views the bodily changes through the alienating and technical jargon of medical data supplied by the narrator and her doctor, surveying herself as an object of scientific knowledge. As her stomach puffs out like the exotic mushrooms which spring up around her cottage, she begins to experience her body as a source of magical power. The novel, however, undercuts the tendency romantically to anthropomorphize nature, presenting the pro-cesses at work inside Liffey's body as blind forces. Her identification with the puffballs ultimately, however, allows her to perceive the extent to which her own body (like theirs) has been dissected: victimized, constructed, appropriated through the discourses of science and romance. As Richard prepares the puffballs for consumption, Liffey recognizes how her own body has been ritualistically prepared for a feast: 'Richard sliced a sharp knife into the biggest puffball and where the cut was the flesh gaped wide, as human flesh gapes under the surgeon's knife and Liffey stared aghast' (p. 228). 'Nature' is a concept which has functioned traditionally to oppress women, for as the narrator of *Praxis* [1978] reflects: 'Nature our friend, is an argument used, quite understandably, by men' (p. 147). Once Liffey grasps this, however, she can begin to use 'nature', use her body, as a source of subversion and connection.

FEMINISM AND UTOPIANISM: THE LIMITS OF DESIRE

The writings of Atwood and Weldon suggest how that desire which is produced in order to regulate social organization may also function as the source of its disruption. Foucault's work has shown the extent to which desire and pleasure have largely replaced overt coercion as the dominant mode of social regulation in the modern state. Utopian impulses, gratified through the department store window and advertising image, have become largely *regulatory* rather than *subversive* in function. Just as Atwood and Weldon, however, have attempted to undo the reification of the female body and reconnect it to a subversive desire, so writers like Doris Lessing, Joanna Russ, Angela Carter, and Marge Piercy have attempted to reconnect the utopian impulses of dissatisfaction to a revolutionary and subversive function. All emphasize that utopia must not be conceived of as an enclosed, regulated, rationalized system (the nightmare world of postmodernist fiction) or space, but as an ongoing process, a mode of relationship between human beings, and not systems, objects, and products. Traditionally, utopia has functioned as the absolute projection of desire which, in its rationalized stasis, is paradoxically the *death* of desire. As Michael Holquist has argued:

> we have recently all too often forgotten, and to our sorrow, that perfection is a game, something available to the mind, but not the state. When we have stopped playing, when we have attempted to instrument the seductive but inhuman logic of games in actual programs, the consequence has inevitably been pogroms. (Holquist 1976, p. 146)

In Piercy's *Woman on the Edge of Time* [1976] or in Lessing's worlds behind the wall, however, there is an attempt to explore the possibility of fulfilling human needs through the formation of a fluid community which might provide an alternative to the present social formation with its training in repression, egotism, and ambition. As Moylan emphasizes, 'if those whose lives are oppressed and unfree are able to dream beyond the present, then the utopian impulse as a non-exclusive activity no longer limited to imposed models will play an increasingly significant role in the oppositional project' (Moylan 1986, p. 212).

Lessing's abandonment of realism (up to *The Good Terrorist* [1985]) is linked to the expansion in her fiction of a utopian vision of a collective mode of existence which, it seems to me, projects the possibility of a community founded on the sort of relational identity which has been associated with women and devalued by the present society. In *The Four-Gated City* [1969], the last volume in the Martha Quest series, Martha walks through London, aware of her cultural difference, her marginality as an ex-colonial and a woman, and experiences a gradual loss of identity. She experiences herself as 'nothing but a soft dark receptive intelligence', feeling that all is space, that 'she could move back in time, annulling time', become the person she was, a little girl, 'really there she was: *she* was, nothing to do with Martha, or any other name she might have attached to her, nothing to do with what she looked like, how she had been shaped' (p. 48). The passage is strikingly similar to the passage (discussed in chapter three) in Woolf's *To the Lighthouse*, where Mrs Ramsay experiences herself expanding to incorporate all and then shrinking down into a 'wedge-shaped core of darkness'. Mrs Ramsay's experience is presented, however, in highly ambiguous terms, as potentially liberating but also, because of her boundary confusion, as annihilating. In Lessing's novel the terms are less ambiguous. Later, when Martha returns to a 'family' structure in order to rework her oedipal transitions through a substitute father/lover Mark and a substitute mother/daughter, Lynda (his wife), she attempts to will herself deliberately into this state of mind, previously experienced *involuntarily* as she wandered through the city:

If she sat quite still, or walked steadily up and down, the space in her head remained steady, or lightening and darkening in a pulse, like the irregular beat of the sea. She had known this lightness and clarity before – yes, walking through London, long ago. And then too, it had been the reward of not-eating, not-sleeping, using her body as an engine to get her out of the small dim prison of everyday. But how could she have allowed herself to forget and not have spent every moment of her time since trying to regain it, to get back where at least one could begin to see the way out, and forward? (*The Four-Gated City*, p. 512)

Lessing has said of the 'Children of Violence' sequence that 'this is a study of the individual conscience in its relations with the collective' (Lessing 1975, p. 14). Even in the first 'realistic' volume, the impulse towards the collective, towards the discovery of an identity in relationship which would allow both connection and autonomy, is linked to a utopian desire which gradually displaces the narrative modes of realism with those of fantasy, dream, and desire. In *Martha Quest* ([1952] volume 1), Martha, struggling with the suffocating repressiveness of her African home, projects the image of the city from which the last volume takes its name. As she stares at the sameness of the distant hills,

> There arose, glimmering whitely over the harsh scrub and the stunted trees a noble city, set foursquare and colonnaded ... its citizens moved, grave and beautiful, black and white and brown together ... fair-skinned children of the North playing hand in hand with the bronze-skinned, dark-eyed children of the South. (p. 17)

Seeking a place in such a city, where races, ages, beliefs, low- and high-born may find community, Martha is forced to throw off the ties of her traditional family, both those of her parents and later those of her husband and child. Initially, she seeks a human community which can realize her vision in organized left-wing party politics. Later she experiments with the physical, with sexuality, as a way through to that 'impersonal current ... the impersonal sea' (p. 511) which she finally comes to experience again in the basement of the Coldridges' loosely knit, Bohemian household.

Martha, like her biblical namesake, comes to serve, and is able through this substitute family to make reparation to her original one, to 'mother' and to receive the mothering which her own censorious mother could not give. She offers Lynda food and milk in her 'madness', and when Lynda, rejecting the polite, formal gesture, sweeps the tray to the floor and kneels down to lap the milk like an animal Martha feels compelled to join her. They 'drank symbolically, not quite lapping' (p. 504). Not quite human either, for often in Lessing's fictions animals are shown to achieve a dignity and intimacy which human beings have lost (Hugo, in *The Memoirs of a Survivor* [1974], for example). Lessing suggests, in fact, that love can exist only outside the possessive and proprietorial demands of the traditional nuclear family or the social dictates of instrumental rationality. Martha can become a 'mother' only in the Coldridge household or to the 'children of violence' at the end, the children who survive the devastation and discover a new, collective identity on the island. Martha comes to view romance and marriage as the *enemies* of love, for their institutionalized inequalities are the breeding ground for neurotic dependency, sado-masochistic behaviour, and the egotistical denial of nurturant human relationship. Even Martha's mother dimly perceives what romantic love has cost her: 'Love, she thought, love – her mind went dark. If that was love, then it had taken her to a hard sad life on first one farm, with her husband, then to another, with a son, hundreds of miles away and up from her real love, the sea' (p. 263).

The sea functions throughout as an image of that impersonal current which Lynda and Martha connect with through their journey into an 'inner space' beyond the rational and temporal. In most of Lessing's fiction, such a space is perceived as an alternative to the egotism bred by an over-rationalized culture and is linked persistently to the socially constructed psychic capacities of women. In *The Golden Notebook* [1962], Anna discusses women's perceptual vision with Tommy, suggesting that she experiences time differently from men because 'When I look at Janet sometimes I see her as a small baby and I *feel* her inside my belly and I see her as various sizes of a small girl, all at the same time. That's how women see things. Everything in a sort of continuous creative stream.' Martha experiences time in this way in her wanderings – she *becomes* the child Martha sitting on the grass of her African home, even as she steps out on to the busy London street. Sarah Ruddick has argued that this maternal capacity to appreciate realistically the continuity of mental life and change could form the basis of a new way of 'studying ... the changing nature of all peoples and communities, for it is not only children who change, grow' (Ruddick 1980, p. 353). Unfortunately, as Lessing sees it, this capacity is undervalued in a culture which prioritizes fixity, stasis, technological precision, and rational control.

In the Preface to *The Golden Notebook*, she writes:

> The way to deal with the problem of 'subjectivity', that shocking business of being preoccupied with the tiny individual who is at the same time caught up in such an explosion of terrible and marvellous possibilities, is to see him as a microcosm and in this way to break through the personal, the subjective, making the personal general, as indeed life always does, transforming a private experience ... into something larger: growing up is after all only the understanding that one's unique experience is what everyone shares.

Martha's 'personal' quest begins with her attempt to identify with the father and is initially conceived in the terms of Eriksonian maturity: development towards an autonomous, rational moral unity. Once Martha has given up her father-identified persona 'Matty' and the critical defensive intelligence, 'the watcher', with which 'Matty' protects herself, a different concept of development and subjectivity emerges. The process is a painful one, for

> when people open up a new area in themselves, start doing something new, then it must be clumsy and raw, like a baby trying to walk. ... She had understood once before that the new, an opening up, had to be through a region of chaos, of conflict. There was no other way of doing it. (*The Four-Gated City*, p. 195)

Martha, instead of feeling threatened by the permeability and malleability of her ego boundaries, as earlier, discovers in the basement a capacity for discovering identity through relationship which need not annihilate her sense of 'inner self'. From experiencing herself and her object relations as a 'smashed mirror' (p. 366), she discovers that the existential fragments 'reflected off the faceted mirror that was one's personality, that responded all the time, every second, to these past selves, past voices, temporary visitors' (p. 369), constitute a dispersed, relational subjectivity which is both part of and separate from others and could form the basis of a new collective mode of social living.

The Golden Notebook reveals the same concern with identity and merger, separateness, and connection which forms the basis of the utopian vision and the subversion of realism in *The Four-Gated City*. Here, these themes are explored through the structural relations between the separate but connected formal parts of the novel itself: the notebooks, the Free Women frames and the explicit cross-referencing of characters, events, and situations. Anna is another woman character who, terrified by her sense of the absence of a central identity, a core being with firm and defined boundaries, has sought modes of existential division and compartmentalization, neurotic defences which will reflect back the required illusion of a unified self. Like Martha, she seeks the connection and nurturance denied her as a female child, but finds in her relationships with other women and men that a 'detached' intelligence is inevitably activated to protect her from the dissolution and mergence threatened by any form of intimacy. Near the end of the affair with Michael, for example, she writes:

> I fought with a feeling that always takes hold of me after one of these exchanges: unreality, as if the substance of myself were thinning and dissolving. And then I thought how ironical it was that in order to recover myself I had to use precisely that Anna which Michael dislikes most; the critical and thinking Anna.

She recognizes that, despite the desire for connection, people stay sane in this world by 'blocking off', and she thus attempts to file her life away into the separate notebooks covering her African past (black), political activities (red), a diary of the present (blue), and a fictionalized version of her emotional attachments (yellow). Aware, too, of her marginal status as a left-wing woman and an anti-colonial ex-colonial, she expresses her dis-ease with language, with the symbolic order, in a series of desperate pastiches, parodies, and stylistic experiments.

She concludes finally that, just as the feminine subject must 'masquerade' in the guises of the (masculine) dominant order, so, too, any attempt to *represent* feminine subjectivity will result in parody: of the 'coy' woman's style of the magazines, of the sentimental fulfilment of romantic desire in the Hollywood movie.

Lessing argued, in fact, that the point of the novel lay in the interrelation of its parts. In the Preface to it, written in 1971, she insisted:

> Throughout the notebooks people have discussed, theorized, dogmatized, labelled, compartmentalized. ... But they have also reflected each other, been aspects of each other, given birth to each other's thoughts and behaviour – *are* each other, form wholes. In the Inner Golden Notebook things have come together, the divisions have broken down, there is formlessness with the end of fragmentation – the triumph of the second theme is that of unity. (p. 7)

This is not, however, the unity of the traditional liberal subject, for what the novel reveals above all is the extent to which self-concepts are constructed through a non-unified and shifting complex of economic, social, historical, and cultural factors. When Molly, appalled, tells Anna that Tommy's self-inflicted blinding has left him, for the first time, all 'in one piece', this confirms Anna's growing belief that simple unity is maintained through a process of 'dividing off'. Anna's notebooks themselves represent the erection of such false ego boundaries in the pursuit of the naïve concept of unity which is exploded in the final, golden notebook. Thus Anna throughout seeks a 'real man' who will 'complete' her, and she compulsively splits off those aspects of her own femininity which she believes do not correspond to masculine desire (for example, the rational, the non-maternal, the non-sexual). Ella, her alter ego of the yellow notebook, similarly splits her lover Paul into the 'good' and the 'bad' and is haunted by the 'shadow of the third', the projection of her own ego ideal on to Paul's wife. Yet Anna recognizes that her 'completion' by a male is also the birth of the 'naïve' Anna. This Anna is freed from the critical detachment which divides her from the external world, but thrown into a state of total dependency for fear of her own disintegration through the loss of the loved object. Unable to recognize this fear and increasingly unable to split it off into the notebooks, Anna projects it on to the world around her, seeing everywhere only political chaos, social disintegration, and international disasters which are experienced as part of her own ego. Indeed, the blue, the most personal of the notebooks, breaks down into a kaleidoscope of world catastrophe and crisis, as Anna's self-analysis gives way to a collage of newspaper cuttings. At this time, her fears begin to surface also in the dreams of the 'principle of joy-in-destruction', the priapic dwarf-figure which she comes to recognize in the later, golden notebook as her own fear of and desire for dissolution.

Initially Anna believes that romantic 'completion' through a man is the only route to wholeness and satisfaction for women, and she explores the nature of this desire through Ella in the yellow notebook. When Paul leaves Ella, she suffers not simply sexual desire but an elemental hunger for return to an impossible pre-oedipal unity, a discovery of self in other which is also an annihilation of self. Anna sees the process as being 'put to sleep':

> her present raging sexual hunger was not for sex, but was fed by all the emotional hungers of her life. That when she loved a man again, she would return to normal: a woman, that is, whose sexuality would ebb and flow in response to his. A woman's sexuality is, so to speak, contained by a man, if he is a real man; she is, in a sense, put to sleep by him. (p. 443)

Even as Anna explores such a belief through Ella, however, she knows it to be simply the phrases of a 'dead and meaningless knowledge', an ideology of romantic fulfilment which promises for women an impossible and illusory 'wholeness'. Anna fights her new awareness, however, clinging even more desperately to the security of the phallocentric order, to the old myths, as the only remaining boundary between herself and dissolution:

> It occurs to me that what is happening is a breakdown of me, Anna, and this is how I am becoming aware of it. For words are form, and if I am at a pitch where shape, form, expression are nothing, then I am nothing, for it has become clear to me, reading the notebooks, that I remain Anna because of a

certain kind of intelligence. This intelligence is dissolving and I am very frightened. (p. 463)

Anna's breakthrough occurs, however, once she ceases to draw on the myths of the symbolic order, the myths of unity and romance, the belief in the necessity for splitting the 'rational' and the 'emotional'; then the solubility of her ego boundaries as a woman can, like Martha's, become a source of utopian strength rather than weakness. As Anna recognizes her displacement and marginalization as a woman, a process of ego dissolution begins where she finds herself merging into others, experiencing a loss of boundaries which no longer expresses the desperate projections of paranoia but a new possibility of connection, of discovering one's identity through others. This discovery comes at first through the sado-masochism, the conventional masculine– feminine patterns of dependency and struggle for independence, which structures the early relationship with Saul. However, as the experience with Saul enables Anna to see the extent to which her masochism is a function of her split-off fear of disintegration, her overwhelming dependency on others, she begins to experience a merging represented in the new, positive terms of the collective, the 'we', rather than the defensive, over-rationalized, egotistic 'I':

> There was a kind of shifting of the balance of my brain. ... I felt this, like a vision, in a new kind of knowing. And I knew that the cruelty and the spite and the I I I I of Saul and Anna were part of the logic of war; and I knew ... in a way that would never leave me, would become part of how I saw the world ... the knowledge isn't in the words I write down now. (p. 568)

Anna 'becomes' part of Saul, part of the African nationalist Charlie Themba, part of an Algerian soldier; she experiences her room not simply as an objective correlative for her own sense of ego but as an aspect, literally, of what she is, as a transitional object. Similarly, recognizing that literature is not simply 'analysis after the event', falsification, she sees that narrative representations, 'making sense', are necessarily metaphorical substitutes, statements of a loss which constructs the 'real' through the fantastic and the imaginary. Indeed, the writing of *The Golden Notebook* resolved Lessing's own writer's block, and afterwards she said in an interview:

> Since writing *The Golden Notebook* I've become less personal. I've floated away from the personal. I've stopped saying, 'This is mine, this is *my* experience. ..' Now, when I start writing, the first thing I ask is, 'who is thinking the same thought? Where are the other people who are like me?' I don't believe anymore that I have a thought. There is a thought around. (Raskin 1970, p. 173)

Utopia, in the novels of Lessing, Russ, and Piercy, is always only ever a possibility, a process to be struggled towards through will or effort, and in Lessing's *The Memoirs of a Survivor* [1974], Piercy's *Woman on the Edge of Time* [1976], and Russ's *The Female Man* [1975] it is presented very largely through a fantastic narrative which is counterpointed by dystopian realism. In Lessing's *Memoirs*, utopia is created not in the material world, which is at the point of collapse after a nuclear disaster, but in the world beyond the wall, a space at the interface of self and other, of the rational 'I' and the disintegrating political unconsious. Gerald and Emily attempt to rebuild the material world on the basis of a communal, collective ethos, only to find themselves burdened and frustrated by the persistence of the 'old forms': the power of the myth of 'romantic love'; the seeming inevitability of hierarchy, of a 'pecking order'; the mysterious 'it' – the principle of joy-in-destruction personified in the Ryans. Their impulse towards the collective is structured, however, through the desires of the individual and their unconscious acceptance of a model of individuation based on difference, autonomy, separateness, and rationalism: Gerald's desire to be 'leader', the one, and Emily's search for the 'unique' dress, the clothing which will transform her into the 'one' object of Gerald's desire. The narrator, another of Lessing's 'house-keepers', journeys meanwhile through the wall, visiting the rooms to turn out the old furniture, cleaning up, making new, seeking to connect this impulse towards the 'rational' and the egotistic with an understanding of the collective, of her socialization as a woman in a traditional family. She seeks, in effect, the sources of human desire in the fantasies of the political unconscious:

As for our thoughts, our intellectual apparatus, our rationalisms and our logics and our deductions, and so on, it can be said with absolute certainty that dogs and cats and monkeys cannot make a rocket or fly to the moon or weave artificial dress materials out of the by-products of petroleum, but as we sit in the ruins of this variety of intelligence, it is hard to give it much value: I suppose we are undervaluing it now as we over-valued it then. It will have to find its place: I believe a pretty low place, at that. (p. 74)

The enigmatic 'we' – the readers? – are addressed by the unnamed narrator who has brought the information in the first pages of the book that her account will begin before 'we were talking about "it"' (p. 9). Both implied and actual reader are thus constructed through this address in terms of an imperceptible merger. The description of events given by the narrator in the first few pages increases this sense of merger. The external world (that of realism) seems to have collapsed with the failure of western rationalism, so that a state of anarchy prevails in which human beings take on the attributes of animals, killing and scavenging for food and hunting in packs, while the animal world represented by the androgynous Hugo comes to represent 'humanist' love, loyalty, devotion, dignity. The narrator, struggling to preserve an order within her own psyche which has disappeared from the world outside, finds herself, however, drawn towards a different kind of merger involving the suspension of the rational, the dissecting consciousness, the urge to individuate:

> I was putting my ear to the wall, as one would to a female egg, listening, waiting ... and then I was through the wall and I knew what was there.... I did not go in, but stood there on the margin between the two worlds. ... I felt the most vivid expectancy, a longing: this place held what I needed, knew was there, had been waiting for ... all my life. I knew this place, recognized it. The rooms were empty. To make them habitable, what work needed to be done. (pp. 15–16)

The desire for merger is not for a collapse into the fragmentation and chaos of the external world, but a perception of the fundamental interdependence of human beings, of the persistence in us of the elemental hunger, the need to be fed, to give food and to receive it, which binds us physically and psychologically to one another.

Emily (the child who appears mysteriously after the narrator has passed through the wall the first time), with her extreme need and hunger, is also the narrator as a child and the child in all of us. Desire 'explodes' (p. 78) in her, and it is expressed largely through images of incorporation and orality: ingesting, eating, licking, sucking, 'mingling constantly with others, as if some giant rite of eating were taking place, everyone tasting and licking and regurgitating everyone else' (p. 78). Emily desires to feed and feed, 'her mouth was always in movement, chewing, tasting, absorbed in itself, so that she seemed all mouth and everything else in her was subordinated to that.' Even sight is experienced as a form of primal incorporation: 'even the intake of words through her eyes was another form of eating, and her daydreaming a consumption of material which was bloating her as much as her food' (p. 50). The oral imagery is strongly reminiscent of Carroll's *Alice through the Looking Glass*, particularly as the plots of both fictions involve the initiating act of stepping through a barrier into a world which reflects the 'real' world but through a distorting lens. In *Memoirs*, the narrator first comes upon a 'personal' world: images of a repressive and sadistic, but historically recurrent, Victorian family life. Here, like Alice, the narrator experiences 'everything very large, overlifesize, difficult: this was again the child's view that I was imprisoned in. Largeness and smallness' (p. 79). Reinforcing the parallel with Alice are references to a Professor White, the narrator's neighbour, who is explicitly called the 'White Rabbit' by Emily, and as in Carroll's work the reader is continuously disoriented in time and space.

Such references appear to be a deliberate attempt to echo the primal world represented through the fantasy in the Alice books in Lessing's own representation of a world behind the wall. In its insistent orality, the novel suggests the need to return towards the pre-oedipal to the moment of separation, the first moments of ego formation in the reflection in the mirror, in order to clear out the decaying, heavy 'personal' furniture. Only then might it become possible to connect and construct an identity through relationship to an 'impersonal' (i.e. non-egotistic) collective mode which involves release from the socially constructed mother–child dyad as it exists both in the nineteenth- and twentieth-century western family. Food is at famine levels not just in the material world, but also in the inner, psychological world. The 'personal' scenes behind the wall reveal the persistent denial of the neediness and hunger of the child Emily, the child who is all of us, as she is precociously sexualized into 'femininity' through the frustrated 'tickling' of her father and the weary reproaches and repressive 'hygiene' of her mother, 'the large cart-horse woman, her tormentor, the world's image' (p. 134). As Emily's 'little arms desperate for comfort' reach out, they become, in their turn, 'those great arms that had never been taught tenderness. ... And smallness, extreme smallness, weakness, a helplessness reaching out and crying for the little crusts of food' (pp. 134–5). Lessing thus reveals the historical and cultural construction of femininity as a process of institutional denial, repression, and marginalization, the repeated castigations of the mother – 'You are a naughty girl' – which will be passed on through the generations, repeating the structures of loss and frustrated desire.

Yet our need for love, shelter, food, and nurturance, born out of our fundamental formation in human relationships, must be met if we are to survive. The most frightening aspect of the new post-holocaust age in *Memoirs* is that its 'children of violence', the wild, anarchic, semi-humans born out of upheaval and brutality, out of the failures of over-rationalized logic, *cannot* recognize each other's needs, *cannot* nurture each other, but have, literally, turned cannibal and are bent on consuming each other. For Lessing, salvation can come only through a profound and full recognition of our relational needs and desires and the attempts to construct a collective world which is not based on the competitive striving of the isolated ego. Through her women questors and housekeepers from Martha to Alice in *The Good Terrorist* [1985], Lessing suggests that the continued existence of the human race will depend upon the displacement of the primacy of the 'masculine' values of war and competition by those such as care and nurturance, at present associated with women and thus regarded as secondary.

The attempt to connect the 'small personal voice' to a vision of a society organized in terms of collective principles which recognize rather than repress knowledge of the fundamental construction of human subjectivity through relationship is a central feature in almost all contemporary 'utopian' writing by women. Marge Piercy's *Woman on the Edge of Time* is typical in that at the 'subjective centre' of the novel is a human being whose marginality in all respects (gender, race, class, economic power) renders her, in fact, a 'non-subject' in terms of the values of the dominant social formation. In Joanna Russ's *The Female Man* the feminine subject disintegrates into multiple voices and dispersed positions which, despite the attempt of the 'real' author 'Joanna' to supply metalingual containment, resist coercion into a unified whole which would conform to liberal definitions of the self. Similarly, the characters in Angela Carter's *The Passion of New Eve* [1977] or Brigid Brophy's *In Transit* [1969] not only defy gender stereotypes but also merge into the projected desires of other characters, change sex, appearance, behaviour, to reveal the subversive collective fantasies which structure human relationships. Whether overtly 'postmodernist' in form (Russ, Carter), or less obviously so (Piercy, Le Guin), such texts share an insistence that freedom, harmony, human dignity, and love lie not in the realization of any 'essence' of the human individual but in the relationships with others which construct our *social* identity.

POSTMODERN PERSONS?

To the extent that most of these novels fragment linear plot, reveal history to be as much the projection of desire as the progression of facts, and problematize the subject, all appear in some ways to conform to the definitions of postmodernism discussed in the first chapter of this book. A typical summary of the 'classic' view of postmodernism suggests, for example:

The constituent elements of the post-modernist text seldom integrate thematically nor do the characters cohere psychologically: discontinuities of narrative and disjunctions of personality cannot be overcome – as they often can with canonical modernism ... – by an appeal to the logic of a unifying symbolic metalanguage, a dominant stable discourse,

209

settled hierarchy or the constituency of the core self. (Currie 1987, p. 54)

The texts discussed in this chapter do indeed undermine the concept of a coherent psychological self – but only when that self is conceived in terms of a unified *inner essence*. What they do *not* reject is the necessity for assuming a self-concept which recognizes the possibility of human agency, the need for personal history, self-reflexiveness, and the capacity for effective action in the world. The 'subject', whether masculine or feminine, clearly *is* historically determined and discursively situated, but human will, subversive desire, and the consolidation of human connectedness can still exist as effective forces of political change. Simpy to deconstruct the subject is not enough for many contemporary women – particularly feminist – writers, for in itself this will not magically produce a collectivist paradise or utopian society. What such a process *can* do is to reveal the inauthenticity of the goal of 'personal unity', expose the contradictions of the liberal definition of subjectivity (particularly as they operate to oppress women), and thus act as a starting-point for the alternative projection of a society founded on a dispersed but rational rather than individualist understanding and construction of the subject.

Currie argues further, discussing mainstream postmodernism in the United States:

Recent American fiction could be broadly defined as characteristically 'characterless' (it is difficult, for example, to think of many novels with a proper name, either for or in their titles). It is a highly deterministic fiction in which the 'human' subject is paradoxically constrained in the freeplay of the text, constructed in the discursive order rather than 'free' in an existential sense. Identity is suggested by the very structure of language itself, a language logically prior to the subject. A stylistic imperium – reign of rhetoric or monarchy of the signifier – has installed itself in place of the hitherto supreme American fiction of the Imperial Self. The subject, in other words, is subjected, its pre-eminent position usurped; no longer sovereign but dethroned, constructed in and through discourse, a creature at the mercy of the monarchical signifier. (Currie 1987, p. 67)

This assertion is even less true than the previous one with regard to most of the fiction by contemporary *women* writers. In their texts, history and subjectivity have *not* dissolved into the hedonistic 'freeplay' of the signifier (in effect the Romantic Imagination reincarnated as language instead of consciousness). Although textuality may, indeed, be foregrounded in various ways (self-conscious reference to the act of creating fictions in Brookner, Drabble, Maggie Gee, Michelle Roberts, Zoë Fairbairns; inclusion of the author in the text in Russ, Gee, Brophy; a whole range of metafictional strategies in Carter; flaunting of authorial omniscience and the construction of plot in Spark), it does not finally displace 'history' and 'character' as *material* constructions which bear a meaningful relationship to actual social practices. In *Woman on the Edge of Time*, for example, the central character Connie (with her impossibly and, therefore, parodically denotative name, yet substantiated and strongly delineated identity) occupies a fictional space which hesitates fantastically between the 'real' world of the present-day psychiatric hospital and the 'possible' future world of Metapoissett.[9] Yet the novel throughout emphasizes the importance of human struggle, will, agency, and establishment of relationship as *acts in the world*, in order that the utopian vision may be achieved through the release of repressed desire. Piercy's psychiatric hospital is the contemporary world of consumer capitalism where human beings function as potential percentages of profit and where those who are economically dysfunctional can simply be controlled (cheaply and with maximum efficiency) through electrodes planted in their brains. The utopian world of Metapoissett is a society organized through a decentralized anarcho-communism which functions in terms of high-tech pastoralism drawing on scientific knowledge in the service of fundamental human needs, desires, and relational impulses. Indeed, Connie at first perceives this society as regressive, 'womanish', infantile. It is a world devoid of that instrumental rationality which ensures the non-resistance of those whom it victimizes through their acceptance of their oppression as natural and inevitable. Connie, however, comes to recognize through Luciente, her guide in Metapoissett, that the morality which she has accepted as 'natural' is the product of relations of power and economic interest which function to deprive her of agency as effectively as electrodes implanted in the brain. What is deemed 'good' in her world becomes its opposite in Metapoissett: 'Our notions of evil center around power and greed – taking from other people their food, their liberty, their health, their land, their customs, their prides' (p. 139). What Connie learns, above all, through the collective, non-competitive, relations of Metapoissett, is that an ideal society must make provision for the human need for personal dignity and autonomy, but conceived as part of a connection and responsibility to others which is recognized actually to construct rather than threaten one's own individual subjectivity.

Joanna Russ's novel *The Female Man*, though more overtly 'postmodernist' in form than Piercy's, also rejects both liberal and post-structuralist conceptualizations of subjectivity. The novel resembles Jorge Luis Borges' 'The Garden of Forking Paths' (in *Labyrinths* [1964]) in structure, offering alternative universes, characters who are, impossibly, aspects of each other, narrative frames which continuously break and merge into one another to undermine any stable concept of 'reality' and to reveal the extent to which plot as 'history' is a projection of human desire determined by relations of power. Like Piercy, though, Russ emphasizes both the subversive potential of such desire and its place in the construction of a human will to action and change. Utopia is, in fact, conceived primarily as change, but change as fluidity, loss of boundaries, connection, rather than the postmodern 'freeplay of the signifier'. The actual form of the novel denies stasis, individual authority and rational systematization, undermining the construction of a stable authorial 'I' ('Joanna') or the categorization of men and women into the fixities of 'masculine' and 'feminine'. 'Whileaway' is *not* utopia as such, for utopia is constructed through the fluid process of reading the whole text itself, forming a relationship which resists the fixed and the static and the attempt to objectify. 'Whileaway' does reveal the utopian impulse, however, to be located in that desire which is created through human dissatisfaction with the present state of affairs. Like Piercy's novel, therefore, *The Female Man* emphasizes the centrality of human will and collective effort in producing historical change or in shifting the relations between women and men:

Whileawayan psychology locates the basis of Whileawayan character in the early indulgence, pleasure, and flowering which is drastically curtailed by the separation from the mothers. This (it says) gives Whileawayan life its characteristic independence, its dissatisfaction, its suspicion, and its tendency towards a rather irritable solipsism.

'Without which' (said the same Dunyasha Bernadetteson, q-v-), 'we would all become contented slobs, nicht wahr?' Eternal optimism hides behind this dissatisfaction, however; Whileawayans cannot forget the early paradise. (p. 52)

Other contemporary women writers locate utopia (conceived as the projection of fundamental human desires and needs) not so much in the future as in past traditions and forms which need to be revisited or revised or 'revisioned', to use Adrienne Rich's term. Thus Angela Carter 'revisits' traditional fairy stories in *The Bloody Chamber* [1979], subverting their stereotypes through the release of that feminine desire entirely suppressed in the original forms. Zoë Fairbairns 'revisions' the family saga in *Stand We At Last* [1983] to explore less the rivalry and conflicts which separate people than the human potential for connection and relationship. Alice Walker's and Toni Morrison's novels explore the racial history of black people in terms of how their oppression is lived out through relationships within the family (or through the black race conceived in itself as a family, as in Walker's *Meridian* [1976], for example) and yet how these same relationships carry the possibility of human dignity and connection. Walker's women characters discover a personal strength through the revalidation of family connection rather than through organized politics (even the 'political' Meridian, like Lessing's Alice in *The Good Terrorist*, conceives of revolutionary action as mothering and nurturance), and through the traditional, communal skills of needlework, patchwork, singing, rather than through the rhetorical finish of political speech or the formal unity of the 'high' literary text. Celie writes in *The Colour Purple* [1983] in order to connect, to find her sister. It is *her* voicing of the rural, uneducated vernacular in the letters which brings about the positive shift in the family, in the relations between women and men, changes which Nettie's stylistic perfection and internalization of white middle-class culture singularly fail to bring about. Similarly, as Celie, Shug, and Sophie stitch and quilt, cook and garden, they produce a *functional* art, establish 'cultural heritage' as a living connectedness not linked to either profit or 'individual talent' but to the human need for warmth, food, beauty, and relationship. Walker herself, in refusing to intrude the authorial voice of 'high culture' into the epistolary structure (which is almost a parody of the early European bourgeois novel), similarly implies that culture must not be elevated above the community, that artistic expression should be a voicing of the establishment of human identity in relationships and connections between equals.

Shug explicitly voices this position as she discusses the concept of God with Celie, rejecting the anthropomorphized figure of traditional Christianity ('When I found out I thought God was white, and a man, I lost interest. ... You mad 'cause he don't seem to listen to your prayers. Humph! Do the mayor listen to anything coloured say?'; p. 166):

My first step from the old white man was trees. Then air. Then birds. Then other people. But one day I was sitting quiet and feeling like a motherless child, which I was, it came to me: that feeling of being part of everything, not separate at all. I knew that if I cut a tree, my arm would bleed. And I laughed and I cried and I run all round the house. (p. 167)

Through Shug, Celie experiences that human love and connection which gives her the strength to begin to resist Albert's brutal treatment. No longer will she feel pressured, through guilt at his emasculation by the dominant white culture, into simply accepting as 'natural' his disregard of her as a human being. Indeed, by the end of the novel she has convinced him not only of her own human worth and dignity as a black woman but of his as a black man, and convinced him also of their mutual need to be both independent of and connected to each other. When Celie first asserts herself and announces that she is leaving him, Albert can only respond: 'Look at you. You black, you poor, you ugly, you a woman, Goddam, he say, you nothing at all' (p. 169). By the end, however, 'us sit sewing and talking and smoking our pipes' (p. 230). Like Morrison's characters (Claudia in *The Bluest Eye* [1970], for example, who destroys the white baby doll with blue eyes, and Macon Dead in *Song of Solomon* [1977], who

214

rejects his father's pursuit of material wealth and profit),
Walker's women characters discover their sense of identity
through rejecting a white middle-class culture in order to
discover the connecting power of their own black cultural forms
and structures. They discover that the vision of the future
utopia is in fact a 're-vision' of the past.

Other women writers have returned to neglected or non-
hegemonous forms, to the popular or the marginal, in order to
explore the structures of human desire. Muriel Spark's novels,
for example, concern themselves with fundamental human
attitudes towards death and mortality which have found covert
expression through a variety of popular modes and genres. In
The Hothouse by the East River [1973], she reverses the structure of
the traditional ghost story so that the inhabitants of contemporary New York are viewed as occupying a deathly world of
regressive fantasy, high-tech automation, and 'real estate', while
the zombie Elsa (a woman who died during the Second World
War but who continues to 'live' in the present with her family
and friends) functions to expose the fears of mortality and the
flesh which motivate the bizarre Manhattan social rituals. Elsa
knows that she is dead. She flaunts the fact through her shadow,
which, recalling Dante's *Purgatorio*, also falls the wrong way and
inspires her husband Paul (also dead) with a desperate fear and
reminder of his own non-existence (Spark wryly, and metafictionally of course, plays with the fact that both are also
characters in a novel, figments of her own imagination). Simply
as a woman, she is a constant reminder of mortality and the
flesh, just as her friend, the Princess Xavier, advertises her
condition when the silkworms hatch and crawl out of her
unmistakably female (and ample) bosom. Neither Paul nor the
Peter Pan culture of middle-class, moneyed Manhattan can
accommodate such reminders, however. Well-heeled New York,
with its obsessional pursuit of psychological theory, real estate,
technological efficiency, and narcissistic gratification, is a culture
which seeks above all to control and to deny knowledge of the
mortal. Thus Paul keeps Elsa effectively imprisoned in the room
above the East River, regarding her as insane, resenting her
'cloud of unknowing', her stubborn, displaced shadow, because
for him only in *knowledge* is there the security of possession and
control.

In such a culture, human connection has become impossible, so that even human bodies dancing together become disembodied 'manicured fingers' engaged in a ritual of radical chic rather than an expression of love or need or desire for each other. The world of *The Driver's Seat* [1968] is similar. Again, women are seen to be the emotional targets of the cultural denial and fear of mortality and the flesh which the whole social façade supports. This world, too, is dominated by images of the unnatural and the synthetic. Everything and everyone must be negotiated through the safety of distances and barriers. The flesh – human desire, in particular – must be packaged, wrapped, or protected. Coverings, 'style', in the shape of book covers, dresses, furnishings, car bodies, jargon, have replaced material substance. People buy books not for their contents but to match the jacket designs to their interior décor; to read, let alone to 'live', is to open oneself, dangerously, to that pity and fear, that acceptance of loss, which is an inevitable aspect of the experience of being human. Lise, as a female, is again a reminder of the pain of being human, of the fact of mortality, and she seeks to disguise and distance herself with the stain-resistant dress, the hysterical over-organization of her office routines, and the dehumanized order of her apartment. She seeks connection, finally, desperately, through arranging her own murder, through the violent dissolution of death which is a *flaunting* of her mortal condition. Lise can no longer live in a package, but neither can she throw off the cultural projections which position her as a victim. She can only advertise her condition through a denial which entails absolute self-annihilation.

In all of Spark's novels the search for connection is always rendered in terms of the pathological. As early as *The Prime of Miss Jean Brodie* [1961], Jean Brodie's possessive and egotistical need for possession, her requirement that a girl be 'hers for life', her passionate involvement with other women (particularly adolescents), and her terror of leaving the pre-oedipal world lead her to consume others, to deny utterly their own autonomy and identity. (When Mr Lowther, the art master, paints the 'Brodie set' he paints them all as Jean Brodie.) All of Spark's novels are, in fact, a lesson in the disastrous consequences for human relationships of desiring connection without respect for the desires and needs of the other. In effect, she dissects the dehumanized 'postmodern condition' to reveal its psychological basis without ever resorting to psychological realism. Her novels, unlike those of Weldon, Atwood, Piercy, Russ, and Walker, are far from optimistic about the possibility of equal, dignified, and caring relationships between human beings, but they certainly do not celebrate the disappearance of the 'subject' as heralding a new age of romantic play. Like the other women writers discussed in this book, Spark embraces neither a complacent liberalism nor an anarchic postmodernism. Her stories, she says, are neither 'true' nor simply 'lies'; they are neither mimetic representation nor simply the play of signification; they neither assume a fixed human moral order nor abjure morality altogether. For these reasons, her novels, too, cannot easily be assimilated to the dominant aesthetic categories of realism, modernism, or postmodernism. Until the restrictiveness of such categories is more generally critically recognized, however, the 'subjects' discussed in this book will remain 'persons?', that is to say, in the mode of the *interrogative* rather than that of the *affirmative* – at least in the eyes of the literary establishment.

NOTES

1 The desire for a penis is simply, then, desire for autonomy, for separation from the mother through the possession of an external sign of difference.

2 See the critical debate on 'Dora' (Moi 1981; Mitchell and Rose 1982) and Freud's own analysis of the Mona Lisa, discussed in Fuller (1980).

3 Why not then see masculine achievement as a substitute for the inability to bear babies, as Karen Horney has suggested?

4 Juliet Mitchell, of course, was one of the first to argue that Freud's theories can be read in provisional and historical rather than universalist and essentialist terms, as descriptions of existing social practices rather than as innate tendencies (see Mitchell 1975).

5 While Klein believed that, despite this 'splitting', the infant is endowed from the first with a rudimentary ego, later object-relations theorists rejected this. For Fairbairns, the ego is formed gradually out of internalizations of the infant's relationship to the mother, and whether these are split into good and bad is not innately determined but dependent upon the mother's handling of the child. Winnicott developed his theory of the 'good-enough mother' from this, ignoring, however, that it may be contradictions not in the mother but in the society in which she is positioned and defined which give rise to splits in the developing ego of the child.

6 The tone and thematic concerns of much mainstream postmodernist fiction express rage, anger, fear, or the omnipotent 'denial' of the ludic text, yet in many women writers (Woolf, Lessing, Atwood) the dominant concern is with loss, desire for connection, discovery of history, and the possibility of human relationship. There is, however, clearly much *anger* in Lessing or Woolf, just as there is a strong desire for connection and history in, for example, Vonnegut. The categories are *not* absolute.

7 As Chodorow argues: 'In a society like ours in which mothers have exclusive care of infants and are isolated from other adults, in which there is physical and social separation of men/fathers from women/

mothers and children, and institutionalized male domination, a mother may impose her reactions to this situation on her son, and confuse her relationship to him as an infant with a sexualized relationship to him as a male. It is precisely such a situation which accounts for the early entrance into the oedipus situation on the part of boys in our society' (Chodorow 1978, p. 108).

8 In Drabble's novels, many of the heroines become mothers themselves, confirming an unconscious solidarity with their own mothers even if their conscious attitude remains ambivalent or negative. Not so in Brookner's.

9 Tzvetan Todorov first used the concept of 'hesitation' to define the fantastic. The essence of this mode he sees as its 'hesitation' of our assumptions about what constitutes the real and its questioning of the 'existence of an irreducible opposition between real and unreal' (Todorov 1973, p. 167).

BIBLIOGRAPHY

PRIMARY SOURCES

The items listed here are presented in two sections: (1) works of fiction or primary sources; (2) works of criticism or theory or secondary sources.

Alther, Lisa [1976] *Kinflicks*, Harmondsworth: Penguin, 1977.
Atwood, Margaret [1969] *The Edible Woman*, London: Virago, 1982.
—— [1972] *Surfacing*, London: Virago, 1979.
—— [1976] *Lady Oracle*, London: Virago, 1982.
—— [1979] *Life before Man*, London: Virago, 1982.
—— [1981] *Bodily Harm*, London: Virago, 1983.
—— [1985] *The Handmaid's Tale*, London: Cape, 1986.
Barth, John [1968] *Lost in the Funhouse*, London: Secker & Warburg, 1969.
—— [1958] *The End of the Road*, Harmondsworth: Penguin, 1967.
—— [1960] *The Sot-Weed Factor*, St Albans: Panther, 1965.
Beckett, Samuel [1959] *Krapp's Last Tape*, London: Faber, 1959.
Borges, Jorge Luis [1964] *Labyrinths*, Harmondsworth: Penguin, 1970.
Brontë, Charlotte [1849] *Shirley*, London: Dent, 1974.
Brookner, Anita [1981] *A Start in Life*, London: Triad/Granada, 1982.
—— [1982] *Look at Me*, London: Traid/Granada, 1983.
—— [1983] *Providence*, London: Triad/Granada, 1985.
—— [1984] *Hotel du Lac*, London: Triad/Granada, 1985.
—— [1985] *Family and Friends*, London: Cape, 1985.
—— [1986] *A Misalliance*, London: Cape, 1985.
Brophy, Brigid [1969] *In Transit*, London: Macdonald.
Carter, Angela [1977] *The Passion of New Eve*, London: Gollancz, 1977.
—— [1979] *The Bloody Chamber*, London: Gollancz, 1979.
—— [1979] *The Sadeian Woman: An Exercise in Cultural History*, London: Virago, 1979.
Drabble, Margaret [1963] *A Summer Birdcage*, Harmondsworth: Penguin, 1980.
—— [1964] *The Garrick Year*, Harmondsworth: Penguin, 1981.

—— [1965] *The Millstone*, Harmondsworth: Penguin, 1980.

—— [1967] *Jerusalem the Golden*, Harmondsworth: Penguin, 1982.

—— [1969] *The Waterfall*, Harmondsworth: Penguin, 1981.

—— [1972] *The Needle's Eye*, Harmondsworth: Penguin, 1981.

—— [1975] *The Realms of Gold*, Harmondsworth: Penguin, 1981.

—— [1977] *The Ice Age*, Harmondsworth: Penguin, 1981.

—— [1980] *The Middle Ground*, Harmondsworth: Penguin, 1982.

Eliot, George [1860] *The Mill on the Floss*, Harmondsworth: Penguin, 1974.

Eliot, T. S. [1923] *The Wasteland*, London: Faber, 1971.

Fairbairns, Zoë [1983] *Stand We At Last*, London: Virago, 1983.

Federman, Raymond [1971] *Double or Nothing*, New York: Swallow Press, 1971.

Frame, Janet [1961] *Faces in the Water*, London: The Women's Press, 1980.

French, Marilyn [1977] *The Women's Room*, New York: Harcourt, Brace, Jovanavich, 1977.

Gee, Maggie [1983] *The Burning Book*, London: Faber, 1985.

Gould, Lois [1976] *A Sea Change*, New York: Avon Books, 1976.

Heller, Joseph [1974] *Something Happened*, London: Corgi, 1976.

Jong, Erica [1974] *Fear of Flying*, London: Panther/Granada, 1978.

—— [1984] *Parachutes and Kisses*, London: Panther/Granada, 1984.

Joyce, James [1939] *Finnegans Wake*, London: Faber, 1939.

Kesey, Ken [1962] *One Flew over the Cuckoo's Nest*, London: Picador/Pan, 1978.

Lawrence, D. H. [1921] *Women in Love*, Harmondsworth: Penguin, 1975.

Lessing, Doris [1952] *Martha Quest*, St Albans: Panther, 1966.

—— [1962] *The Golden Notebook*, St Albans: Panther, 1973.

—— [1969] *The Four-Gated City*, St Albans: Granada/Panther, 1972.

—— [1974] *The Memoirs of a Survivor*, London: Pan/Picador, 1976.

—— [1985] *The Good Terrorist*, London: Grafton, 1986.

Lurie, Alison [1965] *The Nowhere City*, London: Sphere, 1986.

—— [1974] *The War between the Tates*, Harmondsworth: Penguin, 1983.

—— [1979] *Only Children*, Harmondsworth: Penguin, 1983.

Morrison, Toni [1970] *The Bluest Eye*, London: Triad/Grafton, 1986.

—— [1977] *Song of Solomon*, London: Traid/Grafton, 1986.

—— [1981] *Tar Baby*, London: Triad/Grafton, 1986.

Murdoch, Iris [1978] *The Sea, The Sea*, St Albans: Triad/Panther, 1980.

Paley, Grace [1970] *The Little Disturbances of Man*, London: Virago, 1980.

—— [1975] *Enormous Changes at the Last Minute*, London: Virago, 1985.

—— [1985] *Later the Same Day*, London: Virago, 1985.

Piercy, Marge [1976] *Woman on the Edge of Time*, London: The Women's Press, 1979.

Plath, Sylvia [1964] *The Bell Jar*, London: Faber, 1974.

Pynchon, Thomas [1961] *V*, London: Picador/Pan, 1975.

Rossner, Judith [1975] *Looking for Mr Goodbar*, New York: Pocket Books, 1975.

Russ, Joanna [1975] *The Female Man*, London: The Women's Press, 1985.

Shulman, Alix Kates [1972] *Memoirs of an Ex-Prom. Queen*, New York: Bantam, 1972.

Sillitoe, Alan [1958] *Saturday Night and Sunday Morning*, London: Allan and Co., 1968.

Spark, Muriel [1961] *The Prime of Miss Jean Brodie*, Harmondsworth: Penguin, 1965.

—— [1968] *The Driver's Seat*, Harmondsworth: Penguin, 1970.

—— [1973] *The Hothouse by the East River*, Harmondsworth: Penguin, 1975.

Tyler, Ann [1964] *If Morning Ever Comes*, London: Hamlyn, 1983.

—— [1969] *A Slipping Down Life*, London: Hamlyn, 1983.

Vonnegut, Kurt [1969] *Slaughterhouse-Five*, London: Triad/Granada, 1979.

Walker, Alice [1973] *In Love and Trouble*, London: The Women's Press, 1984.

—— [1976] *Meridian*, London: The Women's Press, 1983.

—— [1983] *The Colour Purple*, London: The Women's Press, 1983.

Weldon, Fay [1967] *The Fat Woman's Joke*, London: Coronet, 1982.

—— [1976] *Remember Me*, London: Coronet, 1980.

—— [1978] *Praxis*, London: Coronet, 1980.

—— [1980] *Puffball*, London: Coronet, 1981.

—— [1983] *The Life and Loves of a She-Devil*, London: Coronet, 1984.

Woolf, Virginia [1915] *The Voyage Out*, Harmondsworth: Penguin, 1975.

—— [1918] 'Women novelists', in Michelle Barrett (ed.), *Virginia Woolf: Women and Writing*, London: Women's Press, 1979, pp. 68–71.

—— [1919] *Night and Day*, Harmondsworth: Penguin, 1975.

—— [1925] *Mrs Dalloway*, Harmondsworth: Penguin, 1969.

—— [1927] *To the Lighthouse*, London: Hogarth Press, 1960.

—— [1928] *Orlando*, Harmondsworth: Penguin, 1975.

—— [1928] *A Room of One's Own*, Harmondsworth: Penguin, 1975.

—— [1928] 'Street haunting' in *Collected Essays*, vol. 4, London: Hogarth Press, 1967.

—— [1931] *The Waves*, Harmondsworth: Penguin, 1972.

—— [1931] 'Professions for women', in Michelle Barrett (ed.), *Virginia Woolf: Women and Writing*, London: Women's Press, pp. 57–63.

—— [1937] *The Years*, London: Pan, 1948.

—— [1938] *Three Guineas*, Harmondsworth: Penguin, 1975.

—— [1939] *Moments of Being*, New York, Harcourt Brace Jovanovich, 1976.

—— [1941] *Between the Acts*, Harmondsworth: Penguin, 1953.

—— [1953] *A Writer's Diary*, St Albans: Triad/Panther, 1978.

SECONDARY SOURCES

Abarbenal, Alice (1972) 'Redefining motherhood', in Louise Kapp Howe (ed.), *The Future of the Family*, New York.

Abel, Elizabeth (1981) '(E)merging identities: the dynamics of female friendship in contemporary fiction by women', *Signs*, 6, 3.

—— (ed.) (1982) *Writing and Sexual Difference*, Brighton.

Abel, Elizabeth and Abel, Emily K. (eds) (1983) *The Signs Reader: Women, Gender and Scholarship*, Chicago and London.

Abel, Elizabeth, Hirsch, Marianne, and Langland, Elizabeth (eds) (1983) *The Voyage In: Fictions of Female Development*, Hanover and London.

Adams, P. (1978) 'Representation and sexuality', *M/F*, 1.

Adams, Robert Martin (1978) 'What was modernism?', *Hudson Review*, 31, 1, Spring.

Aldridge, John (1983) *The American Novel and the Way We Live Now*, New York and Oxford.

Allen, Mary (1976) *The Necessary Blankness: Women in Major American Fiction of the Sixties*, Urbana, Chicago, and London.

Althusser, Louis (1969) *For Marx*, Harmondsworth.

—— (1971) *Lenin and Philosophy*, London.

Anderson, Linda (1986) 'At the threshold of the self: women and autobiography', in Moira Monteith (ed.), *Women's Writing*, Brighton, pp. 54–71.

Appignanesi, Lisa (ed.) (1986) *Postmodernism*, ICA Documents 4/5, London.

Armstrong, Nancy (1982) 'The rise of feminine authority in the novel', *Novel*, 15, 2 (Winter), pp. 127–45.

Atkinson, Paul (1979) 'The problem with patriarchy', *Achilles Heel*, 2.

Auerbach, Nina (1978) *Communities of Women: An Idea in Fiction*, Cambridge, Mass. and London.

Balint, Alice (1975) 'Love for the mother and mother love', in Michael Balint (ed.), *Primary Love and Psychoanalytic Technique*, New York.

Barrett, Michelle (ed.) (1979) *Virginia Woolf: Women and Writing*, London.

—— (1980) *Women's Oppression Today: Problems in Marxist Feminist Analysis*, London.

Barth, John (1980) 'The literature of replenishment: postmodern fiction', *Atlantic Monthly*, 245, 1, January, pp. 65–71.

Batsleer, Janet, Davies, Tony, O'Rourke, Rebecca, and Weedon, Chris (1985) *Rewriting English: Cultural Politics of Gender and Class*, London and New York.

Baym, Nina (1986) 'Melodramas of beset manhood', in Elaine Showalter (ed.), *The New Feminist Criticism: Essays on Women, Literature and Society*, London.

Beards, V. K. (1973) 'Margaret Drabble: novels of a cautious feminist', *Critique*, 15, 1, pp. 35–47.

Beauvoir, Simone de (1972) *The Second Sex*, trans. H. M. Parshley, Harmondsworth.

Beja, Morris (ed.) (1970) *To the Lighthouse: A Casebook*, London.

Bell, Michael (1980) *The Context of English Literature: 1900–1930*, London.

Bellamy, Michael (1977) 'Interview with Iris Murdoch', *Contemporary Literature*, 18, 2, Spring.

Belsey, Catherine (1985a) *The Subject of Tragedy: Identity and Difference in Renaissance Drama*, London and New York.

—— (1985b) 'Constructing the subject', in Judith Newton and Deborah Rosenfelt (eds), *Feminist Criticism and Social Change*, New York and London.

Benhabib, Seyla (1984) 'Epistemologies of postmodernism: a rejoinder to Jean-François Lyotard', *New German Critique*, 33, Fall, pp. 103–27.

Benjamin, Jessica (1978) 'Authority and the family revisited: or, a world without fathers?', *New German Critique*, 13, Winter, pp. 35–57.

—— (1980) 'The bonds of love: rational violence and erotic domination', in Hester Eisenstein and Alice Jardine (eds), *The Future of Difference*, Boston, Mass.

Bennett, David (1985) 'Parody, postmodernism and the politics of reading', *Critical Quarterly*, 27, 4, Winter.

Berger, John (1972) *Ways of Seeing*, Harmondsworth.

Bernard, Jessie (1974) *The Future of Motherhood*, New York.

Bersani, Leo (1977) 'The subject of power', *Diacritics*, September, pp. 2–21.

—— (1986) 'The culture of redemption: Marcel Proust and Melanie Klein', *Critical Inquiry*, 12, 2, Winter.

Bion, W. R. (1960) *Second Thoughts: Selected Papers on Psychoanalysis*, London.

Bishop, E. L. (1981) 'Towards the far side of language: Virginia Woolf's *The Voyage Out*', *Twentieth Century Literature*, 27, 4, pp. 343–62.

Blau du Plessis, Rachael (1985) *Writing Beyond the Ending: Narrative Strategies of Twentieth Century Women Writers*, Bloomington.

—— (1986) 'For the Etruscans', in Elaine Showalter (ed.), *The New Feminist Criticism: Essays on Women, Literature and Society*, London.

Bowlby, John (1951) *Maternal Care and Mental Health*, Geneva.

Bradbury, Malcolm (1973) *Possibilities*, Oxford.

—— (ed.) (1977) *The Novel Today: Contemporary Writers on Modern Fiction*, London.

Bradbury, Malcolm and McFarlane, James (eds) (1976) *Modernism 1890–1930*, Harmondsworth.

Bradbury, Malcolm and Palmer, D. (1979) *The Contemporary English Novel*, London

Bradbury, Malcolm and Ro, Sigmund (eds) (1987) *Contemporary American Fiction*, London.

Brake, Michael (ed.) (1982) *Human Sexual Relations: Towards a Redefinition of Sexual Politics*, Harmondsworth.

Brooke-Rose, Christine (1981) *A Rhetoric of the Unreal: Studies in Narrative and Structure, especially of the Fantastic*, Cambridge.

Brown, Richard Harvey (1980) 'The position of the narrative in contemporary society', *New Literary History*, 11, 2, Winter.

Brunt, Rosalind and Cowan, Caroline (eds) (1982) *Feminism, Culture and Politics*, London.

Bürger, Peter (1984) *Theory of the Avant-Garde*, trans. Michael Shaw, Manchester and Minneapolis.

Burgin, Victor (1986) *The End of Art Theory: Criticism and Postmodernity*, London.

Burgin, Victor, Donald, James, and Kaplan, Cora (1986) *Formations of Fantasy*, London.

Burke, Carolyn (1982) 'Rethinking the maternal', in Hester Eisenstein and Alice Jardine (eds), *The Future of Difference*, Boston, Mass.

Butler, Christopher (1980) *After the Wake*, Oxford.

Calinescu, Matei (1986) 'Postmodernism and some paradoxes of periodization', in Douwe Fokkema and Hans Bertens (eds), *Approaching Postmodernism*, Amsterdam and Philadelphia, pp. 239–54.

Chasseguet-Smirgel, Janine (1970) *Female Sexuality: New Psychoanalytic Views*, Ann Arbor.

—— (1976) 'Freud and female sexuality', *International Journal of Psychoanalysis*, 57.

Chernin, Kim (1981) *Womansize: The Tyranny of Slenderness*, London.

—— (1986) *The Hungry Self: Women, Eating and Identity*, London.

Chesler, Phyllis (1972) *Women and Madness*, New York.

Chodorow, Nancy (1978) *The Reproduction of Mothering: Psychoanalysis and the Sociology of Gender*, Berkeley, Los Angeles, and London.

—— (1979) 'Feminism and difference', *Socialist Review*, 9, July/August, pp. 51–69.

—— (1982) 'Gender, relationship and difference in psychoanalytic perspective' in Hester Eisenstein and Alice Jardine (eds), *The Future of Difference*, Boston, Mass., pp. 3–20.

Cixous, Hélène (1976) 'The laugh of the Medusa', *Signs*, 1, 4, pp. 875–93.

—— (1983) 'Portrait of Dora', *Diacritics*, 13, 1, pp. 2–32.

Clarke, Simon, Lovell, Terry, McDonnell, Kevin, Robins, Kevin and Seidler, Viktor Jeleniewski (eds) (1980) *One-Dimensional Marxism: Althusser and the Politics of Culture*, London.

Cohen, Mabel Blake (1973) 'Personal identity and sexual identity', in Jean Baker Miller (ed.), *Psychoanalysis and Women*, Baltimore.

Collins, J., Ray Green, J., Lydon, M., Sachner, M., and Honigskoller, E. (1983) 'Questioning the unconscious: the Dora archive', *Diacritics*, 13, Spring, pp. 37–42.

Cook, Jon (1983) 'Notes on history, politics and sexuality', in Eileen Philips (ed.), *The Left and the Erotic*, London, pp. 83–113.

Corsa, Helen Storm (1971) 'Death, mourning and transfiguration in *To the Lighthouse*', *Literature and Psychology*, 21, 3, pp. 115–31.

Coward, Rosalind (1980) 'This novel changes lives: are women's novels feminist novels? A response to Rebecca O'Rouke's "Summer Reading"', *Feminist Review*, 5, pp. 53–64.
—— (1982) 'Sexual politics and psychoanalysis: some notes on their relation', in Rosalind Brunt and Caroline Cowan (eds), *Feminism, Culture and Politics*, London, pp. 171–89.
—— (1983) *Patriarchal Precedents: Sexuality and Social Relations*, London.
—— (1984) *Female Desire*, London.
Coward, Rosalind, Lipshitz, Sue, and Cowie, Elizabeth (1982) 'Psychoanalysis and patriarchal structures', in Michael Brake (ed.), *Human Sexual Relations: Towards a Redefinition of Sexual Politics*, Harmondsworth, pp. 275–93.
Creighton, Joanne V. (1985) *Margaret Drabble*, London and New York.
Currie, Peter (1987) 'The eccentric self: anti-characterization and the problem of the subject in American postmodernist fiction', in Malcolm Bradbury and Sigmund Ro (eds), *Contemporary American Fiction*, London, pp. 53–71.
Daiches, David (1942) *Virginia Woolf*, New York.
Davidson, Arnold E. and Davidson, Cathy N. (1981) *The Art of Margaret Atwood*, Toronto.
Derrida, Jacques (1978) 'Becoming woman', trans. Barbara Harlow, *Semiotext(e)*, 3, 1.
Deutsch, Helen (1944–5) *The Psychology of Women*, vols 1–2, New York.
—— (1974) 'The psychology of women in relation to the functions of reproduction', in Jean Strouse (ed.), *Women and Analysis: Dialogues on Psychoanalytic Views of Femininity*, New York.
Diamond, Arlyn and Edwards, Lee R. (1977) *The Authority of Experience: Essays in Feminist Criticism*, Amherst.
Dinnerstein, Dorothy (1976) *The Mermaid and the Minotaur: Sexual Arrangements and Human Malaise*, New York and London.
Dollimore, Jonathan (1986) 'The dominant and the deviant: a violent dialectic', *Critical Quarterly*, 28, 1/2, Spring/Summer, pp. 179–91.
Donovan, Josephine (ed.) (1975) *Feminist Literary Criticism: Explorations in Theory*, Kentucky.
Drabble, Margaret (1975) 'The author comments', *Dutch Quarterly Review of Anglo-American Letters*, 5.
Draine, Betsy, (1979) 'Changing frames: Doris Lessing's *Memoirs of a Survivor*', *Studies in the Novel*, 11, 1, Spring.
Eagleton, Terry (1986) 'Capitalism, modernism and postmodernism', in *Against the Grain: Essays 1975–85*, London.
Eichenbaum, Luise and Orbach, Susie (1982) *Outside In Inside Out: Women's Psychology: A Feminist Psychoanalytic Approach*, Harmondsworth.
—— (1984) *What Do Women Want?*, London.
—— (1985) *Understanding Women*, Harmondsworth.
Eisenstein, Hester and Jardine, Alice (eds) (1980) *The Future of Difference*. Boston, Mass.
Elshtain, Jean Bethke (1982) 'Feminist discourse and its discontents:

language, power and meaning', in N. O. Keohane, M. Z. Rosaldo, and B. C. Gelpi (eds), *Feminist Theory: A Critique of Ideology*, Brighton, pp. 127–47.

Erikson, Erik (1959) *Identity and the Life Cycle*, New York.

—— (1964) 'Inner and outer space', *Daedalus*, 93.

—— (1968) *Identity, Youth and Crisis*, New York.

—— (1974) 'Womanhood and the inner space', in Jean Strouse (ed.), *Women and Analysis: Dialogues on Psychoanalytic Views of Femininity*, New York, pp. 291–319.

Ermarth, Elizabeth (1983) *Realism and Consensus in the English Novel*, Princeton.

Fairbairn, W. R. D. (1952) *Psychoanalytic Studies of the Personality*, London.

Farwell, Marilyn (1978) 'Feminist criticism and the concept of the poetic persona', *Bucknell Review*, 24, pp. 139–56.

Felman, Shoshana (1975) 'Women and madness: the critical phallacy', *Diacritics*, 5, Winter, pp. 2–10.

—— (ed.) (1982), *Literature and Psychoanalysis: The Question of Reading: Otherwise*, Baltimore and London.

Féral, Josette (1980) 'The powers of difference', in Hester Eisenstein and Alice Jardine (eds), *The Future of Difference*, Boston, Mass., pp. 88–94.

Fetterley, Judith (1978) *The Resisting Reader: A Feminist Approach to American Fiction*, Bloomington and London.

Fiedler, Leslie A. (1984) *Love and Death in the American Novel*, Harmondsworth.

Firestone, Shulamith (1971) *The Dialectic of Sex*, New York and London.

Flax, Jane (1978) 'The conflict between nurturance and autonomy in mother–daughter relationships and within feminism', *Feminist Studies*, 4, 2, pp. 171–89.

—— (1980) 'Mother–daughter relationships: psycho-dynamics, politics and philosophy', in Hester Eisenstein and Alice Jardine (eds), *The Future of Difference*, Boston, Mass., pp. 20–41.

Fliegel, Zenia Odes (1982) 'Half a century later: current status of Freud's controversial views on women', in Leila Lerner (ed.), *Women and Individuation: Emerging Views*, *The Psychoanalytic Review*, 69, 1, Spring, pp. 7–28.

Fokkema, Douwe W. (1979) 'An interpretation of *To the Lighthouse* with reference to the code of modernism', *Poetics and the Theory of Literature*, 4, 3, pp. 475–500.

Fokkema, Douwe and Bertens, Hans (eds) (1986) *Approaching Postmodernism*, Amsterdam and Philadelphia.

Foreman, Ann (1977) *Femininity as Alienation: Women and the Family in Marxism and Psychoanalysis*, London.

Foster, Hal (1984) '(Post)modern polemics', *New German Critique*, 33, pp. 67–79.

—— (ed.) (1985a) *Postmodern Culture*, London and Sydney.

—— (1985b) *Recodings: Art, Spectacle, Cultural Politics*, Washington.

228

Foucault, Michel (1965) *Madness and Civilization*, trans. R. Howard, New York.
—— (1984) *The History of Sexuality*, Harmondsworth.
Frank, Joseph (1958) 'Spatial form in modern literature', in Mark Schorer, J. Miles, and G. McKenzie (eds), *Criticism: The Foundations of Modern Literary Judgement*, Berkeley, Los Angeles, and London.
Freud, Sigmund (1900) *The Interpretation of Dreams*, Standard Edition, vols 4–5, London, 1953; Penguin Freud Library, vol. 4, Harmondsworth, 1976.
—— (1905a) *Three Essays on the Theory of Sexuality*, Standard Edition, vol. 7, London, 1953; Penguin Freud Library, vol. 7, Harmondsworth, 1977.
—— (1905b) 'Fragment of an analysis of a case of hysteria, Standard Edition, vol. 7, London, 1953.
—— (1908) 'Hysterical phantasies and their relation to bisexuality', Standard Edition, vol. 9, London, 1959.
—— (1914) 'On Narcissism: an introduction', Standard Edition, vol. 14, London, 1957.
—— (1915) 'Instincts and their vicissitudes', Standard Edition, vol. 14, London, 1957.
—— (1917) 'Mourning and melancholia', Standard Edition, vol. 14, London, 1957.
—— (1920) 'The psychogenesis of a case of homosexuality in a woman', Standard Edition, vol. 18, London, 1955.
—— (1923) *The Ego and the Id*, Standard Edition, vol. 19, London, 1961.
—— (1925) 'Some psychical consequences of the anatomical distinction between the sexes', Standard Edition, vol. 19, London, 1961; repr. in Jean Strouse (ed.), *Women and Analysis: Dialogues on Psychoanalytic Views of Femininity*, New York, 1974, with a comment by Juliet Mitchell.
—— (1930) *Civilization and its Discontents*, Standard Edition, vol. 21, London, 1961.
—— (1931) 'Female sexuality', Standard Edition, vol. 21, London, 1961; repr. in Jean Strouse (ed.), *Women and Analysis: Dialogues on Psychoanalytic Views of Femininity*, New York, 1974, with a comment by Elizabeth Janeway.
—— (1933) 'Femininity', Standard Edition, vol. 22, London, 1964; repr. in Jean Strouse (ed.), *Women and Analysis: Dialogues on Psychoanalytic Views of Femininity*, New York, 1974, with a comment by Margaret Mead.
—— (1937) 'Analysis terminable and interminable', Standard Edition, vol. 23, London, 1964.
—— (1940) *An Outline of Psychoanalysis*, Standard Edition, vol. 23, London, 1964.
Freud, Sigmund and Breuer, Josef (1895) *Studies on Hysteria*, Standard Edition, vol. 2, London, 1955.
Fried, Michael (1982) 'How modernism works', *Critical Inquiry*, 9, pp.217–33.

Friedman, Norman (1970) 'Double vision in *To the Lighthouse*', in Morris Beja (ed.), *To the Lighthouse: A Casebook*, London, pp. 149–68.

Fuller, Peter (1980) *Art and Psychoanalysis*, London.

Galen, Amy (1979) 'Rethinking Freud on female sexuality: a look at the new orthodox defense', *Psychological Review*, 62, 2, pp. 173–86.

Gallop, Jane (1982) *Feminism and Psychoanalysis: The Daughter's Seduction*, London.

Gardiner, Judith Kegan (1979) 'Psychoanalytic criticism and the female reader', *Literature and Psychology*, 26, 3, pp. 100–7.

—— (1981) 'The (US)es of I(dentity): a response to Abel on (E)merging Identities', *Signs*, 6, 31.

—— (1982) 'On female identity and writing by women', in Elizabeth Abel (ed.), *Writing and Sexual Difference*, Brighton, pp. 177–93.

—— (1985) 'Mind mother: psychoanalysis and feminism', in Gayle Greene and Coppélia Kahn (eds), *Making a Difference: Feminist Literary Criticism*, London and New York, pp. 113–46.

Garner, Shirley Nelson, Kahane, Claire, and Sprengnether, Madelon (eds) (1985) *The M(other) Tongue: Essays in Feminist Psychoanalytic Interpretation*, Ithaca and London.

Gelpi, Barbara Charlesworth (1974), 'The androgyne', in Jean Strouse (ed.), *Women and Analysis: Dialogues on Psychoanalytic Views of Femininity*, New York.

Gerstenberger, Donna (1976) 'Conceptions literary and otherwise: women writers and the modern imagination', *Novel*, 9, 2, Winter, pp. 141–50.

Giddens, Anthony (1984) 'Modernism and postmodernism', *New German Critique*, 22, Winter, pp. 15–18.

Gilbert, Sandra M. (1982) 'Costumes of the mind: Transvestism as metaphor in modern literature', in Elizabeth Abel (ed.), *Writing and Sexual Difference*, Brighton.

—— (1986) 'What do feminist critics want?' in Elaine Showalter (ed.), *The New Feminist Criticism: Essays on Women, Literature and Society*, London.

Gilbert, Sandra M. and Gubar, Susan (1979) *The Madwoman in the Attic: The Woman Writer and the Nineteenth Century Literary Imagination*, New Haven and London.

Gilligan, Carol (1982) *In a Different Voice: Psychological Theory and Women's Development*, Cambridge, Mass. and London.

Gilman, Richard (1972) 'The idea of the avant-garde', *Partisan Review*, 39, 3.

Gloversmith, Frank (1984) 'Autonomy theory: Ortega y Gasset, Roger Fry, Virginia Woolf', in Frank Gloversmith (ed.), *The Theory of Reading*, Brighton, pp. 147–99.

Gornick, Vivian and Moran, Barbara K. (eds) (1971) *Women in Sexist Society: Studies in Power and Powerlessness*, New York.

Graff, Gerald (1979) *Literature against Itself: Literary Ideas in Modern Society*, Chicago and London.

Greene, Gayle and Kahn, Coppélia (eds) (1985) *Making a Difference: Feminist Literary Criticism*, London and New York.

Gubar, Susan (1986) 'The blank page and the issues of female creativity', in Elaine Showalter (ed.), *The New Feminist Criticism: Essays on Women, Literature and Society*, London.

Guillamin, Colette (1981) 'The practice of power and belief in nature, part one: the appropriation of women', *Feminist Issues*, Winter.

Habermas, Jürgen (1985) 'Modernity – an incomplete project', in Hal Foster (ed.), *Postmodern Culture*, London and Sydney, pp. 3–16.

Haffendon, John (1985) *Novelists in Interview*, London and New York.

Harré, Rom (1983) *Personal Being: A Theory for Individual Psychology*, Oxford.

Hassan, Ihab (1961) *Radical Innocence: Studies in the Contemporary American Novel*, Princeton.

—— (1986) 'Pluralism in postmodern perspective', *Critical Inquiry*, 12, 3, Spring.

Hawthorn, Jeremy (1975) *Virginia Woolf's Mrs Dalloway: A Study in Alienation*, Brighton.

—— (1982) 'Individuality and characterisation in the modernist novel', in Douglas Jefferson and Graham Martin (eds), *The Uses of Fiction: Essays on the Modern Novel in Honour of Arnold Kettle*, Milton Keynes.

—— (1983) *Multiple Personality and the Disintegration of Literary Character*, London.

Heath, Stephen (1982) *The Sexual Fix*, London.

Heilbrun, Carolyn (1973) *Towards Androgyny: Aspects of Male and Female in Literature*, London.

Heilbrun, Carolyn and Higamet, Margaret R. (1983) *The Representation of Women in Fiction*, Baltimore and London.

Henriques, Julian, Holloway, Wendy, Unwin, Cathy, Venn, Couze, and Walkerdine, Valerie (1984) *Changing the Subject: Psychology, Social Regulation and Subjectivity*, London and New York.

Hinshelwood, R. D. (1983) 'Projective identification and Marx's concept of man', *International Review of Psychoanalysis*, 10, pp. 221–6.

Holloway, Wendy (1984) 'Gender difference and the production of subjectivity', in Julian Henriques *et al.*, *Changing the Subject: Psychology, Social Regulation and Subjectivity*, London and New York, pp. 227–64.

Holly, Marcia (1975) 'Consciousness and authenticity: towards a feminist aesthetic', in Josephine Donovan (ed.), *Feminist Literary Criticism: Explorations in Theory*, Kentucky, pp. 38–47.

Holquist, Michael (1976) 'How to play utopia', in Mark Rose (ed.), *Science Fiction: Twentieth Century Views*, Englewood Cliffs, NJ.

Homans, Margaret (1983) 'Her very own howl', *Signs*, 9, 2.

Horney, Karen (1967) 'The dread of women', in Harold Kelman (ed.), *Feminine Psychology*, New York. (First published 1932.)

—— (1974) 'The flight from womanhood: the masculinity complex in women as viewed by men and women', in Jean Strouse (ed.), *Women and Analysis: Dialogues on Psychoanalytic Views of Femininity*, New York, pp. 171–86. (First Published 1926.)

Housman, Judy (1981) 'Mothering, the unconscious and feminism', *Radical America*, 16, 6, pp. 47–61.

Hume, Kathryn (1984) *Fantasy and Mimesis: Responses to Reality in Western Literature*, New York and London.

Hunter, Ian (1983) 'Reading character', *Southern Review*, 16.

Hutcheon, Linda (1983) 'From poetic to narrative structures: the novels of Margaret Atwood', in Sherrill E. Grace and Lorraine Weir (eds), *Language, Text and System*, Vancouver.

—— (1985) *A Theory of Parody: The Teachings of Twentieth Century Art Forms*, London and New York.

—— (1987) 'Beginning to theorize postmodernism', *Textual Practice*, 1, 1, Spring, pp. 10–31.

Huyssen, Andreas (1984) 'Mapping the postmodern', *New German Critique*, 33, Fall, pp. 5–53.

Ingleby, David (1984) 'The ambivalence of psychoanalysis', *Free Associations/Radical Science*, 15, pp. 39–71.

Irigary, Luce (1974) *Speculum de l'autre femme*, Paris.

—— (1981) 'And the one doesn't stir without the other', trans. Hélène Vivienne Wenzel, *Signs*, 7, 1.

Jackson, Rosemary (1981) *Fantasy: The Literature of Subversion*, London and New York.

Jacobus, Mary (1982) 'Is there a woman in this text?' *New Literary History*, 14, 1, Autumn, pp. 117–41.

Jameson, Fredric (1981) *The Political Unconscious: Narrative as a Socially Symbolic Act*, London.

—— (1982) 'Imaginary and symbolic in Lacan: Marxism, psychoanalytic criticism and the problem of the subject' in Shoshana Felman (ed.), *Literature and Psychoanalysis: The Question of Reading: Otherwise*, Baltimore and London.

—— (1983) 'Pleasure: a political issue', *Formations of Pleasure I*, London, Boston, Melbourne, and Henley, pp. 1–14.

—— (1984a) 'Postmodernism, or the cultural logic of late capitalism', *New Left Review*, July/August, pp. 53–92.

—— (1984b) 'The politics of theory: ideological positions in the postmodernism debate', *New German Critique*, 33, Fall, pp. 53–67.

—— (1985) 'Postmodernism and Consumer Society', in Hal Foster (ed.), *Postmodern Culture*, London and Sydney, pp. 111–26.

Jardine, Alice (1980) 'Theories of the feminine', *Enclitic*, 4, 2, Fall, pp. 5–15.

Jefferson, Douglas and Martin, Graham (eds) (1982) *The Uses of Fiction: Essays on the Modern Novel in Honour of Arnold Kettle*, Milton Keynes.

Jehlen, Myra (1983) 'Archimedes and the paradox of feminist criticism', *The Signs Reader*, pp. 69–97.

Jones, Ernest (1961) 'The early development of female sexuality', in *Papers on Psychoanalysis*, Boston, Mass.

Jung, C. J. and Kerenýi, C. (1963) *Essays on a Science of Mythology*, New York.

Kahane, Claire (1980) 'The nuptials of metaphor: self and other in Virginia Woolf', *Literature and Psychology*. 30. 2, pp. 72–87.

Kamuf, Peggy (1982) 'Replacing feminist criticism', *Diacritics*, 12, pp. 42–7.
Kaplan, Cora (1983) 'Wild nights; pleasure/sexuality/feminism', in *Formations of Pleasure I*, London, Boston, Melbourne, and Henley, pp. 15–36.
—— (1985) 'Pandora's Box: subjectivity, class and sexuality in socialist feminist criticism', in Gayle Greene and Coppélia Kahn (eds), *Making a Difference: Feminist Literary Criticism*, London and New York, pp. 146–77.
—— (1986) *Sea Changes: Culture and Feminism*, London.
Kaplan, Sydney Janet (1985) 'Varieties of feminist criticism', in Gayle Greene and Coppélia Kahn (eds), *Making a Difference: Feminist Literary Criticism*, London and New York, pp. 37–59.
Karl, Frederick (1985) *American Fictions 1940–1980*, New York.
Keller, Evelyn Fox (1978) 'Gender and science', *Psychoanalysis and Contemporary Thought*, 1.
—— (1982) 'Feminism and science', *Signs* 7, 3, pp. 589–602.
Keohane, N.O., Rosaldo, M. Z., and Gelpi, B. C. (eds) (1982) *Feminist Theory: A Critique of Ideology*, Brighton.
Kernberg, Otto (1976) *Object-Relations Theory and Clinical Psychoanalysis*, New York.
—— (1977) 'Boundaries and structure in love relations', *Journal of the American Psychological Association*, 25, pp. 81–114.
Klein, Melanie (1932) 'The psychoanalysis of children', in *The Writings of Melanie Klein*, vol. 2, London.
—— (1937) 'Love, guilt and reparation', in *The Writings of Melanie Klein*, vol. 1, London, pp. 306–43.
—— (1940) 'Mourning and its relation to manic-depressive states', in *The Writings of Melanie Klein*, vol. 2, London.
—— (1946) 'Notes on some schizoid mechanisms', in *The Writings of Melanie Klein*, vol. 3, London.
—— (1957) 'Envy and gratitude', in *The Writings of Melanie Klein*, vol. 3, London.
Klinkowitz, Jerome (1987) 'The extra-literary in contemporary American fiction', in Malcolm Bradbury and Sigmund Ro (eds), *Contemporary American Fiction*, London, pp. 19–39.
Kolodny, Annette (1986) 'A map for rereading: gender and the interpretation of literary texts', in Elaine Showalter (ed.), *The New Feminist Criticism: Essays on Women, Literature and Society*, London.
Komter, Aafke (1984) 'Feminism and psychoanalysis', in Anja Meulenbelt *et al.* (eds), *A Creative Tension: Explorations in Socialist Feminism*, trans. Della Couling, London and Sydney.
Kovel, Joel (1974) 'The castration complex reconsidered', in Jean Strouse (ed.), *Women and Analysis: Dialogues on Psychoanalytic Views of Femininity*, New York.
—— (1976) 'The Marxist view of man and psychoanalysis', *Social Research*, 43, 2, Summer.
Kris, Ernst (1964) *Psychoanalytic Explorations in Art*, New York.
Kristeva, Julia (1975) 'The subject in signifying practice', *Semiotext(e)*, 1, 3, pp. 19–26.

—— (1980) *Desire in Language: A Semiotic Approach to Literature and Art*, ed. Leon S. Roudiez, trans. Thomas Gora, Alice Jardine, and Leon S. Roudiez, Oxford.

Krupnick, Mark (ed.) (1983) *Displacement: Derrida and After*, Bloomington.

Kuhns, Richard (1983) *Psychoanalytic Theory of Art: A Philosophy of Art on Developmental Principles*, New York.

Lacan, Jacques (1977) *Ecrits: A Selection*, trans. Alan Sheridan, London.

—— (1986) *The Four Fundamental Concepts of Psychoanalysis*, ed. Jacques Alain Miller, trans. Alan Sheridan, Harmondsworth.

Lachmann, Frank M. (1982) 'Narcissism and female gender identity: a reformulation', in Leila Lerner (ed.), *Women and Individuation: Emerging Views*, *The Psychoanalytic Review*, 69, 1, Spring, pp. 43–61.

Laplanche, J and Pontalis, J.-B. (1973) *The Language of Psychoanalysis*, trans. Donald Nicholson-Smith, ed. Daniel Lagache, New York and London.

—— (1976) *Life and Death in Psychoanalysis*, trans. and introd. Jeffrey Mehlman, Baltimore and London.

Larmore, Charles (1981) 'The concept of a constitutive subject', in Colin MacCabe (ed.), *The Talking Cure: Essays in Psychoanalysis and Language*, London, pp. 108–32.

Lauretis, Teresa de (1984) *Alice Doesn't: Feminism, Semiotics, Cinema*, London.

Leaska, Mitchell (1977) *The Novels of Virginia Woolf from Beginning to Ending*, New York.

Lebe, Doryann (1982) 'Individuation of women', in Leila Lerner (ed.), *Women and Individuation: Emerging Views*, *The Psychoanalytic Review*, 69, 1, Spring, pp. 62–83.

LeClair, Tom and McCaffery, Larry (1983) *Anything Can Happen: Interviews With Contemporary American Novelists*, Urbana, Chicago, and London.

Lerner, Leila (ed.) (1982) *Women and Individuation: Emerging Views*, *The Psychoanalytic Review*, 69, 1, Spring.

Lessing, Doris (1975) *A Small Personal Voice*, New York.

Lilienfield, Jane (1977) 'The deceptiveness of beauty: mother love and mother hate in *To the Lighthouse*', *Twentieth Century Literature*, 23, October, pp. 345–76.

—— (1981) 'Where the spear plants grew: the Ramsays' marriage in *To the Lighthouse*', in Jane Marcus (ed.), *New Feminist Essays on Virginia Woolf*, London, pp. 148–70.

Lloyd, Genevieve (1984) *The Man of Reason*, London.

Lloyd Smith, Alan (1987) 'Brain damage: the word and the world in postmodernist writing', in Malcolm Bradbury and Sigmund Ro (eds), *Contemporary American Fiction*, London, pp. 39–53.

Lodge, David (1977) *The Modes of Modern Writing: Metaphor, Metonymy and the Typology of Modern Literature*, London.

Lorber, J., Coser, R. L., Rossi, A. S., and Chodorow, N. (1981) 'On the reproduction of mothering: a methodological debate', *Signs*, 6, 3, pp. 482–514.

Lyotard, Jean-François (1984) *The Postmodern Condition: A Report on Knowledge*, Manchester and Minneapolis.

MacCabe, Colin (ed.) (1981) *The Talking Cure: Essays in Psychoanalysis and Language*, London.

MacCannell, Juliet Flower (1986) *Figuring Lacan: Criticism and the Cultural Unconscious*, London.

Mackinnon, Catherine (1982) 'Feminism, Marxism, method and the state: an agenda for theory', in N.O. Keohane, M. Z. Rosaldo, and B. C. Gelpi (eds), *Feminist Theory: A Critique of Ideology*, Brighton, pp. 1–31.

Majumdar, Robin and McLaurin, Allen (1975) *Virginia Woolf: The Critical Heritage*, London and Boston.

Manheimer, Joan (1978) 'Margaret Drabble and the journey to the self', *Studies in the Literary Imagination*, 11, 2, Fall, pp. 127–43.

Marcus, Jane (ed.) (1981) *New Feminist Essays on Virginia Woolf*, London.

—— (1982) 'Storming the toolshed', in N. O. Keohane, M. Z. Rosaldo, and B. C. Gelpi (eds), *Feminist Theory: A Critique of Ideology*, Brighton, pp. 217–37.

Markow, Alice Bradley (1974) 'The portrayal of feminine failure in the fiction of Doris Lessing', *Critique*, 16, 1, pp. 88–101.

Martin, Biddy (1982) 'Feminism, criticism and Foucault', *New German Critique*, 27, Fall, pp. 3–30.

May, Keith M. (1977) *Out of the Maelstrom: Psychology and the Novel in the Twentieth Century*, London.

Mead, Margaret (1962) *Deprivation of Maternal Care: A Reassessment of its Effects*, Geneva.

Meisel, Perry (1980) *The Absent Father: Virginia Woolf and Walter Pater*, New Haven and London.

Meissner, William (1978) *The Paranoid Process*, New York.

Menake, Esther (1982) 'Female identity in psychological perspective', *The Psychoanalytic Review*, 1, Spring, pp. 75–83.

Metcalf, A. and Humphries, M. (1985) *The Sexuality of Men*, London and Sydney.

Miller, Jean Baker (1983) *Towards a New Psychology of Women*, Harmondsworth.

Miller, Nancy K. (1981) 'Emphasis added: plots and plausibilities in women's fiction', *PMLA*, 96, 1, January, pp. 36–48.

Millett, Kate (1977) *Sexual Politics*, London.

Mitchell, Juliet (1971) *Women's Estate*, Harmondsworth.

—— (1975) *Psychoanalysis and Feminism*, Harmondsworth.

—— (1984) *Women: The Longest Revolution: Essays in Feminism, Literature and Psychoanalysis*, London.

—— (1986) *The Selected Melanie Klein*, Harmondsworth.

Mitchell, Juliet and Rose, Jacqueline (1982) *Feminine Sexuality: Jacques Lacan and the Ecole Freudienne*, trans. J. Rose, London and Basingstoke.

Modleski, Tania (1985) *Loving with a Vengeance*, New York and London.

BIBLIOGRAPHY

Moi, Toril (1981) 'Representations of patriarchy: sexuality and epistemology in Freud's *Dora*', *Feminist Review*, 9, pp. 60–74.
—— (1985) *Sexual/Textual Politics*, London and New York.
Money, John and Ehrhardt, Anke E. (1972) *Man and Woman, Boy and Girl*, Baltimore.
Monteith, Moira (ed.) (1986) *Women's Writing: A Challenge to Theory*, Brighton.
Moylan, Tom (1986) *Demand the Impossible: Science Fiction and the Utopian Imagination*, New York and London.
Murdoch, Iris (1977) 'Against dryness', in Malcolm Bradbury (ed.), *The Novel Today: Contemporary Writers on Modern Fiction*, London.
New, Caroline and David, Miriam (1985) *For the Children's Sake: Making Childcare more than Women's Business*, Harmondsworth.
Newman, Charles (ed.) (1970) *The Art of Sylvia Plath*, Bloomington.
—— (1985) *The Postmodern Aura: The Act of Faith in an Age of Inflation*, Evanston.
Newton, Judith and Rosenfelt, Deborah (eds) (1985) *Feminist Criticism and Social Change*, New York and London.
Nicholson, Nigel and Trautmann, Joanne (eds) (1975) *The Flight of the Mind: The Letters of Virginia Woolf*, vol. 1: *1880–1912*, New York.
Orbach, Susie (1979) *Fat is a Feminist Issue*, London.
—— (1986) *Hunger Strike: The Anorectic's Struggle as a Metaphor for our Age*, London.
Ortega y Gasset, T. (1968) *The Dehumanization of Art*, Princeton.
Ortner, Sherry (1974) 'Is female to male as nature is to culture?', in Michelle Zimbalist Rosaldo and Louise Lamphère (eds), *Women, Culture and Society*, Stanford. (Repr. in Mary Evans (ed.), *The Woman Question*, London, 1982, pp. 485–508.)
Owens, Craig (1985) 'The discourse of others: feminists and postmodernism', in Hal Foster (ed.), *Postmodern Culture*, London and Sydney, pp. 57–83.
Palmer, Richard E. (1977) 'Postmodernity and hermeneutics', *Boundary*, 2, 5, pp. 363–93.
Person, Ethel Spector (1980) 'Sexuality as the mainstay of identity: psychoanalytic perspectives', *Signs*, 5, Summer, pp. 605–30.
Philips, Eileen (ed.) (1983) *The Left and the Erotic*, London.
Poole, Roger (1978) *The Unknown Virginia Woolf*, Cambridge.
Pratt, Anis (1982) *Archetypal Patterns in Women's Fiction*, Brighton.
Punter, David (1980) *The Literature of Terror: A History of Gothic Fictions from 1765 to the Present Day*, London and New York.
—— (1985) *The Hidden Script: Writing and the Unconscious*, London, Boston, Melbourne, and Henley.
Rabine, Leslie W. (1985) *Reading the Romantic Heroine: Text, History and Ideology*, Ann Arbor.
Radway, Janice (1984) *Reading the Romance: Women, Patriarchy and Popular Literature*, Chapel Hill and London.
Rank, Otto (1941) *Beyond Psychology*, New York.
Raskin, Jonah (1970) 'Doris Lessing at Stony Brook: an interview', *New*

American Review, 8; repr. in *A Small Personal Voice*, New York, 1975.

Rich, Adrienne (1972) 'When we dead awaken: writing as re-vision', *College English*, 34, 1, October.

—— (1977) *Of Woman Born: Motherhood as Experience and Institution*, London.

Riley, Denise (1983) *War in the Nursery*, London.

Rose, Jacqueline (1983) Interview in *M/F*, 8, pp. 15–16.

—— (1986) 'Hamlet – the Mona Lisa of literature', *Critical Quarterly*, 28, 1–2, Spring/Summer.

Rose, Phyllis (1978) *Woman of Letters*, London and Henley.

Rougement, Denis de (1956) *Love in the Western World*, London.

Ruddick, Sarah (1980) 'Maternal thinking', *Feminist Studies*, 6, 2, Summer, pp. 342–67.

Ryan, Michael (1982) *Marxism and Deconstruction: A Critical Articulation*, Baltimore and London.

—— (1983) 'Deconstruction and social theory: the case of liberalism', in Mark Krupnick (ed.), *Displacement: Derrida and After*, Bloomington.

Rycroft, Charles (1985) *Psychoanalysis and Beyond*, ed. Peter Fuller, London.

Sage, Lorna (1986) 'The available space', in Moira Monteith (ed.), *Women's Writing: A Challenge to Theory*, Brighton, pp. 15–33.

Said, Edward W. (1985) 'Opponents, audiences, constituencies and community', in Hal Foster (ed.), *Postmodern Culture*, London and Sydney, pp. 135–59.

Sartre, Jean-Paul (1958) *Being and Nothingness*, trans. H. E. Barnes, London.

Sayers, Janet (1984) 'Feminism and mothering: a Kleinian perspective', *Women's Studies International Forum*, 7, 4, pp. 237–41.

—— (1985) 'Sexual contradictions: on Freud, psychoanalysis and feminism', *Free Associations*, 1.

—— (1986) *Sexual Contradictions: Psychology, Psychoanalysis and Feminism*, London and New York.

Schmidt, Dorey (ed.) (1982) *Margaret Drabble: Golden Realms*, Edinburgh, Texas.

Schor, Naomi (1981) 'Female paranoia: the case for psychoanalytic feminist criticism', *Yale French Studies*, 62, pp. 204–19.

Schorer, Mark, Miles, J., and McKenzie, G. (eds) (1958) *Criticism: The Foundations of Modern Literary Judgement*, Berkeley, Los Angeles, and London.

Segal, Hannah (1978) *Introduction to the Work of Melanie Klein*, London.

Seidler, Victor Jeleniewski (1980) 'Trusting ourselves: Marxism, human needs and sexual politics', in S. Clarke *et al.* (eds), *One-Dimensional Marxism: Althusser and the Politics of Culture*, London, pp. 103–57.

Sevenhuijsen, Selma and deVries, Petra (1984) 'The women's movement and motherhood', in Anja Meulenbelt *et al.* (eds), *A Creative Tension: Explorations in Socialist Feminism*, trans. Della Couling, London and Sydney, pp. 9–26.

Shafer, R. (1974) 'Problems in Freud's psychology of women', *Journal of the American Psychoanalytic Association*, 22, pp. 459–85.
—— (1976) *A New Language for Psychoanalysis*, New Haven and London.
Showalter, Elaine (1978) *A Literature of their Own*, London.
—— (ed.) (1986) *The New Feminist Criticism: Essays on Women, Literature and Society*, London.
Silverman, Kaja (1982) '*Histoire d'O*: the construction of a female subject', in Carole S. Vance (ed.), *Pleasure and Danger: Exploring Female Sexuality*, London, Boston, Melbourne, and Henley.
Sinfield, Alan (1983) *Society and Literature 1945–70*, London.
Smith, Barbara (1986) 'Towards a black feminist criticism', in Elaine Showalter (ed.), *The New Feminist Criticism: Essays on Women, Literature and Society*, London.
Smith, Stan (1981) *A Sadly Contracted Hero: The Comic Self in Post-War American Fiction*, British Association for American Studies.
Snitow, A., Stansell, C., and Thompson, S. (eds) (1984) *Desire: The Politics of Sexuality*, London.
Spacks, Patricia Meyer (1976) *The Female Imagination*, London.
Spillus, Elizabeth Bott (1983) 'Some developments from the work of Melanie Klein', *International Journal of Psychoanalysis*, 64, 3, pp. 321–32.
Spitzer, Susan (1978) 'Fantasy and femaleness in Margaret Drabble's *The Millstone*', *Novel*, 2, Spring, pp. 227–45.
Spivak, Gayatri Chakravorty (1983) 'Displacement and the discourse of women', in Mark Krupnick (ed.), *Displacement: Derrida and After*, Bloomington, pp. 169–97.
Squier, Susan Merrill (1984) *Women Writers and the City: Essays in Feminist Criticism*, Knoxville.
Staley, Thomas F. (ed.) (1982) *Twentieth Century Women Novelists*, London.
Stimpson, Catharine (1979) 'The power to name: some reflections on the avant-garde', in J. A. Sherman and E. T. Beck, *The Prism of Sex: Essays in the Sociology of Knowledge*, Wisconsin.
—— (1983) 'Doris Lessing and the parables of growth', in Elizabeth Abel, Marianne Hirsch, and Elizabeth Langland (eds), *The Voyage In: Fictions of Female Development*, Hanover and London, pp. 186–204.
Stokes, Adrian (1961) *Three Essays on the Painting of our Time*, London.
Stoller, Robert (1975) *The Transsexual Experiment*, London.
Strouse, Jean (ed.) (1974) *Women and Analysis: Dialogues on Psychoanalytic Views of Femininity*, New York.
Stubbs, Patricia (1981) *Women and Fiction: Feminism and the Novel 1880–1920*, London.
Suleiman, Susan Rubin (1985) 'Writing and motherhood', in Shirley Nelson Garner, Claire Kahane, and Madelon Sprengnether (eds), *The M(other) Tongue: Essays in Feminist Psychoanalytic Interpretation*, Ithaca and London, pp. 352–78.
—— (1986) 'Naming and difference: reflections on "modernism *versus* postmodernism" in literature', in Douwe Fokkema and Hans Bertens

(eds), *Approaching Postmodernism*, Amsterdam and Philadelphia, pp. 255–70.

Sullivan, Alan (1980) '*The Memoirs of a Survivor*: Lessing's notes towards a supreme fiction', *Modern Fiction Studies*, 26, 1, Spring.

Sypher, Wylie (1962) *Loss of the Self in Modern Literature and Art*, New York.

Taylor, Jenny (ed.) (1982) *Notebooks, Memoirs, Archives: Reading and Rereading Doris Lessing*, Boston, London, Melbourne, and Henley.

Temperley, Jane (1984) 'Our own worst enemies: unconscious factors in female disadvantage', *Free Associations/Radical Science*, 15, London.

Timpanaro, Sebastiano (1976) *The Freudian Slip*, London.

Todorov, Tzvetan (1973) *The Fantastic: A Structural Approach to a Literary Genre*, trans. Richard Howard, Cleveland, Ohio.

Trilling, Lionel (1967) *Beyond Culture*, Harmondsworth.

Unwin, Cathy (1984) 'Power-relations and the emergence of language', in Julian Henriques *et al.*, *Changing the Subject: Psychology, Social Regulation and Subjectivity*, London and New York.

Vance, Carole S. (ed.) (1982) *Pleasure and Danger: Exploring Female Sexuality*, London, Boston, Melbourne, and Henley.

Waites, Elizabeth A. (1982) 'Female self-representation and the unconscious', in Leila Lerner (ed.), *Women and Individuation: Emerging views*, *The Psychoanalytic Review*, 69, 1, Spring, pp. 29–41.

Walkerdine, Valerie (1984) 'Developmental psychology and child-centred pedagogy: the insertion of Piaget into early education', in Julian Henriques *et al.*, *Changing the Subject: Psychology, Social Regulation and Subjectivity*, London and New York, pp. 153–203.

Weeks, Jeffrey (1986) *Sexuality*, London and New York.

White, Hayden (1980) 'The value of narrativity in the representation of reality', *Critical Inquiry*, 7, 1, pp. 5–27.

Winnicott, D. W. (1958) 'Primary maternal preoccupation', in *Collected Papers*, London.

—— (1965a) *The Family and Individual Development*, London.

—— (1965b) *The Maturational Processes and the Facilitating Environment*, London.

—— (1967) 'Mirror-role of mother and family in child development', in P. Lomas (ed.), *The Predicament of the Family: A Psychoanalytical Symposium*, London.

—— (1982) *Playing and Reality*, Harmondsworth.

Wittig, Monique (1981) 'One is not born a woman', *Feminist Issues*, Winter, pp. 47–54.

Wollstonecraft, Mary (1975) *A Vindication of the Rights of Women*, New York. (First published 1792.)

Wright, Iain (1983) '"What matter who's speaking?" The authorial subject and contemporary critical theory' *Southern Review*, 16, 1, March.

INDEX

INDEX

INDEX

Mansfield, Katherine, 16
Marx, Karl, 20
marxist criticism, 2, 37
masochism, 43, 49–50, 80, 157, 175–6, 191, 194, 204
McKewan, Ian: *The Comfort of Strangers*, 68
McKinnon, C., 150
Mead, M., 62
Miller, Jean Baker, 48, 126–7
mirror phase and identity, 12, 55–9, 126, 136–7, 142, 154–5, 158–9, 169, 178, 200–1, 207–8; *see also* Lacan
Mitchell, Juliet, 54
Modleski, T., 188
Moi, Toril, 25
Moore, G. E., 89
Morrison, Toni, 213, 214
motherhood, 38, 40, 45, 51–2, 61, 62–78, 80, 102–3, 105, 109–115, 119, 127, 129, 130–38, 140–5, 146–7, 149–51, 152–4, 156, 159, 160, 175, 185–6, 187, 189, 193, 199–200, 208
Moylan, Tom, 171, 197
Murdoch, Iris, 81–2; *Under the Net*, 81; *The Sea, The Sea*, 82

narcissism, 43, 44, 54, 144, 145, 157, 178, 215; primary, 51
new criticism, 4, 19, 73
'novel of liberation', 22–33

object-relations theory, 50, 62–78, 94, 109–10; *see also* Chodorow; Eichenbaum; Orbach
Orbach, Susie, 45, 86, 109–10, 176, 177, 178, 181–2
Ortner, Sherry, 192–3

Paley, Grace, 22, 85, 160–7
paranoid–schizoid position, 65–9, 76; *see also* Klein
penis envy, 43–4, 47, 52–3, 130; *see also* Freud on sexuality
phenomenology, 19
Piaget, Jean, 40
Piercy, Marge, 32, 168; *Woman on the Edge of Time*, 197, 205, 209, 211–12, 216
Plath, Sylvia: *The Bell Jar*, 55–6, 61–2, 126, 151–7, 160
Pratt, M. L., 32
Punter, D., 170

Pynchon, Thomas, 32, 51, 68, 169

quest plot, 23, 30, 123, 180
Quin, Ann, 26

Rabine, L., 28
Radway, J., 139
Rank, Otto, 73
Rich, Adrienne, 24, 40, 213
Richards, I. A., 104
Richardson, Dorothy, 16, 78
Roberts, Michelle, 211
romance, 23, 28, 128, 131, 136–8, 139–40, 179, 180, 189, 190–1, 194, 199, 203, 204, 205, 217
Rose, J., 60
Rossner, J., 22
Roth, Philip, 29
Ruddick, Sarah, 199–200
Russ, Janet, 168, 169, 196, 205, 209, 211, 212–13, 216
Russian Formalism, 73
Rycroft, Charles, 52, 65

Sartre, J.-P.: *Being and Nothingness*, 70–1
Sayers, Janet, 37, 39, 59, 63
separation and identity, 21, 42–3, 46, 48, 51, 72–3, 86–7, 102, 105, 116, 118, 120–1, 123–5, 129–31, 143–6, 151–2, 155, 161–2, 182–3, 185, 201–3, 216
Shelley, Mary, 194
Showalter, Elaine, 40, 94
Silverman, Kaja, 149, 171
Spacks, P. M., 18
Spark, Muriel, 26, 168, 211, 215–17; *The Hothouse by the East River*, 215; *The Prime of Miss Jean Brodie*, 216
spatial form, 97–8, 104
Spivak, Gayatri, 24, 183; *see also* deconstruction
splitting, 32, 64–70, 75, 76
Stein, Gertrude, 16
Stokes, Adrian, 84
Strouse, Jean, 39
structuralism, 25, 26, 73
Sukenick, Ronald, 169

Temperley, J., 64
Tennant, Emma, 24
Timpanaro, S., 63